The Complete SketchUp Companion for Interior Design

THE COMPLETE SKETCHUP COMPANION FOR INTERIOR DESIGN

Andrew Brody, AIA

Endicott College

Fairchild Books

An imprint of Bloomsbury Publishing Inc

B L O O M S B U R Y

NEW YORK · LONDON · OXFORD · NEW DELHI · SYDNEY

Fairchild Books

An imprint of Bloomsbury Publishing Inc

1385 Broadway	50 Bedford Square
New York	London
NY 10018	WC1B 3DP
USA	UK

www.bloomsbury.com

FAIRCHILD BOOKS, BLOOMSBURY and the Diana logo are trademarks of Bloomsbury Publishing Plc

This edition published 2018

Library of Congress Cataloging-in-Publication Data

Names: Brody, Andrew (Architect), author.
Title: The complete SketchUp companion for interior design / Andrew Brody, Endicott College, AIA.
Description: New York : Fairchild Books, An imprint of Bloomsbury Publishing Inc, 2018. | Includes index.
Identifiers: LCCN 2017031810 | ISBN 9781501319730 (pbk.)
Subjects: LCSH: Architectural design—Data processing. | Interior decoration—Computer-aided design. | SketchUp.
Classification: LCC NA2728 .B754 2018 | DDC 729.0285—dc23 LC record available at https://lccn.loc.gov/2017031810

ISBN: PB: 978-1-5013-1973-0
ePDF: 978-1-5013-1976-1

Cover design by Jasiek Krzysztofiak
Cover image © Shelley Pass

Typeset by Lachina
Printed and bound in China

To find out more about our authors and books visit www.bloomsbury.com. Here you will find extracts, author interviews, details of forthcoming events, and the option to sign up for our newsletters.

For Dad.

TABLE OF CONTENTS

Preface xv

Unit 1: Getting Started with SketchUp

Chapter 1   SketchUp, Explained 1
Chapter 2   The Basics: Simple Shapes and Objects 16
Chapter 3   Beyond the Basics 36
Chapter 4   Graphical Controls 46
Chapter 5   Creating Furniture 61
Chapter 6   Modeling a Simple Interiors Project 71

Unit 2: Increasing Productivity

Chapter 7   Customize the Interface 90
Chapter 8   Scene Management 107
Chapter 9   Styles Management 116
Chapter 10 Space Planning Tools 127
Chapter 11 Complex Building Elements 143
Chapter 12 Advanced Geometry 162

Unit 3: LayOut

Chapter 13 Simple Design Presentations Using LayOut 175
Chapter 14 Construction Drawings Using LayOut 194
Chapter 15 Advanced Orthographic Drawings 207
Chapter 16 Schedules, Take-Offs, and Charts 219
Chapter 17 Construction Details 229

Unit 4: Beyond SketchUp

Chapter 18 External Media 236
Chapter 19 Interoperability 254
Chapter 20 Photo-Realistic Rendering 265
Chapter 21 Composite SketchUp Views 283

Appendix: Performance Issues 298
Glossary 304
Index 308

EXTENDED TABLE OF CONTENTS

Preface   xv

Unit 1: Getting Started with Sketchup

Chapter 1   SketchUp, Explained   1

Why should interior designers use SketchUp?   3

POINTS FOR SKETCHUP   3

POINTS AGAINST SKETCHUP   5

To BIM or not to BIM?   5

Office-wide decisions   6

Extensions   8

Interoperability   9

What's under the hood?   10

Keyboard graphics shortcuts   10

Of menus and dialogs, inspectors and palettes   12

Installing the software   13

Try it out!   14

Key terms   15

Chapter 2   The Basics: Simple Shapes and Objects   16

Using a template   17

The SketchUp interface   18

Types of tools   20

*Your Friend, **The Instructor***   20

*Viewing the **View tools***   21

What are objects in SketchUp made of, anyway?   23

Drawing stuff   24

LINES   24

CURVES   25

SHAPES   25

THE ERASER   28

Selecting objects   28

Editing tools   29

THE MOVE TOOL   30

TOOL MODIFIERS   30

EXTRUDING SURFACES WITH PUSH/PULL   30

THE OFFSET TOOL   31

THE SCALE TOOL   32

Try it out!   34

Key terms   35

Chapter 3   Beyond the Basics 36

　Model axes 36
　Drawing inferences 37
　Taking the measure of things 38
　Tool tips 39
　Object snap points 39
　Text and leader lines 40
　The **Paint Bucket** tool 41
　Managing content with external applications 42
　　THE 3D WAREHOUSE 42
　　EXTENSION WAREHOUSE 43
　　SEND TO LAYOUT TOOL 44
　　THE EXTENSION MANAGER 44
　Try it out! 45
　Key terms 45

Chapter 4   Graphical Controls 46

　Launching the Large Tool Set 46
　　CUSTOMIZING THE MAC TOOLBAR 47
　　CUSTOMIZING THE WINDOWS TOOLBAR 48
　Slicing open the model 49
　Of section planes and section cuts 51
　Working with styles 52
　Applying a style to a new scene 52
　Scene management 53
　Shadows 55
　Fog 57
　Creating an exterior backdrop 57
　Try it out! 59
　Key terms 60

Chapter 5   Creating Furniture 61

　Create the legs 62
　Copy the legs 64
　Draw the tabletop 64
　Add texture to the table 66

　Save the SketchUp file 69
　Try it out! 70
　Key terms 70

Chapter 6   Modeling a Simple Interiors Project 71

　Document the existing conditions 72
　Model the exterior volume 73
　Insert ready-made components 75
　Position the door 77
　And now, some windows 78
　Layer assignments 80
　Add wall thickness 83
　Save views of the model 85
　Try it out! 88
　Key terms 89

UNIT 2: Increasing Productivity

Chapter 7   Customizing the Interface 90

　SketchUp Preferences 91
　　APPLICATIONS 91
　　DRAWING 91
　　EXTENSIONS 92
　　GENERAL 92
　　OPENGL 93
　　SHORTCUTS 94
　　TEMPLATE 95
　　WORKSPACE 95
　The Model Info menu 96
　　ANIMATIONS 96
　　CLASSIFICATIONS 96
　　COMPONENTS 96
　　CREDITS 96
　　DIMENSIONS 98
　　FILE 98
　　GEOLOCATION 98

RENDERING 101

TEXT 101

UNITS 103

Create a template 103

Try it out! 105

Key terms 106

Chapter 8   Scene Management 107

Composing interior perspectives 107

Updating a scene 109

Creating an orthographic view 111

Creating a section view 112

Elevation drawings 113

Try it out! 115

Key terms 115

Chapter 9   Styles Management 116

Create a style for orthographic views 116

Apply dramatic styles 118

Mix and match style characteristics 120

The Style Builder 121

Create a style all your own 124

Insert the new style 125

Apply styles to multiple scenes 125

Try it out! 126

Key terms 126

Chapter 10   Space Planning Tools 127

Analyze the program 127

Create design options 131

Populate the model 132

Create a circular array 134

Arraying the array 135

The difference between block and component behavior 136

Dimensions 137

Component management 137

Place a painting on the wall 138

Add another design option 140

Lose something? 141

Try it out! 142

Key terms 142

Chapter 11   Complex Building Elements 143

Organize with layering and grouping 143

Model the existing interior 144

Create a stair the old-fashioned way, from scratch 147

Helpful view tools 151

Hide/show components during editing 152

Create a stair the easy way, using an extension 153

Walls and openings 155

Dynamic components 157

Try it out! 161

Key terms 161

Chapter 12   Advanced Geometry 162

Auto-fold 162

Solids tools 164

Groin vault 166

Intersecting objects 167

Sandbox tools 167

Complex curves 169

Warped surfaces 171

Managing extensions 173

Try it out! 174

Key terms 174

Unit 3: LayOut

Chapter 13   Simple Design Presentations Using LayOut 175

Prepare the SketchUp model 176
Send to LayOut 177
Viewport graphics controls 180
Set views to scale 181
Add a viewport 182
Create and edit background graphics 182
LayOut drawing and editing tools 186
Layers 186
Text and titles 188
Edit the title block 189
Insert images 189
Pages 190
Present your masterpiece using LayOut 191
Export file to print 191
Try it out! 192
Key terms 193

Chapter 14   Construction Drawings Using LayOut 194

Choose a template 195
Prepare the SketchUp model 195
Refine the floor plan 195
    CONFIGURE LAYERS 196
    OVERLAY VIEWPORTS 197
    GRAPHIC STANDARDS 201
A finishes plan 201
Add dimensions of model elements 201
Add room names 204
Add notes 205
Try it out! 206
Key terms 206

Chapter 15   Advanced Orthographic Drawings 207

The Scrapbook 208
Section and elevation symbols 209
Floor plan legend 210
Drawing call-outs 212
Creating a clipping mask 213
Adding your own scrapbook 214
Creating the cover page 215
Try it out! 218
Key terms 218

Chapter 16   Schedules, Take-Offs, and Charts 219

Counting components 220
Creating components with embedded metadata 221
Generating a report 222
Measuring the surface area 225
Creating a schedule within LayOut 226
Try it out! 228
Key terms 228

Chapter 17   Construction Details 229

Enlarged floor plan 229
Enlarged section 230
Casework drawings 232
Importing drawings 233
Try it out! 235
Key terms 235

Unit 4: Beyond SketchUp

Chapter 18   External Media 236

Print a perspective view 236
Print a scaled view 238
Export images 241
Create an animation 242
    COMPOSE A LINEAR WALKTHROUGH 243
    CONFIGURE AND PLAY THE ANIMATION 244
    OTHER TYPES OF ANIMATIONS 245
    EXPORT AN ANIMATION FILE 246
3D printing 248
Preparing for a laser cutter 250
Try it out! 253
Key terms 253

Chapter 19   Interoperability 254

Import options 254
Revit 256
    EXPORT FROM SKETCHUP TO REVIT 256
    IMPORT FROM REVIT TO SKETCHUP 259
AutoCAD 259
Trimble Connect 259
Augmented reality 260
Virtual reality 262
Try it out! 264
Key terms 264

Chapter 20   Photo-Realistic Rendering 265

Rendering engine comparison 265
Internal rendering 267
Quickie rendering 268
Interior rendering settings 270
Lighting 272
*The **Capture menu*** 276
Materials 277
Exporting rendered still images 277

Printing target resolution 280
Exporting animation files 281
Try it out! 282
Key terms 282

Chapter 21   Compositing SketchUp Views 283

Preparing the ingredients 283
Rendering recipes 286
    THE FADE 287
    FILTERS 290
    THE OVERLAY 292
    LIGHTING AND LIGHTING EFFECTS 292
Presentations 296
Try it out! 297
Key terms 297

Appendix: Performance Issues 298

System settings 298
SketchUp settings 299
    GENERAL SETTINGS 299
    MODEL SETTINGS 299
Hiding your problems 300
Proxy objects 300
Texture sizes 301
Purging the model 302
What is a Bug Splat? 302
Try it out! 303
Key terms 303

Glossary 304
Index 308

for links to sections of the text where students can dig deeper into the area being discussed.

 for extensions that expand functionality or efficiency.

 for Online Resources, such as videos, web links, and base files.

 for step-by-step sets of instructions, where students are expected to follow along.

Case studies demonstrate how design professionals have adapted SketchUp for use in their offices. Throughout the text, realistic design exercises and whole projects will be used to practice the techniques being discussed. These range from simple residential living room remodels to large commercial space planning projects. No matter your skill level or professional focus, *The Complete SketchUp Companion for Interior Design* is a comprehensive treatment of this handy design software.

Instructor and Student Resources

THE COMPLETE SKETCHUP COMPANION FOR INTERIOR DESIGN STUDiO
We are pleased to offer an online multimedia resource to support this text—*The Complete SketchUp Companion for Interior Design STUDIO*. The online *STUDIO* is specially developed to complement this book with rich media ancillaries that students can adapt to their visual learning styles to better master concepts and improve grades. Within the *STUDIO*, students will be able to:

- Study smarter with self-quizzes featuring scored results and personalized study tips.
- Review concepts with flashcards of terms and definitions.
- Watch video tutorials to learn essential techniques.
- Download template files to practice skills.

STUDIO access cards are offered free with new book purchases and also sold separately through the Fairchild Books website (www.Fairchild Books.com).

- Instructor's Guide provides suggestions for planning the course and using the text in the classroom, along with supplemental assignments and lecture notes.
- Test Bank includes sample test questions for each chapter.

Instructor's Resources may be accessed at www.FairchildBooks.com.

The publisher wishes to gratefully acknowledge and thank the editorial team involved in the publication of this book:

Acquisitions Editor: Noah Schwartzberg
Development Editor: Corey Kahn
Assistant Editor: Kiley Kudrna
Art Development Editor: Edie Weinberg
In-House Designer: Eleanor Rose
Production Manager: Claire Cooper
Project Manager: Chris Black

UNIT 1

GETTING STARTED WITH SKETCHUP

SketchUp, Explained

LEARNING OBJECTIVES

- Describe when and why an interior designer would choose to use SketchUp, as opposed to other applications.
- Identify interior design project types that are best suited for SketchUp, and which are not.
- Configure a computer system that works for your office, and calculate the cost implications of different software and hardware alternatives.
- Install and license SketchUp on either the Mac or Windows operating system.
- Organize a logical filing and back-up system.
- Develop the strategies for using this book that will work best for your skill set and situation.

SketchUp was first developed by @Last Software as a simple three-dimensional architectural modeling tool, and was first released back in August of 2000, by Brad Schell and Joe Esch. The goal was to allow architects and other designers to simply and easily create three-dimensional geometry that represents their ideas, without the clunky, non-intuitive interface typical of 3D modeling software at that point in time. Their unusually clear and intuitive **user interface (UI)**, that is, the manner in which the user and computer system interact, and in particular the use of input devices and software, allowed designers to quickly learn the basics of the application. Their motto was "3D for everyone," meaning that the operation of the program would be as comfortable as using a pen and paper, but with the ability to generate a convincing and accurate 3D model. Navigation through the virtual 3D environment is accomplished through manipulating the mouse buttons, instead of clicking on tools and typing in commands. @Last even has a patent on one of the editing tools they came up with, *Push/Pull*, which takes a selected surface and extrudes it.

Since its first release in 2000, SketchUp has changed only a little, with more or less the same simple interface for creating and modifying shapes and controlling your view. The company has certainly grown over the years, and they often create a 3D scale figure component that immortalizes their team members. In fact, each new release features a new employee in the base template. In 2006, the company was acquired by a tiny little start-up you might have heard of called Google, mainly to help develop 3D content for Google Earth. SketchUp models could be loaded directly into the Google Earth interface, where they could be viewed in their exact geographic location and orientation. **Metadata**, which is further information about a particular drawing, model, or data set, could be attached to, say, a model of an existing building. The SketchUp model would know its geographic location, and when viewed in Google Earth, the three-dimensional neighborhood in which it resides. Other metadata might be as simple as a user photograph of a site, a building permit, occupancy information, and even the **Geographic Information System** (**GIS**) data, which is a vast, constantly growing, organic database of site-specific spatial and geographical knowledge and analysis, used by urban

Figure 1.1 *SketchUp team members, immortalized as components within their own software.*

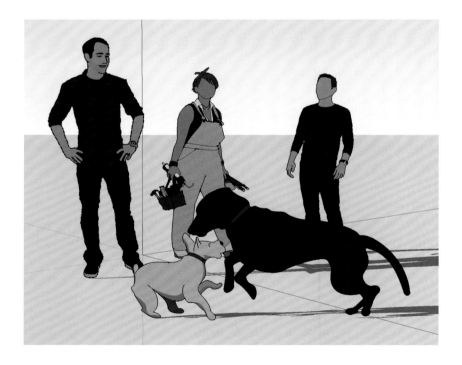

planners, landscape architects, and anyone involved in land use. SketchUp models could also be extracted from Google Earth for further development, or to create architectural projects, site models, and the like.

Apparently, Google decided that their depiction of Earth was completed in 2012, because that's when they sold SketchUp to Trimble, a global supplier of GPS navigation equipment and software. Trimble has kept SketchUp true to its roots as a simple-to-use 3D modeling platform—the basic UI has not really changed all that much since 2000. The biggest change that Trimble has made is to make it much easier to add *Extensions* to SketchUp. These are similar to smartphone apps, adding all sorts of different kinds of intelligent and handy functionality to the base modeling platform. Extensions can be developed by anyone with knowledge of the Ruby programming language, and are often free, although authors can also choose to charge for more robust tools.

 See the Online Resources for links to additional information about the Ruby programming language.

Why should interior designers use SketchUp?

When first starting out, it can be daunting to choose the software for your practice. In school, students are generally exposed to a number of different techniques for representing their projects. The **electronic workflow** that you choose will be based on many things, from the broad scope, such as the types of projects you do, to the more narrowly focused, such as how carefully you need to manage colors when printing.

POINTS FOR SKETCHUP

- *It's easy.* The simplicity of modeling, and the widespread use of the free version, make it easy to find staff who know how to use SketchUp already, or to train new people.
- *It makes the design process more creative.* When compared to Building Information Modeling (BIM) platforms, SketchUp's speed and ease of use allow designers to explore and communicate their ideas quite easily. If a design isn't working well, making changes or exploring options is fast and painless. The typical BIM package requires hours spent hunting through layers of menus to create a simple space plan, which means that users are much less likely to make changes to that plan to improve it.
- *It's cheap.* A single seat of the Pro version is only $695 total for a permanent license, with an annual fee of a little over $100 to update the software; many BIM packages are over $2,000 per year. There is also a free version of SketchUp, which means that it's easy to install on a personal machine, for following along with training videos, sharing with clients, or just playing around.

- *It's good for small projects.* Independent interior designers tend to work on renovations, which have a fairly limited scope, and so probably don't need all the horsepower of a full-on BIM package. If you are not worried about coming up with site plans, complex roof framing plans, wall construction systems, and the like, BIM products are basically overpowered and overpriced.
- *It wants you to learn how to use it.* SketchUp wants you to like using it. There is an internal guide, an interactive feature, called *The Instructor*, which describes how to use each tool as you click on it. There are written and video tutorials online, which is great for when you're hunting for instructions on obscure procedures.

Even the website features a "Get Good Fast" section, which has tips and tutorials. And, aside from all of those reasons, there's this book, which makes it an easy, linear process to learn all about what SketchUp can do!

Figure 1.2 *The SketchUp home page.*

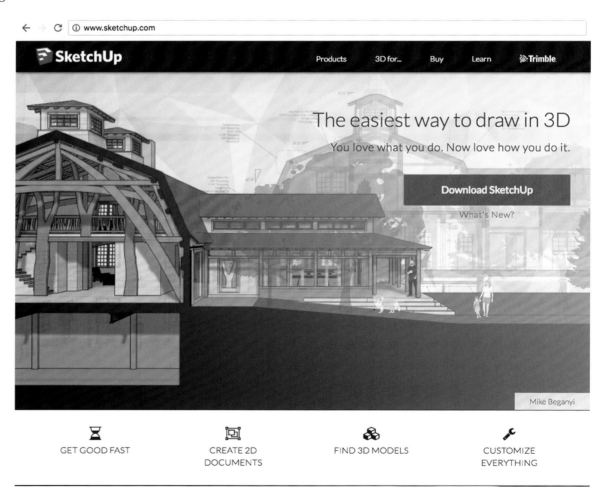

- *You work on big projects.* Small renovations, the size of, say, residential kitchens or small commercial office space, are perfectly suited to model in SketchUp. Multi-story spaces with many different types of schedules and take-offs, or those that need to have a large team working on a single project file, will not work particularly well in SketchUp.
- *You work with furniture systems.* Some systems manufacturers have plugins designed specifically to work with certain applications, such as AutoCAD, that cannot be adapted for SketchUp. Their models can be imported into SketchUp, but most of the attached metadata will be lost, and that is what allows their proprietary plugins to generate purchase orders, bills of materials, and the like.
- *You're loaded.* SketchUp costs less than $1,000, which includes adding a rendering engine and any special purpose and productivity extensions. BIM software can be over $2,000 *per year*, per license, per seat—even with month-to-month leasing—and that can get costly in a hurry. Training to use SketchUp is much simpler, too, and thus cheaper.
- *Your office isn't very busy.* If you have the time to devote to complex training, the more complicated BIM software is more reasonable, because you will be able to train people to use it efficiently. Without that training, your staff will not be able to use the software to its full potential.

To BIM or not to BIM?

Back in the good old days, which was something like the 1990s, you basically had people who still hand-drafted their construction drawings, and you had people using software such as AutoCAD, which was somewhat like an electronic drafting table. Lines were just dumb objects, that didn't know where they were or what they were, either in terms of materials or geometric location within the building. Sheets of construction drawings needed to be carefully cross-checked to make sure that the details matched the overall design, and even the callout symbols for elevations and enlarged drawings had to match what was drawn on the originating plan or section. It was very labor intensive, and consumed a majority of an architect's budget.

The big revolution came with **Building Information Modeling** (**BIM**), which is a digital representation of physical and functional characteristics of a building or facility. This new type of software was a way of creating a design project that was closer to a database of facts about the geometry and construction of a project than to a drawing application for creating a visual representation of a project. In a BIM model,

See the Online Resources for a video tutorial showing a side-by-side comparison of the Mac and Windows versions of SketchUp.

elements in the three-dimensional model store **parameters**, which is information such as dimensions or materials, which could be by instance or across an entire project. These applications create a completely integrated model, so that when you add a window, for example, there is metadata about the manufacturer, catalog number, or anything else that might be available. These applications allow you to go from simple concept models through to entire buildings and site plans, creating sets of construction drawings and documentation, and even rendering, all fully integrated with the software interface. All of this complexity comes at a price, however: it can be hard to create a simple drawing for an idea of a project without knowing a great deal about the construction systems that you intend to use.

SketchUp is, at its core, a face-based 3D modeling tool, and not a BIM type of application. There are ways to extract data from your model in a very BIM-esque manner, however, using *Extensions*. These allow SketchUp to perform most of the automation that BIM software provides, without automatically adding a high degree of complexity to your model.

Office-wide decisions

One of the biggest choices any office manager must make is about their computer **operating system** (**OS**), which is the underlying software that supports all of a computer's basic functions. Most offices will run on either the Windows or Mac OS, although some more technical types may choose Linux, which is open source, and requires a lot more effort to set up. The choice of OS affects both hardware and software, as what is available, and what the final bill will be, can vary significantly. In general, engineering consultants prefer software available on the PC, whereas interior designers lean toward Macs. Architects are more split on the matter, as many will use PC desktops in the office, Mac laptops for stylish and color-accurate presentations, and then iPads for site work and coordination.

There are quite a few expenses that you should consider when making decisions about software—here's a summary of the issues involved in each:

■ *Mac or Windows?* SketchUp works just fine in either platform, but many applications you might want to use are limited to one OS. Revit, for example, is only available on Windows, as is the powerful rendering and animation software 3ds Max. Mac hardware tends to have very high build quality, and looks great in a presentation. As mobile devices, they manage memory and power very well, and the high-quality screens can be color calibrated quite accurately, which is important when trying to render materials and lighting accurately. And of course, Mac comes with very expensive matching accessories, such as a large monitor, a phone, and even a watch! Going with all Windows equipment will probably cut your bill in half, but you may lose some of that money as you add in the extra time needed to calibrate and maintain the system.

■ *SketchUp Pro or SketchUp Make?* Make has most of the modeling and editing tools of Pro, so it's great if you want to have a station or laptop available for training—especially handy when you've hired a staff member. Make lacks a number of features that create producing professional looking drawings, and most importantly, the page setup application LayOut. Without it, you will have a tough time collecting together sets of orthographic drawings with matching title blocks, notes, etc. Instead, you'll have to export image files of your SketchUp model, and assemble presentations in another piece of software, which is tedious. The full Pro version runs about $800, with an annual fee of a little over $100 to update the software. Students can purchase an educational license for $50.

■ *Consultants?* If you work with engineers, architects, lighting designers, and other consultants, it's very handy to be able to import and export DWG files.

■ *In-house rendering?* If your office does a lot of high-end photo-realistic rendering and animations, you probably have some expensive freestanding applications on your system, such as V-Ray or 3ds Mac. You'll need the Pro version of SketchUp to more easily interact with those programs, including exporting geometry.

■ *How is your memory?* If you are the type of person who tends to have five different applications, along with twenty different browser windows and a video chat session, open all at the same time, you are probably going to want to look into a machine with some pretty robust memory capabilities. This tends to force you into choosing a desktop, as many machines, such as the MacBook Pro, cannot have onboard memory expanded.

■ *Storage capacity?* SketchUp files are generally not as big as files created by BIM applications, but they can get upwards of 100 megabytes for a large project. Having a solid-state drive will help to keep things on your computer moving along at a much quicker pace than the older drives that rely on spinning parts. They tend to have less capacity, however, so some sort of external or online backup and archive are critical.

■ *Peripherals?* If you're like me, and your eyes are getting old, you'll probably want a nice big external monitor and an ergonomic keyboard and mouse. Purchasing these items for ten employees at the

Hey, where is the *Extensions* pull-down menu? Sneaky SketchUp won't display the menu until you add your first extension.

SketchUp works best with a mouse with a scroll wheel. There are other ways to navigate the 3D experience, including the touch pad, and even a 3D joystick, from 3dConnexion.

If you sign into Trimble using your Google Account, you may have to verify your identity via email or text message – this is called two-step verification. While this is a little bit irritating, it's worth turning on this feature of Google, for added security.

Apple store will certainly open those aging eyes wide, whereas heading to the local big box store for Windows-based equipment will be less of a shock. That said, if you have clients visiting your office, it may be worth spending the extra money on high quality equipment, no matter who makes it, so that visitors will be impressed with the level of detail of your design aesthetic.

There are, as you might imagine, many other elements that should be considered, especially as an office gets bigger and bigger. A student may be happy with a laptop, because they can use computer labs when they need some extra horsepower for, say, rendering an animation. A large office may be more worried about the ability to have a robust network for file sharing and backup, along with the support staff to manage it. A solo practitioner, however, is more likely to choose a setup based on personal preference and working style, including the impression that their design office is trying to make.

Extensions

SketchUp is more akin to a smartphone, which has plenty of handy dandy features right out of the box, but can be radically expanded using apps. SketchUp's version of apps are called *Extensions*, which *extend* the base functionality of the program—someone was clearly up late to come up with the name "extensions"! Once installed, most of these apps become integrated into the SketchUp interface, either as a toolbar or as a feature that can be called up as needed. Some are meant to extract information out of your file, such as generating lists of components in the model. As in the Apple App store and the Google Play store, many of these are free, whereas other are purchased. Contractors can add tools for modeling the wood framing of a roof, for example, or theatrical producers can add lighting grid tools. There are many, many professions and pursuits that benefit from easy 3D modeling, but are more efficient with special extensions tailored to their needs. As we will see later in this book, extensions are particularly good news for interior designers: there are many special functions that are more common in interior projects, such as generating furnishings and equipment schedules or designing interior lighting, that can require very complicated software packages.

If there isn't an extension, it is possible to write a new one using the Ruby programming language, which happens to be free and open source. SketchUp allows the addition of custom-made apps, so advanced users can really have some fun creating their own tools for special operations.

Interoperability

The Pro version of SketchUp has some export and import options that allow it to better integrate with other applications. If you are using the BIM software, but you want to use SketchUp for quick layouts, furniture modeling, or just experimentation, drawings can be imported directly into a number of different software titles. Sometimes you can use the SKP file format, which is native to SketchUp, or SketchUp drawings can be converted into the AutoCAD DWG file format, which has become a sort-of universal file format for exchanging line drawings or basic geometry. There are also options for importing and exporting geometry to renderers and 3D printers, or in 2D formats that laser cutters can read.

A common workflow is to create a simple model in SketchUp, then bring that model into a more robust rendering engine, which will apply photorealistic lighting and materials. Some of these rendering engines operate within the SketchUp interface, which is certainly convenient for design iterations. Others require that you import the model geometry

SketchUp Features	Make	Pro
Build 3D models	✓	✓
Import CAD files	✗	✓
Export CAD and PDF files	✗	✓
Create multi-page presentation sets	✗	✓
Produce construction drawings	✗	✓
Export animation videos of any size	✗	✓
Present files and full-screen presentations	✗	✓
Add custom attributes and behaviors	✗	✓
Generate lists and reports	✗	✓
Use solid modeling tools	✗	✓
Make hand-drawn rendering styles	✗	✓
Work with simulated film cameras	✗	✓
Email technical support	✗	✓
Licensed for commercial use	✗	✓
Import, Export, and Create IFC Files	✗	✓

Figure 1.3 *Feature comparison between the Make and Pro versions of SketchUp.*

Trimble recently released a web-based app for viewing and editing models, called my.SketchUp. It may not be as ergonometric as working on a desktop, but it would be handy for, say, quick views on a work site.

and materials into an outside application, sometimes requiring conversion to a different file format. Some tech savvy offices will take their BIM models and clean them up in SketchUp, removing extraneous geometry that is typical of those types of models, and then render the simplified model in yet another application.

What's under the hood?

These days it is easy to be a platform atheist, because neither OS has a clear advantage, at least in terms of the functionality of SketchUp. Nor is there an alternative OS, such as Linux, which will work with SketchUp. Either way, once you've chosen an OS, you also need to think about the hardware that typically comes with it. SketchUp and some of its plugins make heavy use of the **Graphics Processing Unit** (**GPU**), which is the part of the computer that takes whatever information it has and tries to display it on the screen. The more rich and complex your 3D environment is, the more challenging it can be for the GPU to keep up. Also worth considering is the **Central Processing Unit** (**CPU**), which is sort of like the brain of the computer. In a general sense, bigger really is better—although, with CPUs, it's actually the total number of processors that's important.

Keyboard graphics shortcuts

As mentioned earlier, interior designers seem to have a preference for Mac systems. To this end, different keys and keyboard combinations will follow an iconography based on the standard Mac keyboard.

Certain keys are repeated endlessly, so instead of having to type out "Hit Enter" (Mac) or "Hit Return" (Windows) twenty times in a long set of instructions, the text will use the ↵ icon in place of the text. The text will use the ⌘ symbol for the *Command* button, which is generally replaced with the *CTRL* button in Windows. The *Option* button on Mac, which is generally replaced by the *ALT* button in Windows, will use the ⌥ symbol. If the keystroke for Windows varies from these standards, it will be noted in the text, but it is otherwise assumed that the standard substitution applies.

When two keys need to be pressed at the same time, the text will show them in sequence, which is also how they're indicated in the SketchUp pull-down menus. Thus, the system *Copy* command, where you must hold down the *Command* button and tap the C key, will look like this: ⌘C (or CTRL C in Windows). For some commands, it's only necessary to tap on a key to activate the feature, without holding it down, which will be indicated as such in the step-by-step instructions.

Case Study: The Architectural Team, in Chelsea, MA, is a full-service architecture firm. They tend to use SketchUp during the schematic design phase, where the ease of use allows even senior members of the design team to manipulate the model and explore design options. The office must decide when it's time to finish designing and migrate the project to their BIM platform, Revit, to produce construction documentation.

Case Study 1.1 The Sibley Building, Rochester, NY.
From http://www.architecturalteam.com.

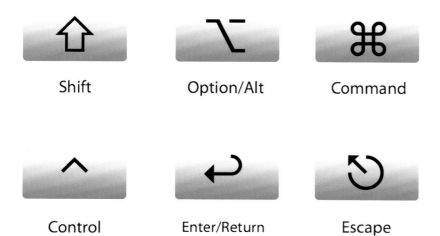

Shift   Option/Alt   Command

Control   Enter/Return   Escape

Figure 1.4 *Keyboard key graphic symbols.*

For those visual learners out there, knowledge about SketchUp can be expressed as a mind map. See the Online Resources.

Menu items (and nested menu items) from the pull-down menus will be indicated with a right-pointing arrow (>), as in *View < Component Edit > Hide Rest of Model*. When there is an ellipsis (. . .) after a command, it means that choice will open up some sort of menu or dialog box, e.g., *File > Open. . .*

Of menus and dialogs, inspectors and palettes

There are a number of different terms for the types of boxes that open up at various points while you are using SketchUp, and these terms can vary depending on where and when the **dialog box** shows up. In general, Mac dialog boxes are called up one by one, and on Windows, they all reside in a default **Tray**. Either way, some are referred to as a **browser**, others as a **palette**, and one, *The Instructor*, is called the **inspector**, presumably because it is always inspecting what you are doing. Most of these dialog boxes are modeless, and so can sit happily on the side of your screen. Some are true dialog boxes, and are waiting for you to input some sort of response, after which you'll have to click OK or Apply.

If you are running a system with two monitors, collect all of the tool palettes and browsers and inspectors over to the extra monitor—this will save having to open or maximize them every time you want to enter a value or get information about something.

When you right-click on some object or selection set, the menu that pops up is called a **context menu**, and it is generally a set of options

Figure 1.5 *A secondary monitor, with browsers, toolbars, and menus galore.*

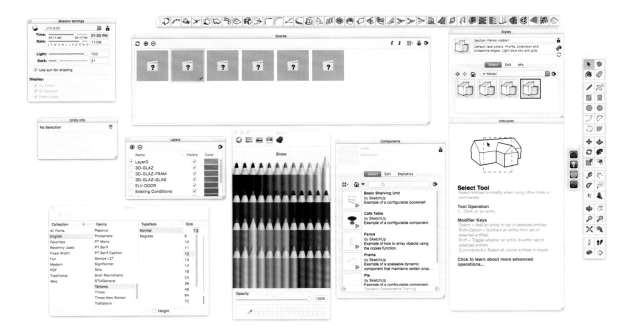

related specifically to whatever it was that you clicked on. The written menus that span the top of your interface are known as the **pull-down menus**. Most tools can be accessed by a spot in the pull-down menu, some have a keyboard shortcut, and some also have a button on a toolbar somewhere. Note that, on a Mac, the context menu can also be accessed by tapping the touch pad with two fingers, or holding down the *Option* key and clicking. Many Windows machines will allow CTRL-clicking to access the context menu, and some even have a right-side mouse button next to the touch pad.

Installing the software

So you don't even have SketchUp installed yet, do you? The SketchUp website, www.sketchup.com, makes it fairly easy to download the software for whichever operating system you have. If you want SketchUp Make, the free version, the licence is valid forever. SketchUp Pro comes with a thirty-day free trial, so after that time, the license will revert to the functionality of the free version. If you decide you like Pro, you can accept a terms of use, pay for the license, and you're good to go. If you are a student or educator, you should just go straight to the educational licensing section, where you can get SketchUp Pro at a significant discount: $49, as of this writing. Either way, fill out the brief form explaining who you are and how you plan to use SketchUp, and then download the installation file.

On Mac, open the installation file, which is usally downloaded either onto your desktop or into your downloads folder.

Once installed, you can drag the installation package from the desktop (or Downloads folder) into the trash. To uninstall SketchUp, drag the icon in the Applications folder into the trash.

Ergonomics is the study of the mechanics of the human body. Configure your work station to be ergonomically correct for the best posture, eye level, and arm support.

See the Online Resources for a side-by-side comparison of the Mac and Windows versions of SketchUp Pro.

Figure 1.6 *Installing the software on Mac.*

Install the software by dragging the application into your Applications folder—it might take a few minutes to complete this operation. At that point, SketchUp will probably open right up, but if it doesn't, navigate using the Finder to your Applications folder and double-click on the SketchUp icon. To make the application icon stay permanently in the dock, right-click on it, and choose *Options > Keep in Dock* from the context menu.

On Windows, you have to run the executable file downloaded from the website, which will install the software on your computer. As on Mac, it will probably be in the Downloads folder, so use Windows Explorer to find it. Double-click on the EXE file, and you will be presented with a series of dialog boxes to click through.

Once installed, the software should open right up. When all is said and done, there is typically an icon that shows up on your desktop, or even in a tile, if you are using the Windows 10 interface. You can even drag the application shortcut directly onto the quick-launch toolbar, so that it's quickly available.

Figure 1.7 *Installing the software on Windows*

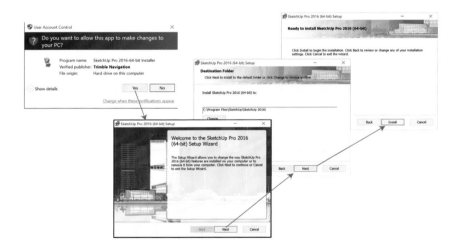

Try it out!

- Make a chart indicating the pros and cons that an interior designer might consider when deciding whether to use SketchUp.
- List five different types of common interior design projects, and indicate which ones are or are not suitable for SketchUp.
- Develop a list of equipment and software needed to get started using SketchUp for both the Mac and Windows operating systems. Calculate the cost implications of different software and hardware alternatives, and develop a rationale for choosing one over the other.

- Purge your computer of old documents and software and configure a file management system that is logical and easy to back up.
- Adjust power usage and graphics settings on your computer for optimal performance.
- Configure your hardware so that your eye height, head angle, and arm positioning are optimal for comfort and ergonometric performance.

Key terms

- Browser
- Building Information Modeling (BIM)
- Central Processing Unit (CPU)
- Context menu
- Dialog box
- Electronic workflow
- Geographic Information System (GIS)
- Graphics Processing Unit (GPU)
- Inspector
- Metadata
- Operating system
- Palette
- Parameters
- Pull-down menu
- Tray
- User interface

CHAPTER 2

The Basics: Simple Shapes and Objects

LEARNING OBJECTIVES

- Identify the function of the different areas of the SketchUp interface.
- Demonstrate the creation and modification of basic drawing elements using the default tool set.
- Develop *Selection Sets* using a number of different techniques.
- Modify the view using various *Zoom* tools and techniques.
- Use *The Instructor* to learn about drawing and editing tools interactively.

Modeling with SketchUp is meant to be as intuitive as drawing with a pencil on paper. In fact, one of the default tools is the *Pencil* tool, and it works in basically the same way as a real pencil—without needing sharpening, of course. The big difference from hand-drawing, however, is that in SketchUp, you create three-dimensional geometry, and not just lines. Three-dimensional modeling requires tools for sculpting objects, in addition to ones for drawing individual elements. You'll also need to navigate in and around these virtual creations, creating perspective compositions by re-orienting the view of the model.

Models for interior designs or architectural projects are all made of the same elemental parts, so we'll learn those first. To get started, SketchUp provides us with a set of default tools, the use of which we will go over in this chapter. So now that you've got the software installed, let's open it up, choose a template to work with, and take the basic tools for a spin.

 Any template can be converted to metric from feet and inches, or vice versa. This setting is under *Preferences > Units.*

Using a template

When you open SketchUp for the first time, you will see a dialog box prompting you to choose a template. There are a number of different types of templates to choose from, depending on what type of project you plan to create. These range from general use (perhaps a playground, or a UFO), architecture (for buildings), landscape architecture, construction documentation, even kitchen design. There are templates for urban planning, woodworking, and 3D printing, and for the metric and standard measurement systems.

Most of the templates will display colors and any image-based materials that you've painted on surfaces, which in SketchUp-land are called **Textures**, along with colors for the ground and sky. Others will force the model to be only in black and white, which is better for construction drawings. For a typical interior design project done here in the United States, the best one to use is the *Architectural Design—Feet and Inches* template, so choose that one, and click the *Start Using SketchUp* button.

If your office does mainly the same types of projects over and over, you really only need to choose a template once, so un-check the radio button for *Always Show on Startup*. Interior design projects in particular

Once you create a new model, the visibility settings inherited from the template can be tweaked in any number of ways. See Chapter 9 for more information.

Figure 2.1 *Splash screen.*

Where you go to find online videos and help

Where you go to authorize the software

Choose a template

Only needed the first time you open SketchUp

The Mac version has a full-screen mode, which hides the menu bar. Choose *View > Enter Full Screen* to maximize the application. Hover your mouse at the top of the screen to reveal the menu again. Choose *View > Exit Full Screen* if you'd rather see the menus all the time.

You can create your own template, which is handy when you've gotten your SketchUp models configured for the types of projects that you tend to do. See the section on creating a template in Chapter 7 for instructions.

It's an annoyance to have the template selection dialog box pop every time you launch the application. Uncheck the radio button next to *Always Show on Startup;* and it will never trouble you again.

There are several mysterious buttons on the left side of the Status Bar. Click on these to geo-locate your model, claim credit for your model, or log in to your Trimble account, which will synch any *Extensions* that you might add, and call up *The Instructor.*

rely on a large number of components and complicated view controls, but those are not part of any of the standard templates. Later, we'll discuss the most valuable things to include in an interiors template.

The SketchUp interface

The SketchUp **user interface** (**UI**), which is the on-screen layout of application features that you interact with, will probably look familiar if you've used any drawing or modeling software before. Most prominent is a large drawing area, where all the object creation and editing happens. This area is ringed by a menu bar, which has the pull-down menus that come with most applications. There is a row of buttons just below this, which are how you activate the basic drawing and editing tools. To the right, you'll find various **inspectors**, which are self-contained menus that change based on what you've selected, and other palettes for changing characteristics of your model or the elements within it.

As with most applications these days, tools can be activated in a number of ways: you can click on the button in the default toolbar, select it from somewhere in a pull-down menu, or type the keyboard shortcut. So, for example, the *Line* tool has a button, but you could also choose *Draw > Lines > Line* from the drop-down menu, or just type the letter L. Some users will prefer a less cluttered drawing area, hiding the menu bar and all the toolbars, whereas others might prefer to have every button visible all at once—it's a matter of personal preference. In general, however, basic creation and editing of 3D geometry is done with all the drawing and modeling tools on the default toolbar, labeled *Getting Started*, at least until you learn the more advanced tools.

Palettes for choosing and modifying different model features, such as *Styles*, *Scenes*, and *Entity Information*, are known variously as **browsers**, **inspectors**, or even just **information windows**. These can be called up individually, by choosing them from the *Window* pull-down menu. Many users choose to leave them all open, but minimized into a small stack—just click on the top bar of any browser to collapse it.

On Mac, menus can be **floating menus**, on their own anywhere on your computer screen, or even on an external monitor, if one is available. They can also can be **docked menus**, which is to say, connected one under the other, so that they can all be moved simultaneously. Just click and drag on the top bar of a menu, sliding it under another one, until the two snap together in a neat stack. This is particularly nice if you're working on the limited screen space of a laptop.

On Windows, all of these bars are collected into a menu **tray**, which moves all of the menus at once. They can still be expanded and collapsed individually, but they can't float. To change which menus are visible, choose *Window > Manage Tray*. The whole tray can be shifted to an external monitor.

The first concept to know about SketchUp is that it is a three-dimensional modeling environment. The architectural template has a vast gray expanse, with some lightly colored lines that define the X (red), Y (green), and Z (blue) directions in this virtual 3D world. Whenever you draw, SketchUp likes to follow along one or another of these axial directions, although it's also possible to draw off axis or force drawing along only one particular axis. By default, there is one model of a person standing in this empty three-dimensional world, which helps you to judge the scale of the objects that you are about to draw. As you move around the model, the figure keeps looking at you, in a creepy sort of way.

Modeling in SketchUp is a matter of creating two-dimensional objects, either individual lines or surfaces, and then extruding them and manipulating them into three-dimensional shapes. The edges, endpoints, and surfaces of these objects can be manipulated in a number of ways, to create ever-more-complex geometry.

You forgot what keys those keystroke symbols represent, didn't you? They are used in SketchUp throughout the menus and preferences. Here they are:

Command:	⌘
Option/Alt:	⌥
Control:	^
Shift:	⇧
Caps lock:	⇪
Tab:	→|
Esc:	↺
Enter/Return:	↵

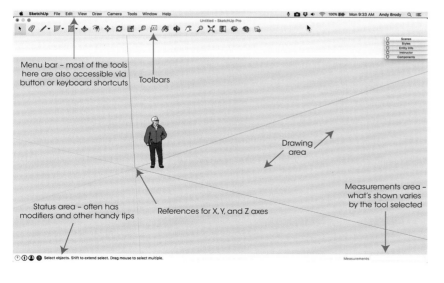

Figure 2.2 *The software interface.*

Menu bar – most of the tools here are also accessible via button or keyboard shortcuts

Toolbars

Drawing area

Measurements area – what's shown varies by the tool selected

Status area – often has modifiers and other handy tips

References for X, Y, and Z axes

Types of tools

The default toolbar has all the tools you'll need to get started modeling in SketchUp, which is probably why it's called the *Getting Started* toolbar. It's divided up into groups of tools based on their general function: object creation, object editing, getting information, changing a view, and managing content with external applications. Rather than read them left to right, we'll review the operation of each group of tools based on the operations you need to learn in the software: first are the tools for modifying the view, so that you can navigate around the 3D space of the model. Then we'll learn to create linear objects and faces, and edit them in a number of ways.

SketchUp can display both the tool icon and its name in the **tool tip**— just go to *View > Tool Palettes > Customize Toolbar*. On a PC, just right-click an empty area of the toolbar and choose *Toolbars*, and then *Options*. From the bottom of this menu, you can choose to display both icon and text, and also check the *Use Small Size* option, if you'd prefer smaller icons.

Your Friend, *The Instructor*

Sometimes the best way to learn a new application is to just start clicking on tools to see what they do. It would be nice to have an expert looking over your shoulder, however, to give you hints and gentle guidance as you explore. For this, SketchUp has its own little teacher built right into the interface, called *The Instructor*, which by default is open as a separate window when you open a new document. Click on any tool, and *The Instructor* will show you a brief video demonstrating the basic elements of how that tool works, along with any keystrokes or other elements that modify the behavior of the tool. For those of you who are visual learners, this little animation is a great way to see how a tool operates before actually trying it out. If you prefer to read instructions carefully before using a new tool, there are written-out steps for showing how to operate the tool. If there are *Modifier Keys*, which we will learn about later in the text, they are listed here, along with a link to advanced operations, which will bring you to the vast online help area.

For students who like exploring software in a more freeform manner, especially those who have some familiarity with other 3D modeling

Figure 2.3 *The* Getting Started *toolbar, showing tool groupings.*

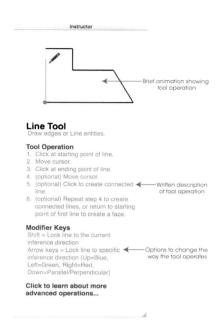

Figure 2.4 The Instructor, *instructing how to use the* Line *tool.*

If you plan to use SketchUp for anything other than simple shapes, purchase a three-button mouse. To zoom, just scroll in or out.

Zoom and orbit will orient around whatever objects you have selected. You can also right-click on the object or objects and choose *Zoom Selection.*

platforms, *The Instructor* allows you to quickly get a sense of the capabilities of different tools. If you accidentally closed *The Instructor*, just click on the question mark in the lower left corner of the SketchUp window to open up the *Help* window.

Viewing the *View tools*

To modify the view of a typical drawing application, users can either **zoom** in to the content on the screen, or zoom out to display more of the drawing area, making details of the drawing very large or very small on the screen, They can also **pan**, dragging the view on your screen left or right, or up or down. For those users with a scroll-wheel-enabled mouse, these basic zooming tasks are accomplished with various mouse buttons. Scroll in or out to zoom, and click and drag the scroll wheel and left mouse button to pan.

SketchUp models are three-dimensional, so you need to be able to navigate above, below, and inside the models, and not just in and out. This will allow users to create geometry in different locations, and evaluate the design from different perspectives. However, these views tend to be more complex to configure than just moving around the outside of a building or piece of furniture. There are only a few tools needed, which are all on the *Getting Started* toolbar.

The left-most button is the *Orbit* tool, which allows you to spin the model around whatever point you happen to click on. Click the *Orbit* tool, and then click and drag with your left mouse in one or another

Figure 2.5 *The basic* View *tools.*

Some view options are available only in context menus. Right-click on some selected objects and choose *Zoom Selection*.

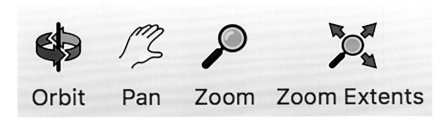

direction to spin the model around the cursor. With a three-button mouse, just click and drag with your scroll wheel. On a laptop, click and hold on the left side of the trackpad, and drag your other finger to spin the model. This works, but can lead to some tangling, depending on where you are in the model. Another way to activate the command is to put down that cup of coffee in your other hand, and instead hold down ⌃⌘ while clicking and dragging the left button.

Why does the *Pan* tool look like a hand? The visual metaphor is that it's similar to when you place your hand on a piece of paper and drag it around your desk. Click on the *Pan* tool, and then click and drag in any direction to slide your view over. On a mouse, you'll need to click and drag both your scroll wheel and your left mouse button, which requires a strong grip, but makes it easy to switch back and forth between the *Pan* and *Orbit* tools. Another way to activate the *Pan* tool is to hold down ⌃⌘⇧ while clicking and dragging the left button. This is only needed if you are using a mouse without a scroll wheel.

To get closer or farther away from your model, use the *Zoom* tool, which looks suspiciously like a magnifying glass. Click the *Zoom* button, and then click and drag with your left mouse button, which is to say, hold down the left button while moving the mouse up or down. Move either up or down to zoom in to or away from whatever happens to be under your cursor at that time. Click and drag either left or right to zoom in or out a bit more slowly.

Zoom Extents, the remaining tool, will automatically zoom out to display everything in the model, centering all visible geometry on the middle of the screen and fitting it to the width of your window. This is handy

Just to be irritating, Mac and Windows scrolling directions are opposite from each other.

Note here that Mac trackpads can be configured to have custom gestures. Different PC manufacturers will often have their own settings for their hardware, so you'll have to do some homework to find out which ones work on your system.

if the view is stuck inside a piece of geometry and can't scroll out, or if the view is zoomed so far out that the model isn't visible anymore.

Without a mouse, use the gestures programmed into the Mac trackpad: drag two fingers up or down to *Zoom*, or left and right to zoom a bit more slowly. To *Orbit*, hold down ^⌘ and click and drag. To *Pan*, hold down ⌘^⇧ and click and drag. Alas, this technique works better for right-handed people, because of the layout of the typical Mac touchpad.

SketchUp Pro can understand 3D models in several file formats, including DWG, IFC, and 3ds, which many other modeling applications can create. Imported information can be 2D lines or whole 3D models.

What are objects in SketchUp made of, anyway?

SketchUp is a **surface modeler**, which is to say that everything you build is composed of edges and colored areas that fill in when edges form a loop. These filled areas, called **faces**, automatically fill in a closed loop of linear objects, so long as all the objects are drawn in the same plane. Thus, a three-dimensional object is more like a shoebox than, say, a block of cheese—hollow inside, rather than filled with material. The other type of 3D modeling application is called a **solid modeler**, where every object is completely filled in. These are handy for applications such as 3D printing and fabrication.

This difference in model structure has implications for how many tools work: in SketchUp, most tools are for creating and manipulating surfaces, rather than mashing together or separating solid objects. For interior designers, this type of structure means that you can get inside any shape that you create, which is how architectural volumes are built up. In a general sense, there are several ways to create objects:

- Draw linear elements such as lines and arcs that, when connected, form the bounding edges of a **face**.
- Draw pre-defined objects, such as rectangles and circles, which have edges and faces.
- Add linear elements onto existing faces, to divide them up.
- Manipulate points and edges using a variety of editing tools, and let SketchUp add the necessary geometry to complete the action.
- Manipulate faces using a variety of editing tools, and let SketchUp add the necessary geometry to complete the action.

You can't have a face without a complete loop of bounding edges, so erasing just one edge line will delete the entire face too. Add that linear element back in, and SketchUp will re-draw the face, which is handy when trying to get a model to fill in missing faces. There are many other tools within SketchUp to create 3D geometry, and additional tools available through the *Extension Warehouse*, which we'll learn about later on in the book. There is also my favorite way of creating geometry, which is borrowing it from other people, through the 3D Warehouse, or through other exchange websites.

Figure 2.6 *Bounding elements and faces.*

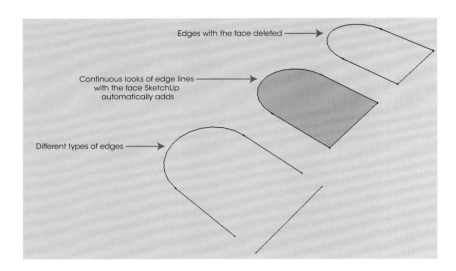

Want to draw a power cord? Try the *Ropefall* extension, which creates ropes out of individual lines. It even has a sort of gravity effect that can be fun to play with. Or go to www.sketchrope.com for more details.

Drawing stuff

There are really only four basic drawing tools that you need to get started, and it's pretty easy to glean from their names what exactly they do. The *Pencil* tool draws lines, and the *Eraser* tool erases them; the *Arc* tool draws arcs, and, following along with the theme, the *Rectangle* tool draws rectangles. As the text describes the process for using each tool, try to draw the same shape indicated. If you're feeling confident, leave *The Instructor* open, to see a short animation of how the tool works, and also for tips on advanced features that the tools might have.

Advanced users might be happy to just click on a tool to try it out. Be sure to look down in the *Status* area for any modifiers or other prompts that pertain to this particular tool.

LINES

Let's start with the most basic drawing tool there is: the *Line* tool. Click on the button that looks suspiciously like a pencil, and then click once to start drawing a line—don't click and drag. You will see a line connected

Figure 2.7 *The basic drawing tools.*

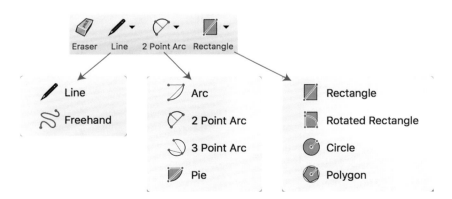

to your initial start point, following around your cursor—this is called a **rubber band line**. Just click again somewhere else on the screen, and you've made your first line!

Like a lot of applications, SketchUp will hide other tools underneath the buttons on top. There is a little black down-facing arrow next to the *Line* tool, called a **caret**—click and drag on the arrow to reveal any hidden goodies, which is, in this case, the *Freehand* tool. This tool can draw a polyline, which is basically a series of short line segments glued together—click and drag with your left mouse, and a somewhat smooth polyline with very small linear segments will be drawn along the path you trace. As soon as you release the button, the polyline sketch is finished. If you happen to end up in the same place that you start, SketchUp will complete a loop, and fill the inside with a face. Not exactly an architectural triumph, but it is a start.

CURVES

Drawing an arc can be complicated, because three points need to be defined, and there are, in fact, a number of different ways to accomplish it. The default version, which is the one visible in the *Getting Started* toolbar, uses three points to define the arc: one endpoint, the radius, and the arc length. Click on the *Arc* tool, and click in the drawing area to indicate the start of the arc. Click again for the length of the radius, and a third time to indicate the arc length. If you study carefully the icon for the *Arc* tool, you will see that the red dots indicate each click location, and the lines indicate the motion of your mouse in between those clicks—a handy bit of graphic design.

Like the *Line* tool, there are other options hidden under the tiny black caret on the right side of the tool icon. Click the down arrow to see several other options for drawing an arc: *2 Point Arc*, *3 Point Arc*, and the *Pie* method. Each of these might be appropriate in different situations, depending on where you are trying to draw in an arc. Click on the *2 Point Arc* tool, and then click the first time to define one end of the arc; click again to define the endpoint of the arc; and click one last time to define the length of the radius. The *3 Point Arc* tool uses the start point, center of the arc, and the endpoint to generate the geometry. The *Pie* tool will draw an arc in the same manner as the default *Arc* tool, but also creates a line at the other endpoint that returns to the center point of the arc and fills in the area with a face.

SHAPES

It's possible to build up just about any shape using linear elements, but there are a few types of geometry that are common enough to warrant

Arcs can sometimes be difficult to keep on the ground as you draw—move the cursor around as you draw to preview which direction it's going.

There are a number of different geometric inferences specific to arcs, including the usual axes, and also *Half-Circle* and *Tangent at Vertex.*

Want to draw that rectangle an exact dimension? After drawing it, type in [width],[length] ↵, and the shape will adjust to that dimension. You can keep changing your mind, typing in a new set of values, until you activate the next tool, and then you'll need to edit the shape using other tools.

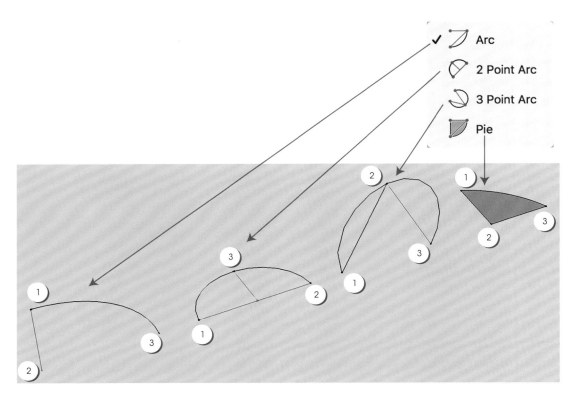

Figure 2.8 *The different* Arc
tools.

their own tool. As you can probably guess from the icon, and the name, the *Rectangle* tool will draw a rectangle. Just click once to start the base of the rectangle, and again to finish the rectangle—give it a try.

The rectangle you just drew consists of four independent edges and a face that's in the middle of them. Select any one edge, and then hit the Delete key, and you'll see the face disappear. As with other tools that have a little arrow next to them, the *Rectangle* tool has hidden beneath it some other handy button. In this case, you'll find the *Rotated Rectangle*, *Circle*, and *Polygon* tools. The *Rotated Rectangle* tool is actually the most complex of the bunch, as it allows you to draw off the ground plane.

1. Click on the *Rotated Rectangle* tool.
2. Click once to indicate the first corner of the rectangle.
3. Click again to indicate the angle that the rectangle is rotated in the horizontal plane.
4. Click again to indicate the angle that the rectangle is rotated in the vertical plane.
5. Click one last time to indicate the second corner of the rectangle.

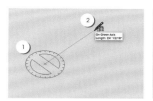 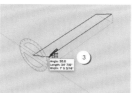 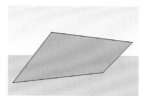

Figure 2.9 *A rotated rectangle.*

When typing in a dimension, leave out the dash. *So, 2'6"↵, rather than 2'-6"↵. SketchUp will treat the dash as a minus sign, and subtract the second value from the first.*

Hold down Shift while using the *Eraser* tool to hide objects instead of erasing them. They can be revealed later, by choosing *View > Hidden Geometry.*

Drawing a circle is, by comparison, relatively simple—activate the tool, click once to define the center point, and then one more time to indicate the radius. To specify an exact dimension for the radius, immediately after you have drawn the circle, take note of the value in the measurements box at the lower right of the SketchUp window. It's telling you the dimension of the line you just drew in full 1:1 scale. To change the dimension, just type a different number—no need to click in the box, or anywhere else. So, for a 1-foot radius, type 1'↵, and notice how the circle changes size. You could also type 12"↵, and get the same result—SketchUp can cope with feet or inch dimensions. Many tools have values that can be entered in this manner, either after the drawing operation is completed, or sometimes, before you start.

The *Polygon* tool works in a similar manner to *Circle*, clicking once to define the center point, and again to define the radius. Before starting to draw, however, you can type in the number of sides that you would like on the polygon—the number will show up in the measurements box, as with the value for the radius of the circle. Experiment with drawing polygons with different numbers of sides, and also with typing in a dimension for the inscribed radius.

Figure 2.10 *Various shape tools.*

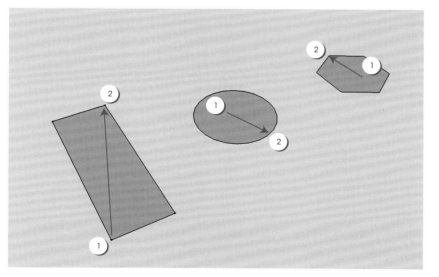

Metric dimensions are somewhat simpler to enter. Use meters, or move the decimal place to specify fractions of a meter—e.g., type in .1↵ to specify 100 cm. You can even type in a fraction, and SketchUp will do the math for you.

All of these modifiers only work immediately after you complete an operation. As soon as you click on a new tool, you won't be able to change the dimension for the number of copies.

THE ERASER

We all make mistakes, and nothing beats being able to make them go away instantly. The eraser allows us to do that—click on the button to activate the tool, and click directly on the offending object. You can also click and drag across several objects, just like a real eraser, and erase them all. Erasing one of the edges of a face will make the face disappear—but it will leave any remaining edges as lines. It is also possible to select a variety of entities by using the *Select* tool discussed below and tapping the Delete key.

Selecting objects

You've created quite a few interesting drawing elements, but what can you do with them? You generally need to select objects to edit them (although not always), so click on the *Select* tool to begin (or tap on the Space Bar, which is the keyboard shortcut). Need to select more than just a single object? Double-click in the middle of a face anywhere in the model, and SketchUp will select the surface and its bounding edges. Now try triple-clicking on a single face of, say, a box. This will select the surface, its bounding edge, and any geometry that's touching the original surface, even if it's through an interstitial piece. Now try quadruple-clicking on the surface, and observe what happens. Just kidding—nothing happens when you quadruple-click on something! But it's fun to make students try it.

There are a number of ways to build your **selection set**, which is the collection of object(s) you'd like to modify: use the left mouse button to click directly on a single object, such as an edge or a surface, to select it. There are also a few keystroke modifiers that will help you build the selection set: hold down ⇧ to add or subtract elements (you'll see a little +/- symbol next to the cursor), ^ to only add elements, or ⇧^ to only remove elements from the selection set. ⌘A will select everything that's visible anywhere in the model (but not objects hidden in one way or another).

Have a lot of objects to select? Try clicking and dragging on an empty area of the model, which will create a virtual window. Drag to the right to create a *selection window*, where only objects that fall entirely within

The Mac version supports multiple file windows within a single instance of the application. In the Windows version, you'll have to open multiple instances of SketchUp, which can tax system resources quite a bit.

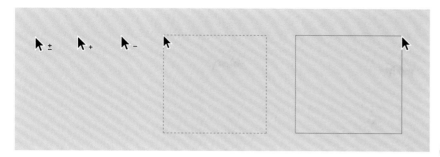

Figure 2.11 *The Selection* tool *with different modifiers, a crossing window, and a selection window.*

As we saw when creating objects, you can force movement along a particular axis by tapping on one of the arrow keys. The cursor will show a funny little folded plate icon, with a tooltip that says *Constrained on Line.*

the box will be selected. Drag to the left for a *crossing window*, where any objects that fall within or touch the box will be selected.

Try to select several of the objects that you've created, including a single face and a single edge. Add another edge to the selection set, and use a *Selection Window* to add a whole polygon. With all those different entities selected, the simplest thing you can do with selected objects is to delete them—just tap the *Delete* button (the backspace key will work too, if you have one). You can also use the operating system clipboard, which is handy if you want to, say, copy from one model into another. Select whatever you'd like to copy, tap ⌘C, which is the system *Copy* command. If you want to eliminate the geometry from the model, type ⌘X, which is the system *Cut* tool. Switch to your other drawing and then tap ⌘V to paste the selected objects into the new drawing. Note that, because this clipboard belongs to the operating system, you won't have any of the handy modifiers that enhance the SketchUp *Copy* tool.

Editing tools

Once you have created a healthy selection of objects, it is possible to modify them using the editing tools. In fact, much more geometry in a model is created by manipulating lines and faces that are already there than is created using the drawing tools. As with the drawing tools, editing tools have dimensions and other parameters that can be typed in at various points.

Figure 2.12 *The editing tools.*

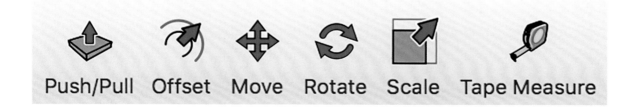

Keep an eye on the status bar as you draw, as that's how SketchUp will indicate the next step you need to take, as well as any modifiers that might be available.

In the case of *Push/Pull*, tapping ⌥ (CTRL in Windows) will make a copy of the surface you're editing.

THE MOVE TOOL

The most common tool is *Move*, which, as you can imagine, takes whatever you've selected and moves it somewhere else in the model. The first step is to select whatever it is that you want to move, using the techniques mentioned above, and then tap on the *Move* tool. Click once to define the **base point** for the move, which is the starting point in 3D space from which you'll measure the distance and angle of the move. This point doesn't even have to be on the object itself, but can be anywhere in the drawing area. Move your cursor around, and you will see the objects glued to it, connected by a rubber band line that starts at the base point you defined.

You can move the selection anywhere in 3D space, but the cursor tends to snap to the cardinal directions, either left to right, front to back, or up and down. These directions can be inferred by the graphic axes in the model, which are colored red, green, or blue. As the cursor approaches one of those axes, the rubber band line will turn the color of that direction, making it easier to draw along the orthogonal grid. Click again to define the endpoint for the move—it's as simple as that!

TOOL MODIFIERS

One of the quirks of SketchUp is that there is no separate *Copy* command. Instead, you use a modifier with the *Move* tool to create either single or multiple copies. A modifier changes the way a particular command works, either by enhancing it or defining some feature. We have already seen one in action when we change the number of sides while using the *Polygon* tool. There is no need to type anywhere; values show up in the measurements box by default. Activate the *Move* tool again, and click to provide a base point as before. This time, however, before clicking on the second point, tap ⌥ (CTRL in Windows), and you will see a tiny little plus sign next to your cursor. This indicates that you will now be making copies instead of just moving—you can toggle this on and off by continuing to tap the modifier key.

Now, when you click on the endpoint, you will see you have two objects instead of one. There are even more modifiers that you can use after you make a copy: type *3↵, and you will make an array of three objects, spaced the same dimension as the first one. Type /3↵, and you will see three copies squeezed in between the first and last ones that you made. Type in a dimension, and you will see all of the copies adjust their spacing to match this new dimension. This is a quick way to create a linear **array**, which is a series of copies, all spaced equally.

EXTRUDING SURFACES WITH PUSH/PULL

Of all the basic tools, *Push/Pull* is probably the most fun to play with. The icon gives a graphical indication of what the tool does: it takes a

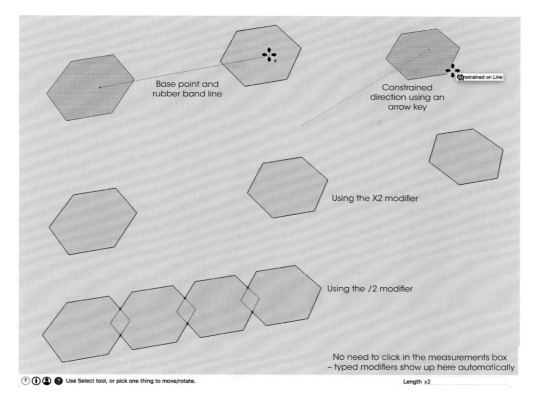

Base point and
rubber band line

Constrained
direction using an
arrow key

Constrained on Line

Using the X2 modifier

Using the /2 modifier

No need to click in the measurements box
– typed modifiers show up here automatically

Use Select tool, or pick one thing to move/rotate.

Length x2

Figure 2.13 *Using the* Move *tool with the* Copy *modifier to make an array of objects.*

surface that you click on and extrudes it in the direction that your mouse goes. It's sort of like a PlayDoh® extruding machine that kids use, which pushes dough through a cutout of a particular profile, so that you can make whatever length you'd like of, say, a tube shape. For this tool, you can either select the face you want to modify first (handy in a crowded model), or just move your mouse over any face in the model, and it will become highlighted when SketchUp anticipates that you want to modify it.

Let's select the polygon that we drew earlier—the face, not the edge. When the *Push/Pull* tool is activated, the surface becomes connected to the cursor—the extrusion grows or shrinks in the direction you move. Click to place the extruded circle some height above, or below, the original shape. As with other tools, you can type a dimension in the measurements box.

For any tool that requires a click to define a displacement, there is no need for the second click—just type in a value. Avoiding this second click will save a lot of time, over the course of a lifetime.

THE OFFSET TOOL

Want to make a hollow box or a ring? The *Offset* tool will make a copy of any bounding edge that you choose, which you can then *Push/Pull* up to make a ring of sorts. To learn this tool, let's go step-by-step to create a telescope-like structure, by creating a series of concentric extrusions.

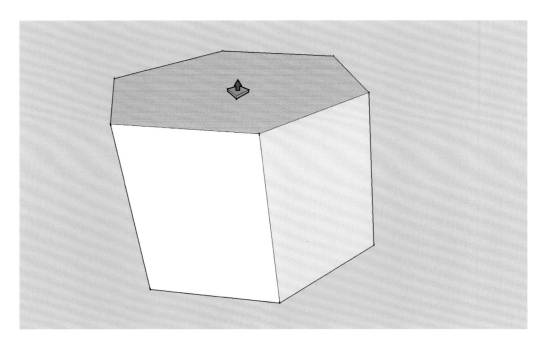

Figure 2.14 *The* Push/Pull *tool in action.*

Select individual linear elements instead of entire bounding edges for different offset effects.

Are you a visual learner? Go to the Online Resources, and watch the "Basic Tools" video, which demonstrates each of the tools described in this chapter.

1. Draw a circle.
2. Type in 4↵ to define the radius.
3. *Push/Pull* the circle up 12".
4. Click on the *Offset* tool, and then click on the top edge of the tube—SketchUp will highlight the edge, and show the tool tip *On Edge*.
5. Click and drag the edge toward the center of the circle.
6. Type 1↵ to indicate the distance for the copy of the edge—it should snap to that position.
7. *Push/Pull* up the inner circle.
8. Type 12".
9. Repeat steps 4–8 another three times.

THE SCALE TOOL

The *Scale* tool allows you to change the size of a selected object or objects, either proportionally or along a particular axis. Let's start with the 2D operation first. Draw a rectangle, and then double-click to select it. Activate the *Scale* tool, and you will see a series of green squares at each of the main geometric nodes—the endpoint and midpoints of each

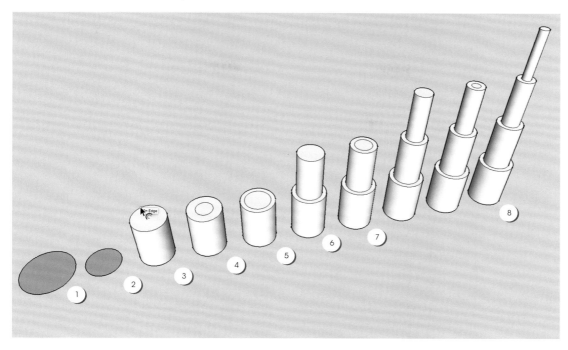

Figure 2.15 *Creating a tube-like structure.*

of the edge lines. Click and drag on any of these handles to rescale the model in one direction or another—give it a try.

Three-dimensional objects have additional handles at the edges and center of each plane of the object. You can drag in a random direction to distort the shape in an irregular manner, or hold down ⇧ to re-size proportionally. Irregular objects also have the same set of grips on a bounding box-shaped outline. Give it a try: draw a polygon of any flavor that you find interesting, and use *Push/Pull* to extrude it to some height. Then, click on the *Scale* tool, and stretch the object from a corner, the middle of a side, and one of the edges, to see the different effects.

You can even use the *Scale* tool on just one surface of a simple shape to create cones, wedges, and other more complex geometry. In fact, many editing tools, such as *Move* and *Rotate*, will work on single surfaces, edges, and sometimes even points.

Note also that, like other tools, you can type in a value during or immediately after the operation of the tool. For the *Scale* tool, the number you enter will determine the size relative to the original. So, typing .5↵, for example, will result in 50 percent of the original dimension, and typing 2↵ will result in the equivalent to 2X of the original. After typing in a number, a dialog box will pop up asking if you want to rescale the entire model. Click *No*, unless you're sure that every entity in the entire model needs to be adjusted.

Some entities, such as components, will not work directly with the *Scale* tool. You'll need to edit the component first, and then change the elements.

Want to modify only one segment of a polygon? Right-click on it, and choose *Explode Curve* from the context menu.

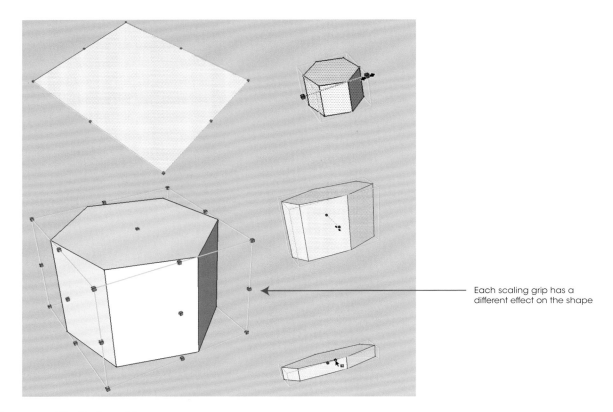

Each scaling grip has a different effect on the shape

Figure 2.16 *The* Scale *tool in action.*

Figure 2.17 *Scaling one face of a shape.*

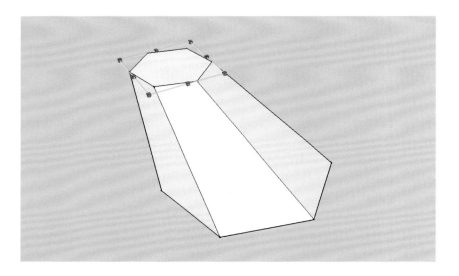

Try it out!

■ Print a screenshot of your SketchUp interface and label the toolbar area, pull-down menus, tool palettes, information bar, and measurements box.

- Print a copy of your keyboard reference (Mac or Windows) from the Online Resources, and memorize the shortcuts for your system.
- One by one, create a rectangle, a rotated rectangle, a circle, an octagon, an arc, a line, and a squiggle.
- Select the objects you drew in the exercise above, both by clicking on them directly and by using selection and crossing windows. Make a copy 20' away.
- Create a cube with an edge dimension of 1'. Draw a circle on the underside, and extrude it into a handle.
- Create a pyramid and a cone.
- Create a simple rectangular building, give it a gabled roof, and then draw a shed roof dormer.
- Draw the letters of your name using lines, arcs, and squiggles. *Push/Pull* to give the letters some thickness.

Key terms

- Array
- Base point
- Caret
- Docked menu
- Face
- Floating menu
- Information windows
- Inspector
- Menu
- Origin
- Pan
- Rubber band line
- Selection set
- Solid modeler
- Surface modeler
- Template
- Textures
- Tool tip
- Tray
- User interface (UI)
- Zoom

Beyond the Basics

- Identify the origin and the three axes of the SketchUp drawing environment, and how they are used for drawing.
- Identify the geometric object snapping points on rectilinear and circular objects.
- Annotate drawings with text.
- Apply textures to surfaces in a model.
- Import components from the 3D Warehouse.

SketchUp models use certain organizational systems to make drawing easier, particularly for architectural types of objects. Buildings, furnishings, and materials are, more often than not, drawn making reference to an orthogonal grid, which helps in both planning and construction. Objects also need to be connected with each other, often with a high degree of precision. Many building elements are standardized, so an integral library is provided with access to vast collections of objects and materials.

Model axes

Every SketchUp model represents the three-dimensional world, and so uses a three-dimensional graphing system to locate objects precisely. This virtual world is defined by the three axes you probably learned in

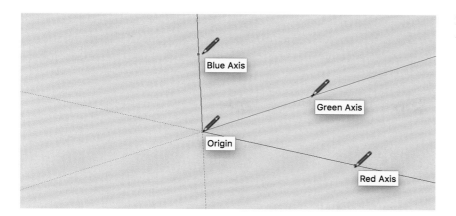

Figure 3.1 *The color-coded axes in SketchUp.*

middle school geometry: x, y, and z. In SketchUp, however, the axes are given a visual identity, each having their own color: red, green, and blue, respectively. Points along this three-dimensional grid can in fact be referenced by their geometric coordinates, with the 0, 0, 0 point as the central location, or origin.

Drawing inferences

As you draw lines, move objects, and are otherwise in the middle of commands, you will notice that the rubber band line connected to the base point will turn green it gets close to the green axis, red near red axis, and blue near the blue axis. And have a tendency to snap to those directions. This is a feature of SketchUp called **Inferences**, where the application tries to anticipate in which direction along the orthogonal grid you'd like to draw. It's also possible to draw or move objects at random angles, and SketchUp can draw lines parallel to those non-orthographic angles, too.

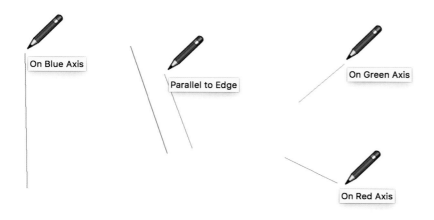

Figure 3.2 *SketchUp inferring the direction of a line.*

You can force a line to be drawn along any of the three axes in the model. After starting a line, hold down ⇧ and one of the arrow keys at the same time, and your cursor will be forced along either the red, green, or blue axis, depending on the arrow. Click again to complete the line in that direction.

Taking the measure of things

As you might imagine, the *Tape Measure* tool will help you find the distance between points in a model. Click on one endpoint of a line, and then the other, and you will see the distance between these points indicated in the measurements box. If you click in the middle of a line, however, SketchUp will prompt you specify an offset length and direction from the starting point, either by clicking or by typing in a value. Doing this leaves a gray dashed **reference line** at that location, parallel to the original line. These reference lines are not model geometry per se, but instead are infinitely long line-like entities that can be used to draw and to measure the location of objects. For example, you could draw a reference column grid this way, or a centerline around which to place lighting. These lines can be hidden for printing if needed.

Figure 3.3 *The* Tape Measure *tool, measuring.*

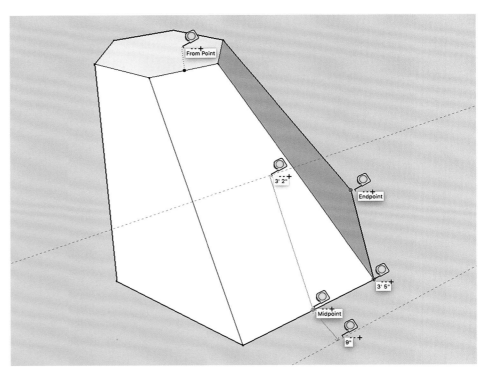

Tool tips

SketchUp has a number of tools to help you draw more accurately. Leave your mouse over some object, and you will see various **tool tips** pop up, depending on what you are hovering over, and if you are in the middle of the operation. These help you in a number of instances, including when you are trying to align with different parts of objects in the model.

Object snap points

As you draw and modify objects and move over different parts of the model, the cursor tool tip will display references to a number of different geometric points. On lines, those points are *Endpoint*, *Midpoint*, and *On Edge*. You can also be *On Face*, or, as we saw when we learned about the *Line* tool, you can draw *Parallel to Edge*. Leave your mouse over a point for a moment, and then move it in either the red, green, or blue direction, and you will see the *From Point* tool tip. As with the *Line* tool, you can use the arrow keys to constrain references, and you'll see the *Constrained on Line* tool tip. You can even combine the above techniques, move your mouse over another object snap, and see the *Constrained on Line from Point* tool tip.

Figure 3.4 *Object snapping points.*

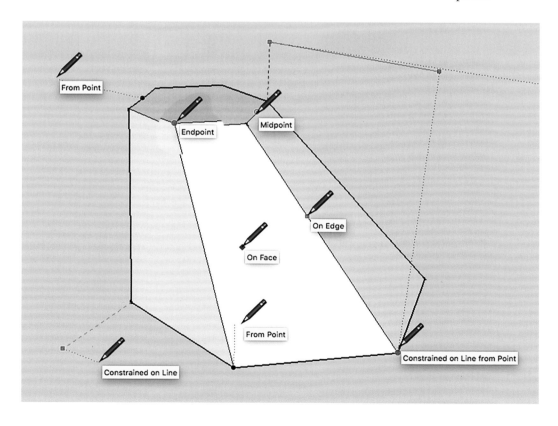

It's possible to import new collections from, say, a manufacturer, by dragging the collection file into the Macintosh HD/Library/Application Support/SketchUp 2017/ SketchUp folder. Custom collections in Windows can be added using the fly-out menu.

Text and leader lines

The *Text* tool works in a manner that is fairly similar to other applications, although in SketchUp, it usually adds a leader line, and the default text that populates the text edit window will try to describe whatever you pointed at. Click on the *Text* tool, and then click again to place the leader line—let's try right in the middle of a surface. As you move your mouse away, you will see that an arrow is left behind, and a leader line from the arrow is connected with a rubber band to your cursor. Click again to place the text—it shows up in a text edit box already highlighted, so you can just begin typing to change the default values that come out. Notice, however, that the default value, in this case, is the area of that face you pointed at—handy, right? If you try clicking on other objects, such as an edge, or a component, you will get relevant information about those objects.

If you happen to click on an area where there is no object, SketchUp will place a piece of anchored text on that location on the screen—give it a try. This can be both handy, as the text will remain in place, no matter how much you zoom in or out or pan around, but also aggravating, as the text can get in the way of a particular view.

Figure 3.5 *Text, with and without leader lines.*

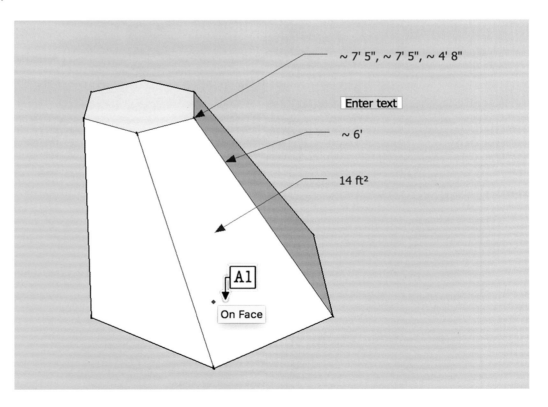

The *Paint Bucket* tool

Okay, who doesn't like the *Paint Bucket*? It's fun to take a monochromatic model and bring it to life with colors and image-based textures. The most basic rule about the paint bucket is that you can only paint faces. You can paint with colors, images, or even imported images. Click on the *Paint Bucket* tool, and you should see the *Colors* menu pop up. Navigate through the tabs and collections to find a color or image that you like, click on it, and then click on a surface to apply the material texture or color. The Mac and Windows versions of SketchUp have the same library of colors and textures, but organize them differently, as you can see in Figure 3.6.

SketchUp faces have two sides, and it is possible to paint each of those sides with a different material. This is particularly important when you are creating objects that people can get inside of, such as a box for a room, or even in a piece of furniture that you might see from many angles. Colors can be chosen using menus that have a color wheel, RGB sliders, or crayons. The Windows version, however, doesn't have the colors displayed using pencils or a color wheel. Click on the brick icon to see a list of all of the categories of colors and textures in the system, called **collections**.

Click on the *Home* button to see which colors and textures are used in the current model. To modify a material, right-click on its icon in the menu and choose *Edit* from the context menu. This adds a section to the bottom of the *Colors* menu, where you can change a number of different properties of the material. If it's a color, you can change the RGB value,

Figure 3.6 *Mac and Windows versions of the* Colors *menu.*

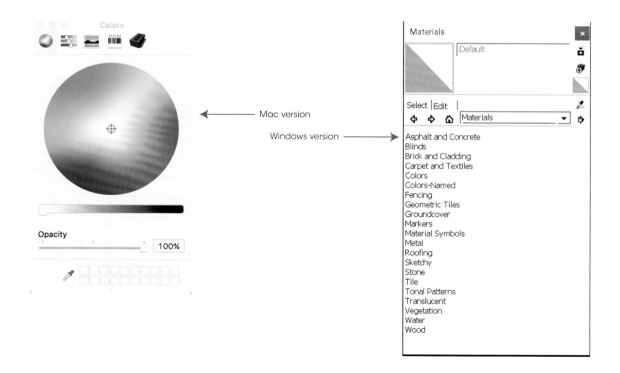

or rename it, if you want. Click on the *Texture* button to add an image file. If there already is an image file, you can change the scaling that makes it either larger or smaller when applied to a surface, or replace it with another image. When you're done, click the *Close* button.

If you want to use a material that's already in your model, click the *Eyedropper* tool at the bottom of the *Texture Palettes* tab, or just hold down ⌘ (ALT on a PC). This will give you an eyedropper cursor that you can use to suck up a copy of any texture used on any surface in the model—this is known as **sampling**. Whichever material you sample will become the active one, and you will see the *Paint Bucket* cursor appear again, so you can paint to your heart's delight.

Managing content with external applications

There are a number of tools related to interactivity with the other applications and libraries at the end of the toolbar. One accesses an online database of SketchUp content, another adds apps on top of the basic SketchUp interface, and the last sends your model to a page layout program.

Figure 3.7 *Those other tools at the end of the toolbar.*

3D Warehouse   Extension Warehouse   Send to LayOut

THE 3D WAREHOUSE

The next tool is probably the biggest time-saver you'll find: an online library of free, ready-made components of all sorts. Just tap on the tool to bring up the 3D Warehouse interface, where you can search, browse, and download any of tens of thousands of models users have posted, all for free. You can even upload your creations to share with the SketchUp world.

Many of these models are quite extensive and carefully done, but some are complete garbage, so be careful to check the scale and configuration of the model to make sure it's what you were expecting. Even the ones that are not so great, though, will provide you with a starting point that you can modify to suit your needs, so that you don't have to re-create every single piece of furniture in your project.

Click on the large image preview to import—SketchUp will prompt you to choose between opening the selected component as a separate file or importing it directly into your model. If you're confident that the component will work, by all means, load it directly into your model. If it appears that there are some extraneous elements inside the component, such as scale figures, or unwanted pieces of furniture, open it separately to remove these elements first—this will keep the complexity of your main

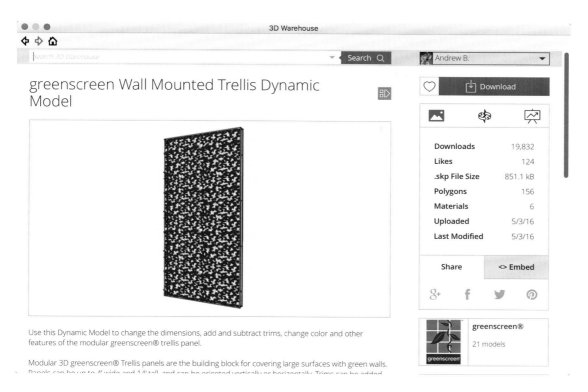

greenscreen Wall Mounted Trellis Dynamic Model

Downloads 19,832
Likes 124
.skp File Size 851.1 kB
Polygons 156
Materials 6
Uploaded 5/3/16
Last Modified 5/3/16

Share <> Embed

greenscreen®
21 models

Use this Dynamic Model to change the dimensions, add and subtract trims, change color and other features of the modular greenscreen® trellis panel.

Modular 3D greenscreen® Trellis panels are the building block for covering large surfaces with green walls. Panels can be up to 4' wide and 14' tall, and can be oriented vertically or horizontally. Trims can be added.

model more manageable. Save the purged component into your project folder, and choose *File > Import* to bring it into your current model.

Figure 3.8 *The 3D Warehouse browser.*

EXTENSION WAREHOUSE

The Extension Warehouse is another online library that you can access—an app store of sorts for plugins that you can add to SketchUp, many of which are free, and some of which can be purchased. There is a search bar where you can look for handy tools to add to SketchUp. You'll need a Trimble or Google account (a legacy of Google's ownership of SketchUp a while back) to log in and download apps. Information about which extensions you've added will be attached to your account, so if and when you upgrade SketchUp, it'll be easier to find all of your favorite apps. All through the text, references are given to extensions that might be useful for the task at hand.

The library is constantly growing and changing, so there are always new ones to try, and a majority are free, or at least free to try. There is a whole category of extensions specific to interior design, which can help manage furniture components in your model, for example, or generate schedules. Other extensions will help model types of geometry, such as soap bubbles or Bezier curves, or will add photo-realistic rendering and lighting calculation capabilities.

You can browse through the entire library, search, or take a look at the top extensions within a given industry. For interior design, there are

Extensions are written in a special, object-oriented programming language called Ruby. The language is open source, and only requires some sort of text editor to use, so give it a try.

Just finished making a really cool component? Log in to the 3D Warehouse using your Google account, and you can upload yours for other people to use.

extensions that range from helping you create furniture, stairs, and walls, to helping you create furniture counts and materials take-offs.

SEND TO LAYOUT TOOL

The last tool, *Send to LayOut*, opens up your SketchUp model in a page composition application that comes free with SketchUp Pro (it is not included with the free Make version). This software is very important for producing presentation boards from SketchUp, especially orthographic drawings like plans and sections. Once your model is linked to a LayOut file, any changes you make in the design will be reflected in the final page compositions. This is where you can draw up construction details and lay out whole sheets of construction drawings, too. It's pretty complex, though, and so all of Unit III is dedicated to the uses of LayOut.

THE EXTENSION MANAGER

You might be tempted to accumulate quite a few extensions for SketchUp, just like you might overload your phone with too many apps. SketchUp has a built-in function called the Extension Manager to help you choose which extensions you'd like to run and keep those apps up to date. If you're finding that your system is slowing down, uninstalling an app will help SketchUp boot up faster. Note that it's not possible to completely

Figure 3.9 *The Extension Warehouse.*

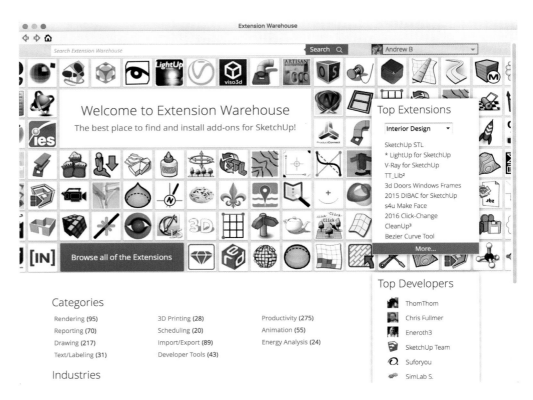

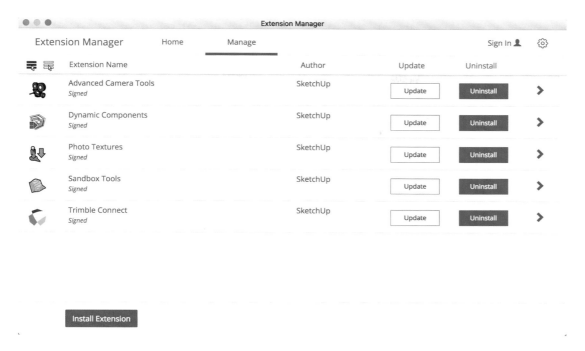

remove an extension from your library here—you'll find the option on the My Extensions section of the Extension Warehouse interface.

Figure 3.10 *The Extension Manager.*

Try it out!

- Print a screenshot of your SketchUp drawing area and label the three axes and the origin.
- Print an image of a tube and a box shape. Label every possible object snapping point.
- Download a model of a sofa from the 3D Warehouse and use text notes to indicate the different finishes used.
- Download a seating grouping from the 3D Warehouse and choose all different materials.

Key terms

- Collections
- Inferences
- Reference line
- Sampling
- Tool tips

Graphical Controls

LEARNING OBJECTIVES

- Manage toolbars, including the Large Tool Set.
- Compose interior perspective views.
- Create and manage scenes of your model.
- Create section planes to cut away parts of your model.
- Identify the characteristics of standard **orthographic** views.
- Apply basic styles to your views.

SketchUp is a lot like a smartphone, in that there are a lot of features, but many of them are not apparent at first glance, or until you install specialized apps. The default user interface has only the *Getting Started* toolbar, which, as we've seen, is a great way to introduce yourself to the capabilities of SketchUp. There are quite a few additional tools that we'll need to create more complicated geometry and views. Sections through a model are particularly important when evaluating interiors projects, as they help to compose the ceiling plane as it relates to what's happening at the floor plan level. Interior perspectives require some additional controls to create compelling compositions.

Launching the Large Tool Set

This is the one aspect of SketchUp where the Windows and Mac versions are arranged quite differently. In general, tools on the Mac version are mostly added one by one, whereas on the Windows version, whole toolbars are added or removed.

See the Online Resources for a printable sheet of keyboard shortcuts for both Mac and Windows.

CUSTOMIZING THE MAC TOOLBAR

On Mac, choose *View > Tool Palettes > Large Tool Set* to call up a larger collection of tools. Many of these tools duplicate the ones that are on the default tool bar.

Other tools visible on this toolset were actually hidden underneath other stacked tools, such as the *Arc* tool. To customize which tools are visible, right-click on a blank area of the toolbar, and choose *Customize Toolbar* from the context menu.

Drag any tool that you'd like up onto the toolbar area, or down into the default toolbar. You can also drag tools off the toolbar at the top of your screen—there's a cute puff-of-smoke animation as they disappear—to remove all of the default tools that are duplicated on the Large Tool Set, which is all the drawing and editing tools. Many users will prefer smaller buttons, to better take advantage of a small screen—every pixel counts! Click *Done* to apply the new settings and exit.

If a particular tool has a keyboard shortcut, you'll see it where the tool is found in the pull-down menus. If there isn't one, you can assign one—see the section on shortcuts in Chapter 7 for instructions.

Figure 4.1 *The Large Tool Set.*

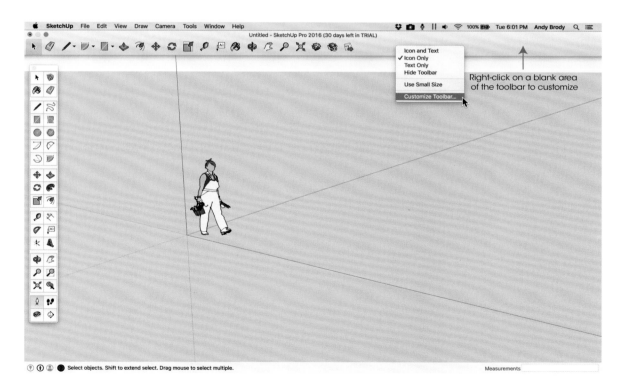

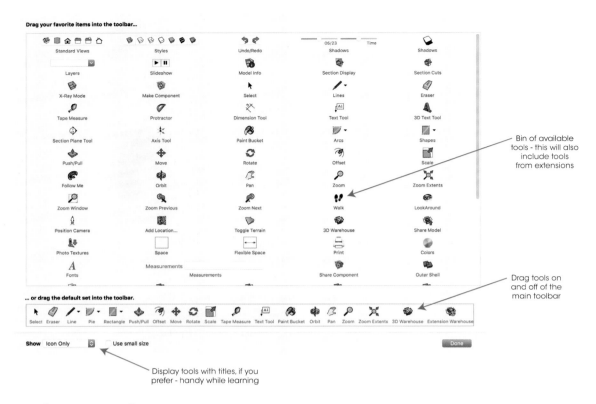

Figure 4.2 *The customize toolbar dialog box.*

CUSTOMIZING THE WINDOWS TOOLBAR

On the Windows version, choose *View > Toolbars*, and you'll call up a dialog box where you can check off the Large Tool Set and un-check the *Getting Started* toolbar. While here, you can also click on the *Advanced* tab and choose the option for small buttons, if you prefer.

One of the other toolbars you might want to add is the standard toolbar, which has all of those familiar buttons such as *Copy*, *Paste*, and *Save*.

Figure 4.3 *The Windows toolbars dialog box.*

All of these tools are available from the drop-down lists, and you can also assign keyboard shortcuts to them, if you're a typing kind of person, so it's possible to work in a clean screen type of mode.

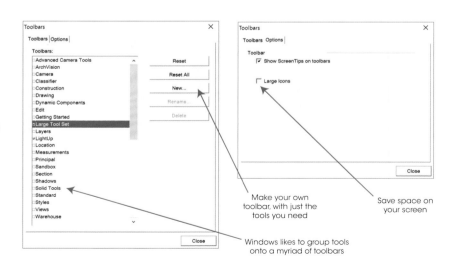

As you gain skills in SketchUp, you will find that you'll add or subtract toolbars depending on what you're doing. This is particularly true when you add extensions to the application, which are like mini app collections, to do specialized activities. You can also add a new toolbar here, which is handy if there is a very particular set of tools that you use. Just drag tools onto the new toolbar to populate it. Note that you need to find out which toolbars the tools you want are hiding on, open them up, and then drag them onto your new toolbar.

Looking to waste some time creating organic shapes? Activate the *Sandbox* toolbar and try out some of the tools. You can create a grid, and then *Smoove* it up, which is sort of like *Push/Pull*, only more cool.

Slicing open the model

Section planes are a special drawing element that slice away a part of the model hiding whatever is behind the location of the plane. They will also change the line weight of anything they slice through, making it much darker than elements seen in the background. They are very handy for creating floor plans, reflected ceiling plans, sections, and elevations. Like other objects, they infer their direction as you are inserting them from the drawing elements that your mouse happens to be over. But also like other objects, as you create them, you can force them to go along one or another axis, using either the arrow keys, or by holding down **Shift** to lock the inference at that point. Here's how to do it:

The top tool in a stack is always the last one used.

1. Go to the exterior overview of your model by clicking on the scene tab at the top of your screen.
2. Then, click on the *Section Plane* tool in the lower right of the Large Tool Set.
3. Move your mouse into the drawing area and over part of the model. You will see a green box with four arrows, one at each corner. Normally it's facing down, but as you move your mouse over vertical surfaces it will face in the direction normal to those surfaces.
4. Click on the left side wall of the model, and you will see the side wall disappear. The section plane is now a sort of orange color.
5. Click on the *Select* tool.
6. Click on the edge of the section plane to select it—it should turn blue.
7. Click on the *Move* tool.
8. Click somewhere on the section plane for a base point.
9. Click again in the middle of the windows to move the section plane over.

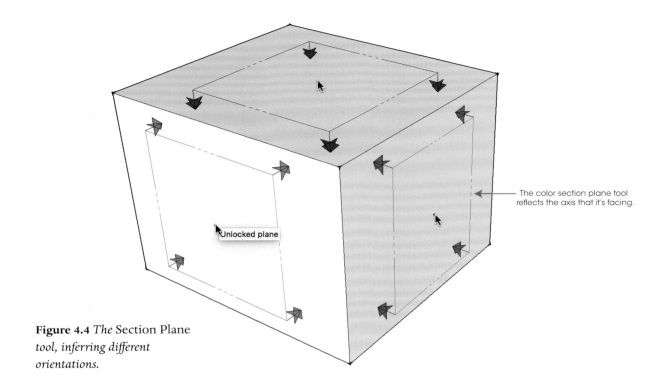

The color section plane tool reflects the axis that it's facing.

Unlocked plane

Figure 4.4 *The* Section Plane *tool, inferring different orientations.*

Section planes can also be rotated, their visibility and status can be saved as part of a scene, and they can even be part of animations.

Figure 4.5 *The section plane in the model.*

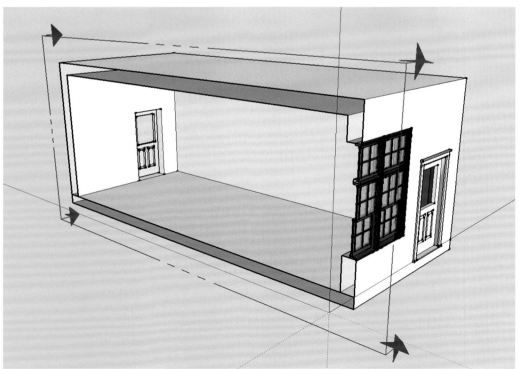

Figure 4.10 *The* Scenes *palette.*

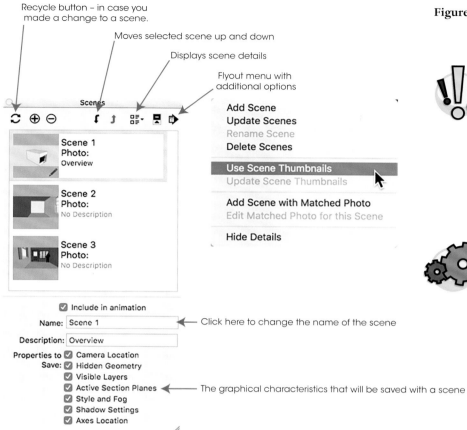

Recycle button – in case you made a change to a scene.

Moves selected scene up and down

Displays scene details

Flyout menu with additional options

Add Scene
Update Scenes
Rename Scene
Delete Scenes

Use Scene Thumbnails
Update Scene Thumbnails

Add Scene with Matched Photo
Edit Matched Photo for this Scene

Hide Details

Click here to change the name of the scene

The graphical characteristics that will be saved with a scene

Sometimes imported components can modify a scene so that it doesn't remember all the properties—they will be un-checked when you update. This can be frustrating if you've just saved a dozen scenes, but they don't reflect view changes.

Most places where you can select from a list, such as in the *Scenes* palette, allow certain selection modifiers, such as ⌘A to select all. You can also click on the top item in the list, hold down *Shift*, and click on another item further down—this will select the first, last, and all interstitial items. Holding down ⌘ adds or subtracts from the selection set.

This menu is very handy to have open when creating and editing views of a model. You can add and subtract scenes and also change the order, which is useful when creating an animation. It's handy to leave the details visible, by clicking on the *Details* button, to see what SketchUp is remembering about this scene. Sometimes, when you import components, they have scene settings with them, and this can muddle up your settings.

See the section in Chapter 7 titled "Geolocation" for instructions on how to define the exact location for your model, which will make the shadows accurate.

Daylighting settings, including if the sun is out or not, can be saved as part of a scene.

Shadows

SketchUp will not produce photo-realistic drawings without an extension, but it does have one very realistic option: shadows. They are based on the geolocation of the model and also time of day. To turn them on, choose *View > Shadows*, and just like that, the sun is out.

Some nice shadows cast by window mullions or furnishings can add some interest to a view, as well as critical depth cues. If your model has been geolocated and oriented realistically, this sort of view can give you a good idea of locations in your project that might be prone to glare at different

Figure 4.11 *Here comes the sun.*

Interior views are, by their nature, inside the building, and so will need electric lighting to appear realistic. See Chapter 20 to learn how photo-realistic rendering can be accomplished.

times of day, and which ones can have brightness easily controlled by window treatments, for example. To set the time of day and the date, you'll need to open the full set of sun controls: choose *Window > Shadows*. From here, it is possible to have very precise control of daylighting conditions.

Click the *Display Secondary Selection Pane* button to expose all the controls available. From here, it's possible to adjust most characteristics of the daylighting scheme. Set the time zone, known as the Universal Time Coordinated (UTC) to your location—the default is for Boulder, Colorado, where SketchUp was created. Adjust the shadows to produce an interesting view or to check for glare. It is also possible to do still and animated daylighting studies, comparing the lighting conditions at different times of the day and the year.

Because SketchUp supports transparent textures, it is also possible to study the effect of different types of window treatments, including shades that let in different percentages of daylight, sheer materials, and other types of fabrics. This is particularly important to control glare and to anticipate the deterioration of materials due to direct sunlight exposure.

In Windows, choose *View > Toolbars*, and then check the box next to *Shadows*.

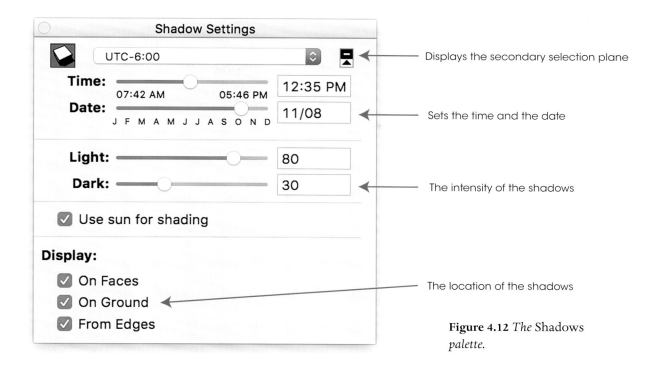

Displays the secondary selection plane

Sets the time and the date

The intensity of the shadows

The location of the shadows

Figure 4.12 *The* Shadows *palette.*

Fog

This is another one of those features that may not be the most realistic, but adds some mystery and a sense of depth to a view. It is especially effective in a large space, where it can be used to slightly obscure deeper parts of the room. It can also be used to make the view out of a window appear foggy, which is nice if you're using an image file for a backdrop. Choose *View > Fog* to activate. Fog density is based on distance from the **station point**. Fog settings are global, so they will apply to every scene in an animation. Preview the animation to make sure it doesn't obscure details you were hoping to see along your path. As with shadows, the depth and density of the fog can be controlled using a special palette—choose *Window > Fog* to activate.

From here, you can control the front and rear cut-off of the fog, which makes it possible to adjust for larger or smaller spaces. You can also make the color blue or red or whatever you want, which can be creepy, but also interesting.

Creating an exterior backdrop

Sometimes it adds an element of realism to put an image in behind a window. You can't add images automatically to any view, but you can insert images that are attached to shapes, like a rectangle.

Use two different scenes of the same view, one in the morning and one in the evening, to study the lighting during the day. See the Online Resources for an example of a daylighting study animation using these scenes.

See the section on filters in Chapter 21 to find out how to use blurring to achieve a similar sort of effect.

For fog to work, make sure *Use Hardware Acceleration* is turned on in the SketchUp Preferences.

Figure 4.13 *The foggy room.*

Figure 4.14 *The Fog palette.*

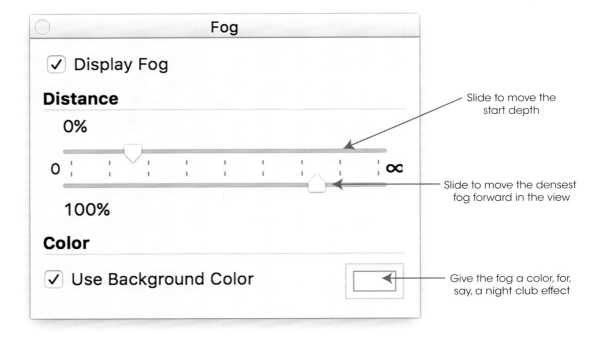

1. Draw a rectangle about 100' away from the front window.
2. Search for a high-resolution image where the camera height above the ground appears to be more or less the same eye height as in your view from SketchUp. Save the image to your project folder.
3. Insert your image file so that it is organized vertically.
4. Move the image up or down until the horizon line in the image matches the ground line in the model. This will make it appear more or less normal when viewed from inside the model.
5. Check your interior view to make sure it looks realistic.

This method works better than just, say, painting an image directly on a window, because the exterior view will shift as the camera moves. It's not as realistic as a rendered dome over your project, but for most still images, this works well.

Want to extrude an image file so that it has some depth? Right-click on the inserted image and choose *Explode* from the context menu. It can now be edited like any face in SketchUp. If you just want to be able to paint that image on other surfaces, choose *Use As Material* from the context menu.

Can't seem to select your image file? Make sure you have Image Files selected as the file type.

Figure 4.15 *The model with an image behind the window.*

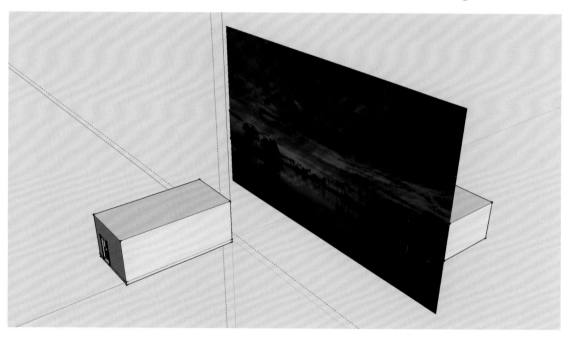

Try it out!

- Open the Large Tool Set. On Mac, delete repeated tools, and add *Save*, *Undo*, and *Redo* to the standard toolbar. On a PC, deactivate the default toolbar and activate the standard toolbar.

- Create an interior perspective with a 55° **field of view**. Orient it so that there's a balance of floor, ceiling, and walls.
- Insert a section plane along the north-south axis of the model.
- Create true, orthographic floor plans and section views, and save each as a scene.
- Create scenes for three different perspectives, the plan, and a section in your project.
- Create a style for sections that are active but not visible, and another where sections are inactive but visible.
- Create bird's-eye and worm's-eye views of your model and save them to scenes.

Key terms

- Field of view
- Orthographic
- Section plane
- Station point

Creating Furniture

LEARNING OBJECTIVES

- Identify the key geometric parts of a piece of furniture.
- Assemble a furniture model using multiple pieces.
- Modify entity properties by entering a measurement.
- Organize objects using groups and components where appropriate.
- Design and draw complex architectural edge profiles.
- Explain the procedure for painting objects inside a component.
- Create a custom image-based texture.
- Summarize differences between components and groups.

While many interior designers never get the opportunity to create a custom piece of furniture for a client, most will have to specify pieces from standard manufacturers and designers. There are many, many ready-made models for these sorts of interior elements, but sometimes it's necessary to create a new one from scratch, making this a basic skill for an interior designer. The techniques involved are a good vehicle for learning SketchUp, and will also help when working with furnishings and equipment models created by others.

Modeling a piece of furniture in SketchUp involves all of the basic drawing and editing skills learned in the last two chapters, and also a means of organizing the geometry you create for ease of use. Let's create a simple coffee table, with four tapered metal legs and a top made out of wood with a profiled edge. Figure 5.1 shows an image of a handsome table we will try to reproduce in this chapter.

This table has some nice, simple features, including tapered legs, an edge with a profile, and a very nice wood grain. To re-create any object

See the Online Resources for a video demonstrating the creation of this model.

Figure 5.1 *Inspiration for our coffee table.*

Top is a rectangular shape with a profiled edge

Rails are rectangular shapes

Legs are round and tapered

in SketchUp, it's best to study the object first and try to determine which drawing techniques will be needed for each part. For the table, let's build it from the ground up, drawing the approximate size using the scale figure that comes with SketchUp. The basic steps are going to be: create a leg component, create the tabletop, give it a profiled edge, and then paint everything the different textures.

Create the legs

Let's start with a simple extruded circle, give it a tapered profile, and then convert it into a component. Once the leg component is created, we can make the copies.

1. Activate the *Circle* tool as before.

   Notice the measurements box on the lower right—it will show the diameter of the circle you just drew (see Figure 2.2 for the location). To change that value, just type the number you want, and then hit *Enter*—no need to click anywhere. This trick will only work immediately after completing the circle—you can't come back and change it after you've activated another tool. Make the circle have a 1" radius by typing 1↵. SketchUp assumes inches, so there's no need to type in the apostrophe.

2. Activate the *Push/Pull* tool to pull up the circle into a tube.

3. Click once on the circle to define which surface will be *Push/Pulled*, and then move your mouse vertically just a bit to indicate the direction for the surface to extrude.

4. Rather than click a second time, just type in 17↵ for the distance now. As with the circle radius, the number will show up in the measurements box, drawing the line 17" in the direction that your mouse was heading. This technique saves one whole click—over the course of a lifetime of drawing, this could be significant!

Some drawing entities can be changed by changing their properties numerically instead of graphically. Every object in the SketchUp environment has some sort of information about it, and many have properties that can be changed by typing in values, rather than using drawing and editing tools.

Lathed profiles are much harder to make. See the Online Resources for a video tutorial.

5. Using the *Select* command, select the bottom circle that forms the lower part of the leg.
6. Right-click on the circle and choose *Entity Info*. This will bring up a menu with information about the circle, and if you have a larger selection set, shared properties of all the objects you have selected.
7. Change the radius of the bottom circle to one quarter of an inch. Now you have a tapered leg!

Note that SketchUp objects can be placed on different layers, which can be quite handy for complex models and for things like creating design options within a given space. See Chapter 10 for more information about layers and applying layers to objects.

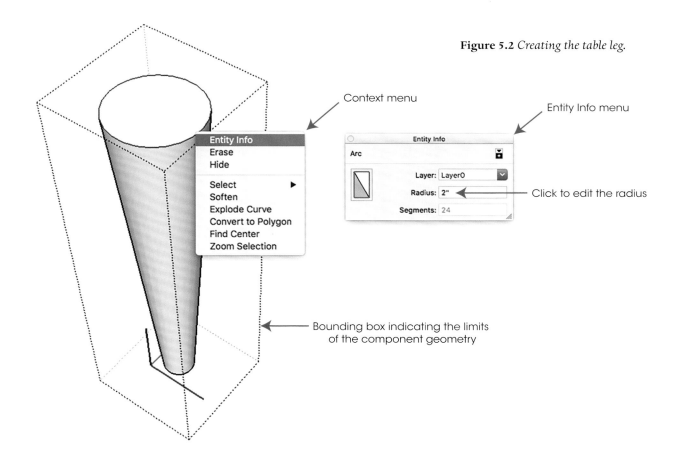

Figure 5.2 *Creating the table leg.*

Some objects can be quite tricky to select if there are many building elements in the background. Remember to orbit, zoom in, or zoom out as needed to get the easiest view to work in.

In addition to typing in a value, you can also use modifiers with certain tools. An example is creating an array (see Chapter 10).

Copy the legs

When creating repeated parts like the legs, we want to consider the optimal behavior for the copies have. We could just select the objects, and use the copy feature of the *Move* tool to make several copies, but each one would just be a collection of unique lines, arcs, and faces, so any changes would have to be made to each leg. We could convert the objects into a **group**, which is a collection of model entities glued together into one easily manipulated macro element. This would make them easier to move and copy without getting "sticky." Each group is unique, though, so changing the properties of one leg will only affect that one group. To have them all match, even after a change is made, we need to turn the tapered tube into a **component**, which, like a group, is a collection of drawing elements. The difference is that all instances of a component will reflect any changes made to any one of them. As designers, this last method will give us the most flexibility.

Select the leg using the *Select* tool and whichever selection technique you prefer—triple-click on the legs or use a selection or crossing window. Right-click on the selection and choose *Make Component* from the context sensitive menu. Give it a name—something clever, like "leg." Now, select the newly created component, click the *Move* command, and then tap ^ to make a copy. Click once anywhere in the model to define the **base point** for the operation, which is one of the two points needed to define the displacement and angular direction of the tool. Then, move your mouse a few feet over and click again to define the displacement. The angle is defined by the location of the second click relative to the first click. In this case, also allow SketchUp to snap to the red axis, and place the leg some distance away. Once again, you can type in a distance using the measurements box, or just estimate, using the scale figure in the background as a reference, as we did in the previous chapter.

Draw the tabletop

Because the legs are components, objects that touch them won't stick to them in the way that they would if the legs were just free objects. We can draw the tabletop right on top of the legs, create an overhang, and then apply an edge profile without affecting the legs at all.

1. Activate the *Rectangle* tool and then draw from the top of one leg across to the catty-corner leg top.

2. Push/Pull to give it some thickness—1" looks about right. Since we only have the photo to go on, use your aesthetic judgment here, along with your knowledge of materials and ergonomics.

3. Push/Pull the perimeter of the leg tabletop to create the overhang.

That's the basic geometric shape of your tabletop—now let's add a profile to the edge of the tabletop. Rather than make an exact copy, let's add a few arcs and a square corner—feel free to use your aesthetic judgment and experiment.

4. Draw the profile along one corner.

5. Choose the *Follow Me* tool, which is listed under the *Tools* pull-down menu.

6. Click on the profile that you would like to leave around the perimeter of the table.

7. Similar to the *Push/Pull* tool, the selected profile will extrude along your mouse path. This tool, however, allows you to continue around the edges—just move your mouse along the top and then along an adjacent side edge to see the extrusion continue.

8. To quickly make it wrap all the way around the table, hold the ALT key while dragging your mouse, and the profile will wrap entirely around the tabletop. Either way, just click to complete the operation.

Now let's use the *Offset* tool to create the geometry of the rails.

9. Select just the tabletop, and not the legs, using the *Select* tool.

10. Right-click on the selection and choose *Make a Group* from the context menu.

11. Double-click on the new group in order to edit.

12. Orbit the tabletop so that you can see the bottom surface.

13. Activate the *Offset* tool and then click on the bottom edge of the tabletop to select it.

Don't remember how to make a copy of an object? See Chapter 2 to refresh your memory.

The angles that SketchUp prefers to snap to can be changed under the *Units* tab of the model info dialog box.

Do your arcs seem a little faceted, instead of smooth? See Chapter 12 to learn how to smooth the edges.

Having a really bad day? If you want to quickly undo all changes since your last save, choose *File > Revert*.

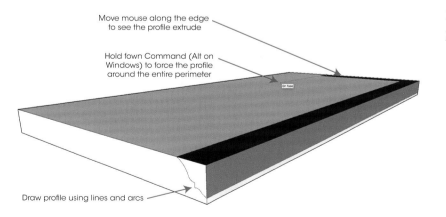

Move mouse along the edge to see the profile extrude

Hold fown Command (Alt on Windows) to force the profile around the entire perimeter

On Face

Draw profile using lines and arcs

Figure 5.3 *Creating an edge profile.*

You can control whether or not you see the rest of the model during an editing operation by using *Toggle View > Component Edit > Hide Rest of Model.*

14. Move the profile in from the edge until it appears to overlap the leg, and click to place the offset profile.
15. Activate the *Offset* tool again, this time selecting the inner profile and using an offset of approximately an inch.
16. Use the *Push/Pull* tool to stretch this new rectilinear profile down approximately 2.5" to create the rails.
17. Click outside of the group editing bounding box to close the editor.

Add texture to the table

In the computer modeling world, a **texture** is any image-based material applied to one or both sides of a face in the model. This is different than a **solid color**, which is generally defined by its mix of **red, green, and blue (RGB)** pigments. Components and groups, however, need special consideration, because the objects within them can be a different material from whatever the overall entity is painted. Dumping paint on a single component only paints that component, so we need to "open" up the component by editing it, and paint the individual objects inside it. Just double-click on one of the legs to edit—it doesn't matter which one. The rest of the model will display as gray, with a bounding box to indicate the limit of the component you're working on (see Figure 5.5). Use the paint bucket to completely cover the leg with a chrome texture from the material library. The other instances of the component, if they are visible, will reflect this change.

Figure 5.4 *Adding the rails.*

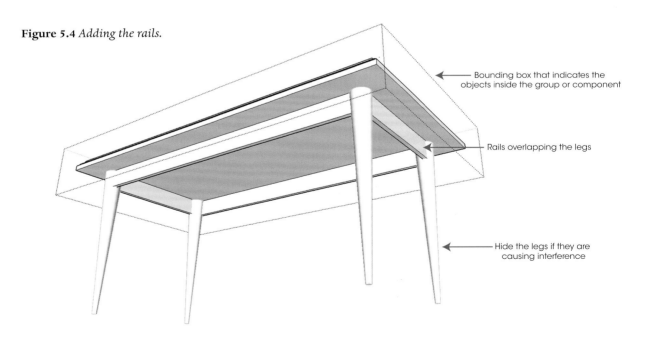

Bounding box that indicates the objects inside the group or component

Rails overlapping the legs

Hide the legs if they are causing interference

The tabletop is a bit trickier to paint, because there aren't any great solid wood textures that come with SketchUp, so we'll have to create our own.

Faces that overlap in the middle, rather than along an edge, don't produce an edge line. To create one where the legs and rails overlap, right-click on the rails and choose *Intersect > With Model* from the context menu.

1. Open your favorite internet search engine.
2. Switch to searching for image files.
3. Look for search options—most search engines will allow you to filter the results for higher resolution images, either by a pixel value or by selecting "large" files.
4. Search for a seamless image—this indicates an image where the left edge matches up graphically with the right edge, and the top edge also matches the bottom edge.

See the Online Resources for a video tutorial showing how to create a round tabletop with a profile edge.

Image-based textures in SketchUp **tile**, which is to say that they will repeat with copies of the original image to fill up whatever face you are trying to cover, even if that face is larger than the original image. If the image is not seamless, it will be possible to see the joint where one image butts up against one of the copies.

See the Online Resources for links to sources of seamless textures.

5. Save the file into your project folder and re-name it if it's not clear what it is.
6. Back in SketchUp, choose *File > Import*.
7. Browse to find the file you saved, and be sure to check the option for *Use as Texture* so that the image is used to paint in the model.
8. Click once on the tabletop to plant the lower left corner of the image, and then a second time to define to the overall size of the image. For now, just cover part of the tabletop.

Figure 5.5 *Painting the leg component.*

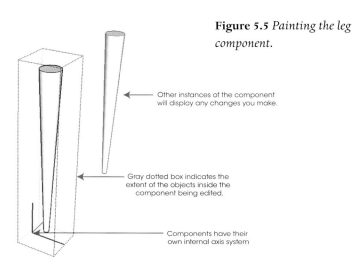

Other instances of the component will display any changes you make.

Gray dotted box indicates the extent of the objects inside the component being edited.

Components have their own internal axis system

Want to paint a shape with complex ins and outs? Select the entire shape before applying a texture with the paint bucket.

Rendering textures based on imported image files can sometimes lead to unexpected results. See the section on texture sizes in the Appendix for further information.

9. Open the materials library, either by clicking on the *Paint Bucket* tool, or by choosing *Window > Materials*.

10. Click on the home icon and you should see all of the materials used in the project. If you have a specific size board for the wood, this is where you would type in the dimension. You can also re-name the material now and colorize the image if you'd like to adjust the appearance.

11. Click OK to exit the menu and close the Materials Browser.

12. This texture needs some additional tweaking to look right on the tabletop, but it would be better to see the changes live on the model, to make a better design decision. Set the model in a view where you can see the wood clearly.

13. Right-click on the tabletop and choose *Texture > Position* from the context menu.

14. The rest of the model will become gray, and you'll see a series of pins on the corners of your original image. These will allow you to stretch, move, or distort the texture, right on the model. Rotate the image file so that the long axis is parallel to the length of the tabletop.

15. Tap ↺ to exit texture modification.

If you happen to be using that same texture somewhere else in the model, be sure that you haven't just messed up some other element. If

Figure 5.6 *Editing the wood material.*

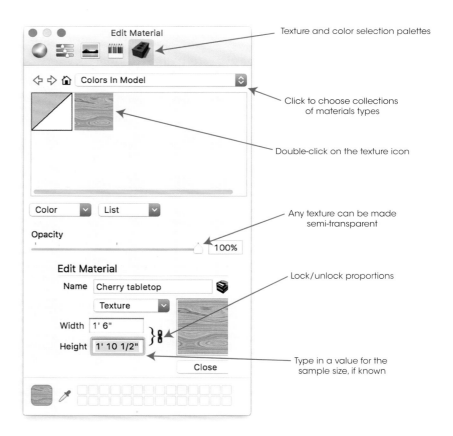

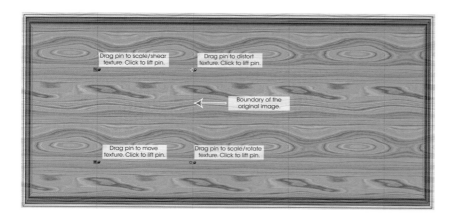

Figure 5.7 *Modifying a texture.*

Want the grain to be a book-matched version of this texture? You'll have to use Photoshop to create this special texture. See the Online Resources for a video on how to do this.

you're not sure, before editing the image, select it in the Materials menu, right-click on it, and choose Duplicate from the context menu. Then just make sure you use that new texture on the object where you plan to modify its dimensions.

Save the SketchUp file

Do we really need to talk about how to save a document? Well, probably not the basic operation, which is the same for almost any application you'll use: ⌘S brings up the *Save As* menu (or just saves the document, if you've already saved it once before). From there, you should choose a location within your filing system that makes sense.

SketchUp files have their own **file extension**, which is a special set of letters appended to a file name that the OS uses to determine which application to use to view and open the file. SketchUp file names all end with the SKP extension, although both the Mac OS and Windows like to hide those extensions, perhaps because it's a little too easy to change them by accident, along with the file name. SketchUp will also automatically save a backup file in same location as your main file, with a special file extension, SKB. If something horrible happens and your original file gets corrupted, you can use this backup to replace the original. The trick is that you won't be able to open it until you change the file extension from SKB to SKP—this will tell your OS that the file should be opened with SketchUp. Then the file should open up without a problem.

Most medium to large offices have a shared folder on their internal network where homemade components and other project standards are

To see the full file name on Mac, open the Finder Preferences, and on the advanced panel, check the radio button next to *Show All Filename Extensions*. In Windows, open Windows Explorer, and on the *View* ribbon, check the radio button next to *File Name Extensions*.

There are a number of different extensions that can help with managing components in your models, such as Project Sketch, and inserting groups of new ones, such as DeskMakers.

saved. These are often locked, so that consistency from model to model and project to project can be enforced. For students and solo practitioners, it's still a good idea to save components into a personal library that you can draw on. This folder would be a good one to have as part of an automatic backup system, such as a mirrored drive or through an online service, so that you never lose any of your hard work.

If you plan to share this component, delete any extraneous geometry in the model—especially anything hidden. This includes the scale figure and any other elements you might have drawn. A nice touch is to force the component to be glued to the horizontal plane, so that it automatically ends up in the correct orientation when someone inserts it into their model. You can find this option under the *File* tab of the model info dialog box. Be sure to save the file in a location and with a name that you will remember, and that is also descriptive.

Try it out!

- Print out a photo of a piece of furniture you'd like to model and identify the basic geometric shapes that it could be modeled from. Indicate which parts might benefit from being in a group or a component.
- Model the piece of furniture in the above exercise.
- Create a box for a room and add a complex crown molding profile along the entire perimeter of the ceiling.
- Download an image of a laminate pattern from a manufacturer's catalog and apply it to the table component.
- Create a round tabletop with an edge profile and tapered legs.
- Create table legs with a turned profile.
- Create a table with a drawer.

Key Terms

- Base point
- Component
- File extension
- Group
- Red, green, and blue (RGB) color
- Solid color
- Texture
- Tile

Modeling a Simple
Interiors Project

LEARNING OBJECTIVES

- Identify the difference between exterior and interior architectural models.
- Explain the north-south orientation of SketchUp's model axes.
- Create the interior volume of a project from basic planar shapes.
- Manage geometry with layers.
- Search 3D Warehouse for door and window components to populate the model.
- Create and save views of the model for quick access.

Starting a new project is always an exciting time in a design office—an empty volume from which your design will emerge. There is a difference in strategy when modeling a project for interiors versus something like site planning or an architectural model. If you were designing, say, an entire building, you could begin by modeling the exterior skin of the project, using various modeling and editing tools. You wouldn't have to worry about wall thicknesses, since all you'd see is the outside of the shapes you draw. Interiors projects, on the other hand, require that you model the interior volume that you'll be renovating, requiring much more precision and detail from the base model, just to get started on the project.

In either case, certain basic strategies can be used to keep the model organized, to make it relatively easy to view and manipulate the model during design, and to create the output needed for presentations and construction drawings. We will see that this has implications for how

We will use this project for a few chapters. If there is another project that you'd like to use, by all means, go ahead. There is nothing magical about the configuration of this building or space.

Can't get inside a building to measure? Modeling existing buildings using photos of their exterior and some critical measurements can be quite easy using the *Photo Match* tool.

you take measurements of the existing conditions, how you model the space, how you add built-in elements such as windows, and how you set up views of the design.

The basic steps for generating the existing conditions start with getting good field measurements. Draw the exterior walls first and then any existing interior partitions. Add components for doors and windows and any other existing elements. Put everything on a layer, to help keep things organized, and then save some handy views to make navigating the model a little easier.

Document the existing conditions

Because an interiors project often involves manipulating complex, sometimes historic existing finishes, greater precision can be needed when creating existing conditions drawings. In particular, the distance between the finished faces of surfaces is the critical measurement, since things like tile patterns or paneling spacing can be impacted. These measurements are actually critical to a good design, because they allow us to determine the clearances for furnishings, accessibility, and the patterns of materials.

Figure 6.1 *A model of our retail site.*

Our empty storefront has a nice interior space, and will allow us to explore best practices for modeling for a simple renovation project. The scope of this project will only be **FF&E**, or furnishings, finishes, and equipment, meaning that the project will only involve those elements, and not any parts that affect the structure or skin of the building. We will renovate the front room and create a small café, leaving the rear areas untouched. If this was a real project, then this would be the time to send out the poor, suffering intern to make some precise **field measurements**, which are a set of exact dimensions of a space, including the overall volume and the sizes and arrangement of any elements, such as doors, windows, recesses, soffits, and anything else. All these measurements we will need typically show up in a sketch plan and section, which is then traced in SketchUp to create the empty volume for the project.

Note that it's important, from a design standpoint, to take measurements from a viable substrate—sometimes interior finish systems, such as wainscoting, can actually throw your measurements off quite a bit.

OK, while it's not technically an extension to SketchUp, you can use the Room-Scan app to use your Apple mobile devices to measure existing conditions. It can export a DWG file that SketchUp Pro can import to scale, saving you a lot of time, especially for a large interior.

Trouble getting measurements of a building? Try taking a photo of the egress plan, which is supposed to be posted in a prominent location.

Model the exterior volume

SketchUp can only draw individual faces, which might seem just fine for an interiors-only project. Since we are planning to have floor plans and sections, though, we need to model more than just a single surface for the space—we need to model wall thickness. The problem is that door and window components are designed to cut a hole through only the single surfaces they are placed in. We will need to start by modeling the exterior of the building, adding doors and windows. Later on, we will add in wall thickness, which means we'll have to cut openings into the walls we built.

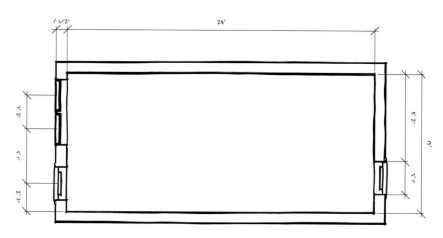

Figure 6.2 *Sketch of the existing conditions.*

Figure 6.3 *The basic shape of the floor plan.*

Building on what we have learned from the last chapter, let's draw the plan shape using a rectangle.

1. Open a new SketchUp model using the *Architectural* template.
2. Click on the *Rectangle* tool.
3. Click on the **origin**, which is the intersection of the red, green, and blue axes, as the first point of displacement.
4. There's no need to click a second time to define the dimension—just type in 15',30'↵ and the rectangle should be drawn correctly.

We learned in an earlier chapter that all SketchUp models are all geo-located, so whatever we draw will be oriented based on that location. In SketchUp, the north-south direction corresponds to the green axis, and the east-west direction corresponds to the red axis, so make sure that you've got the rectangle oriented properly. Fortunately, the poor suffering intern that we sent out to do these measurements oriented their sketch correctly, which is to say, north is facing up.

5. All we need to do now is create the vertical portion of the interior volume. Tap the *Push/Pull* tool.
6. Extrude the rectangle up—once again, we can just type in the dimension, 12'↵, without actually having to click a second time—and create our space.

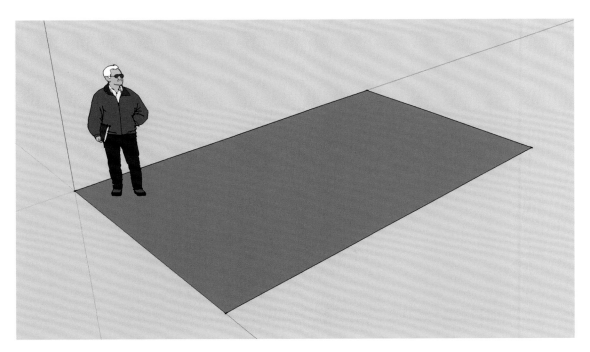

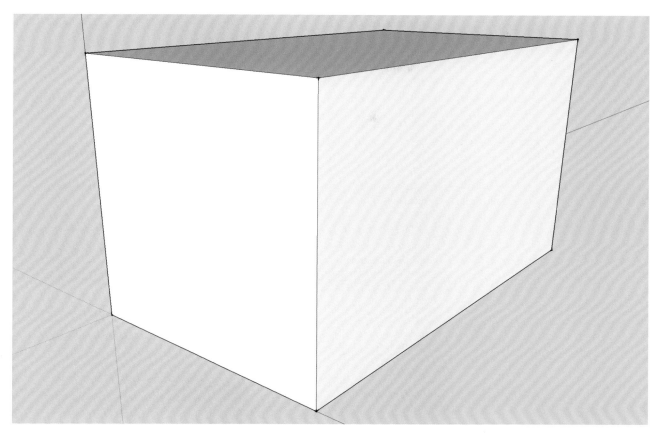

Figure 6.4 *The building volume, from the outside.*

Insert ready-made components

So far, we have created our own objects—a coffee table, and now the interior volume—which is loads of fun, but you wouldn't want to have to create every single building element, and certainly not for standardized elements such as windows and doors. Fortunately, SketchUp has a whole library filled with ready-made objects that we can use. Go to *Menu > Components* to open the Components Inspector. Tap the *Home* button, which cleverly looks like a little house, to see what's loaded onto your computer.

See the Online Resources for a video demonstrating the creation of this model.

In the Windows version, inspectors may already be visible, as Windows prefers to have them all open. On Mac, it's much more of a clean-screen type of environment, so you have to call up these inspectors as needed. If you need more screen space, click on the top bar to minimize the inspector without actually closing it.

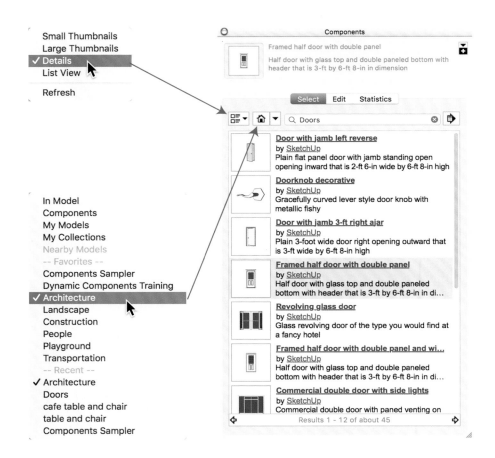

Figure 6.5 *The Components Inspector.*

In the Components Inspector, clicking on the sub-collection icon will jump to placing the new component in your model. If you happen to click on the written name instead of the icon, the 3D Warehouse menu will pop up—see a discussion about how this works in Chapter 2.

There are different groupings of components, which SketchUp calls **collections**. Click on the little down arrow next to the tiny house icon, and then choose *Architecture* from the drop-down list. The architecture library has some of the basic interior elements that are good for getting you started. Many of these are fairly basic in nature, and of course are not tied to exact manufacturers' products. But they are a good way to get started. Click on the *Doors* sub-collection, and you should see a long stack of different kinds of doors that are available. Most of these doors come with a frame, although not all. Let's choose a door component a few down from the top, labeled *Framed Half Door with Double Panel*. Click on the icon, and the door will be connected to your cursor in the model. Click on the exterior wall on the front, along the right bottom edge, to place the door.

Once inserted, the door component remains glued to your cursor until you activate another tool, so you can move it around by moving your mouse. Notice how the door cuts an opening in the wall, allowing you to see into the interior. Note that SketchUp Make, the free version of the software, does not automatically install the whole library of components, so you may have to search for a door that more or less matches what's shown here.

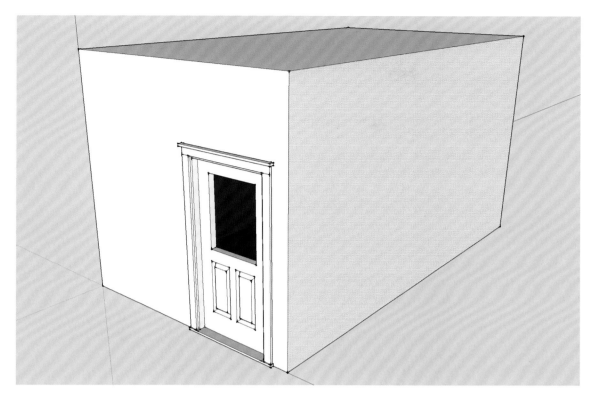

Figure 6.6 *The inserted door.*

Position the door

If this was just an architectural project, we could position the door wherever we thought it would work well. Because it's an interior renovation, however, we actually have dimensions from our field work, so we should use those. Let's draw in a **reference line**, using the *Tape Measure* tool—tap on the tool, and then click in the middle of the front right corner of the building to start measuring. The door opening starts 23" off the exterior corner of the building, but it's easiest to position the door using its center position, which adds another 30", making a total of 51", so type 51↵. A dashed gray reference line should appear where the center of the door should be.

Now, select the door using the *Select* tool, tap the *Move* tool, and then use midpoint of the top of the door as a base point—this may take some zooming and orbiting to be able to see well enough to select. Let's make sure that the door doesn't move up or down, but only left or right—tap the right arrow to force it to move only along the red axis. Now, just move your mouse anywhere on the reference line, and you should see the *Constrained on Line* tool tip. Click, and the door should snap into the correct position.

Some doors and windows will not automatically cut an opening in a face. If that happens, draw a rectangle on the wall first, and then delete that rectangle.

Using your scroll wheel while another tool is active is called a transparent command. The operation of the other tool will be unaffected, so you can make reference to model elements that were not visible when you started the tool. If you were to click on the *Orbit* tool, however, it would interrupt the Copy operation.

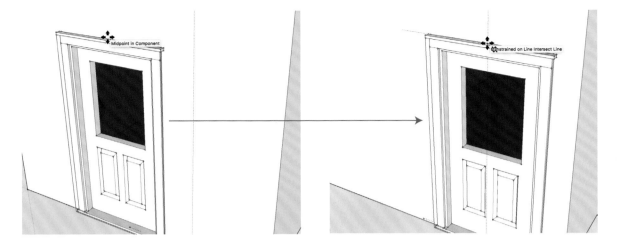

Figure 6.7 *Placing a reference line with the* Tape Measure *tool.*

That was so fun, let's place a copy of the door in the back of the space, for access to the rest of the building—the toilet, storage room, and the rear exit.

1. Select the door.
2. Type ⌘ C to copy it to the system clipboard.
3. Type ⌘ V to paste it from the system clipboard.
4. The door will be attached to your cursor, as before. Click on the rear wall to place it.
5. Click the *Move* tool.
6. Use the upper right corner of the door as a base point.
7. Using the left arrow key, force movement in the red direction.
8. Click and drag your scroll wheel to orbit your model so that you can see the front door.
9. Move your mouse over the corresponding corner in the front door.
10. Click to complete the move.

And now, some windows

There are a couple of double-hung windows in this building, but we'll use another one of the ready-made components. We could draw in reference lines as we did when placing the door, but it's probably easier to use the *Move* tool, in conjunction with the ability to force movement along particular axes. This will allow us to align the window precisely with the trim on the door.

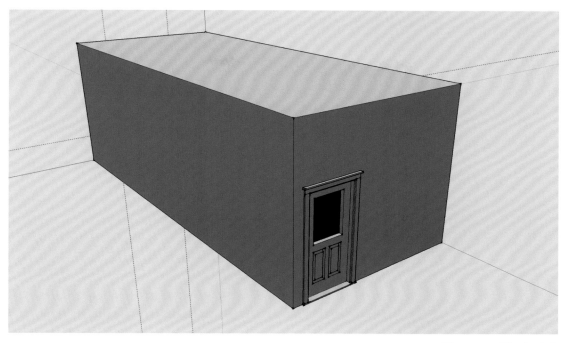

Figure 6.8 *The back door.*

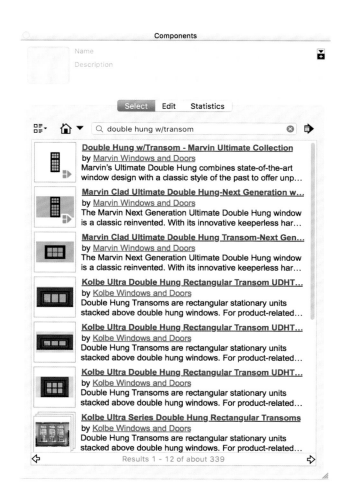

Figure 6.9 *The window search results.*

In SketchUp, layers are mainly used for organization. In LayOut, a particular layer can be isolated and then given unique graphic properties, such as being dashed at red. Overlay this on top of a base plan, and this is how demolition plans, for example, are created.

1. Let's go back to our Component Browser.
2. In the search bar, type in Double Hung w/Transom↵.
3. Let's choose the top one. It's not that I'm getting a kick-back from Marvin Industries—they just happen to make very nice SketchUp components of their products.
4. Click to place the window in the front wall, to the left of the door, but in no particular spot right now.
5. Using the *Tape Measure* tool, draw reference lines 5'1" off the left side wall, and 2'5" above the bottom of the space.
6. Click the *Move* tool so that we can place the window more precisely.
7. Use the lower right corner of the window as the base point—you should see the tool tip *Endpoint in Component*.
8. Move your mouse intersection of the two reference lines—you should see the *Intersection* tool tip. Click to place the window.
9. Click on the *Move* tool again.
10. Tap to ⌥ make a copy.
11. Grab the window by the lower left corner as the base point.
12. Click on the lower right side of the first window to place the copy.

Using locked inferences is much faster than drawing out reference lines. In general, this method is very fast, although it often means that you have to place things incorrectly at first and then fix them later, which can be counterintuitive.

Layer assignments

It's a good idea to try to keep existing geometry separate from the new design elements that you are planning to model. The easiest way to do that is to use the *Layers* feature in SketchUp, which will seem very familiar to users of AutoCAD. Each element in SketchUp, from lines, arcs,

Figure 6.10 *Constraining movement in the blue direction.*

Figure 6.11 *Copying the window using inferences.*

Figure 6.12 *The properly placed window and door.*

and faces, to components and groups, can be assigned to a layer, and these layers can be turned on and off as needed. To see what layers are in your drawing, choose *Window > Layers* to bring up the Layers Inspector.

By default, there is only one layer in an empty SketchUp model, Layer0. This model has a few others, which happened to be imported along with my door and window components. For now, let's leave those alone, and click on the big plus sign to add a new layer, called, cleverly, *Existing Conditions*. Objects can be selected in a number of different ways, but because we don't have anything other than existing objects in our model, let's select all, by typing ⌘A. To add the objects to a

Push/Pulling a surface all the way to the opposite side of a shape will automatically delete the surfaces at both ends. If you wanted to keep both surfaces, tap ⌥ first, and SketchUp will make a copy in both locations.

Figure 6.13 *The Layers Inspector.*

Remember that you can minimize these inspectors by clicking on their top bar.

Your view is upside down and sideways now, isn't it? Choose *Camera > Standard Views > Iso.* This will zoom you out so that the limits of your model will fill the screen, and re-orient you vertically.

Is a piece of text getting in the way of a particular view, but you need it in another view? Place the text on a layer, which can be turned on and off independently. See the section on layers in Chapter 14 for more information on the uses of layers.

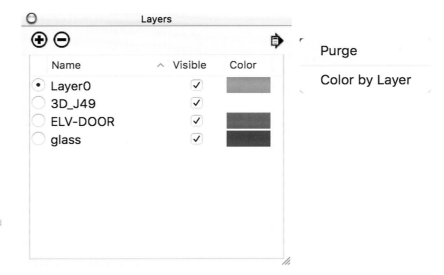

particular layer, right select them, and choose *Entity Info* from the context menu. That brings up another menu, which you can have alongside your *Layers* menu, for those times when you're making layer assignments. Choose the new layer from the drop-down list in the dialog box, and all those objects will now be on the new layer.

Unlike AutoCAD, there aren't many properties associated with a layer, except for the ability to color objects by their layer. It's more of a convenient organizational tool. Why didn't we just start this whole ordeal by making the current layer *Existing Conditions*, and then create the model? Well, yeah, we could have done it that way, too. It's common to forget that step, or to forget to change the current layer back after drawing the existing conditions, which leads to other problems.

Figure 6.14 *Changing the layer of objects.*

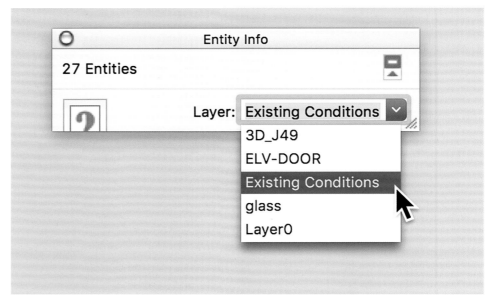

Add wall thickness

The time has come to give our walls the thickness they deserve. The general strategy is to create a rectangular opening using a rectangle, and then *Push/Pull* it to match the components we've chosen.

1. Open the model and navigate to the Exterior Overview scene.
2. Click the *Select* tool.
3. Click on the top face, which is the ceiling, to select it.
4. Click on the *Offset* tool.
5. Click on the edge of the ceiling for the base point—anywhere along the perimeter will do.
6. Move your mouse toward the center of the ceiling and type 12↵ to define the offset distance.
7. Click the *Push/Pull* tool.
8. Move your mouse over the center volume until it is highlighted, and click to define the base point.
9. Move your mouse over the outside lower corner of the model until your cursor says *Endpoint*, and click to define the second point of displacement. This will hollow out our building, leaving just a perimeter of 12" thick walls.
10. The *Push/Pull* tool made our floor go away. We can bring it back by tracing over one of the edges, so click on the *Line* tool.
11. Choose any edge of the floor and click on one endpoint.
12. Click on the opposite endpoint and the floor should re-appear.
13. Now the door opening: click on the rectangle tool.
14. Draw a roughly rectangular opening.
15. Make sure you have nothing selected. Then, activate the *Push/Pull* tool.
16. Make sure you have nothing selected. Move your mouse over the new rectangle until it is highlighted, and click to define the base point.
17. Move your mouse over any point along the edge of the exterior wall, until the tool tip reads *On Edge*, and click to define the second point of displacement. As with the wall thickness, you'll create a hollow opening.
18. The *Push/Pull* tool is still active, so move your mouse over the edge of the door opening until that face is highlighted.
19. Click to define the base point.
20. Move your mouse over the edge of the window frame—you will probably have to zoom in to see this—and, when the tool tip reads *On Edge*, click to define the second point of displacement.

The *Eraser* tool does not actually erase faces, but just edges, groups, and components. To delete only faces, but leave the bounding edges, you must select them and tap the *Delete* button.

Sometimes good inspectors go bad, or at least they go missing, especially when using two monitors. If you can't find or resize a menu, you might need to reset your workspace. Open your SketchUp Preferences, click on the *Workspaces* pane, and then click on the *Reset Workspace* button.

We traced over one edge to make the floor face return. We could have used any of the linear drawing tools, but it's critical that all edge lines be coplanar and that they form a continuous loop.

Several tools will auto-select if you activate them without any previously selected drawing elements. If you have a lot of objects to move, and the model isn't too crowded, this method can be quite fast.

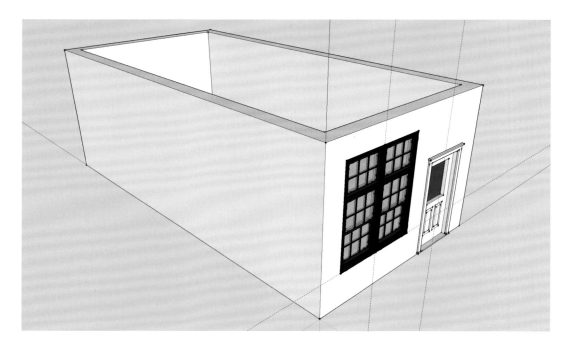

Figure 6.15 *The hollow building.*

If you deleted the door threshold, use a line to draw it back in. Sometimes doing this will add back in the face in front of the door—you'll have to delete that.

Figure 6.16 *Cleaning up the door frame.*

21. Repeat this last step for each edge of the door frame that is out of alignment.
22. Repeat steps 13–22 for the window openings.
23. For the ceiling thickness, we'll use a similar technique. Click on the *Select* tool and then click on one edge of the ceiling boundary.
24. Click the *Move* tool and tap ⌥ to make a copy.
25. Click on a point on the line to define the base point.
26. Move your mouse down in the blue direction and type 12 to define the second point of displacement.
27. Click the *Push/Pull* tool.

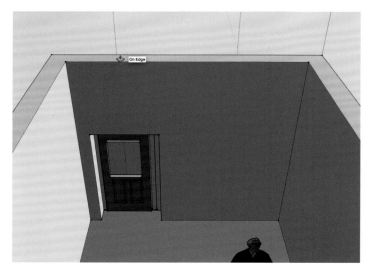

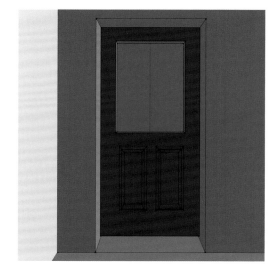

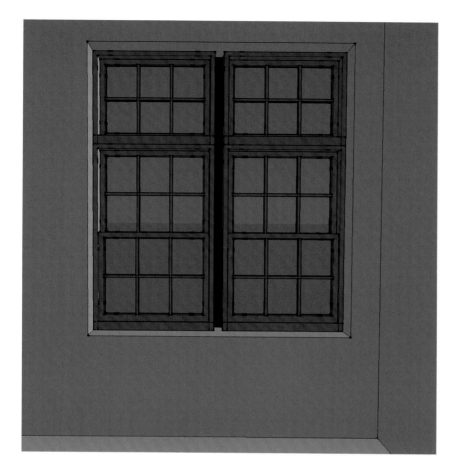

See the Online Resources for a video demonstrating the creation of the Existing Conditions model.

Figure 6.17 *Cleaning up the window frame.*

28. Click on the newly created rectangle.
29. Move your mouse over the opposite edge of the ceiling, until the tool tip reads *On Edge*, and click to fill in the ceiling volume.
30. For the floor, the thickness should go underneath the ground level. Activate the *Push/Pull* tool.
31. Tap on ⌥ to force the creation of a copy.
32. Click on the floor face to select it and give a base point all at once.
33. Move your mouse down, which might require some zooming and orbiting, and type 12 to define the second point of displacement.
34. This volume needs to go all the way to the outside face of the building—clean up using *Push/Pull*, as you did with the door and window openings.

Save views of the model

SketchUp models are easiest to view from the outside, which is why they're so handy for doing things like the exteriors of buildings, the

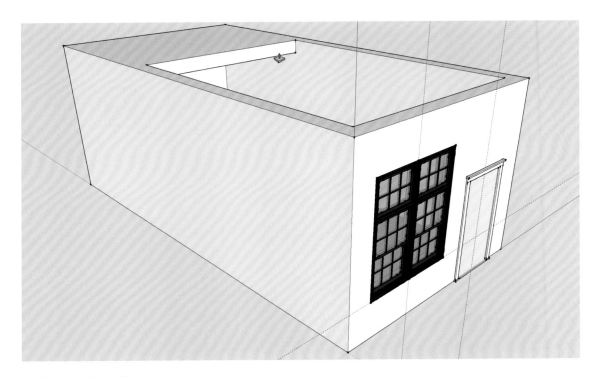

Figure 6.18 *Drawing the ceiling thickness.*

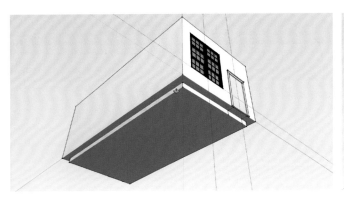
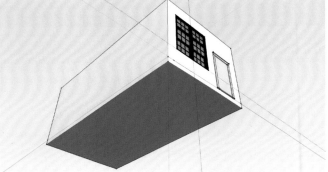

Figure 6.19 *The floor thickness.*

See the Online Resources for a video demonstrating how to use an image file of a floor plan to trace the basic volume of a space.

site that surrounds them, furniture, or even wedding cakes. Interior design however, requires being able to see inside these three-dimensional models, because that's what you're designing. Getting inside a SketchUp model is not as easy as it could be—it's actually hard to walk through walls in the virtual world, too. This is why it's nice to save some interior views of your model, so that you can come back to those spots later on. While we're at it, we can save some handy views that will make space planning, and also things like lighting layout and ceiling design, a bit easier.

On the Windows version of SketchUp, scene tabs are left-justified.

First, let's save an overview of the model: zoom out using the *Zoom* tool (the scroll wheel) in conjunction with the *Orbit* tool (click and drag the scroll wheel), so that you can see the whole model, preferably from a view where you can see the front facade. Once you have a well-composed view, choose *View > Animation > Add Scene*. You will then see a tab show up on the center of your screen, labeled *Scene 1*.

Because we have created a solid object, there's no way to see the interior of the project without somehow zooming inside. The simplest way to get inside a model is to use the *Zoom* tool and zoom right in through the front door. Click on the little magnifying glass up in the main toolbar, and then click and drag up—start with your mouse over the front door to zoom into it. You can also use the scroll wheel for this, although this can be a little too fast, once you're inside. It might take a few clicks and drags to make it through the door geometry—SketchUp will hesitate, because it doesn't like to move through a solid surface. SketchUp also has the funny habit of bumping the camera up as you have to jump over different elements, such as a door threshold or a piece of furniture, which is sort of funny when it shows up in an animation.

Clicking and dragging down will zoom you out. Clicking and dragging left will also zoom you out, but a little bit more slowly, which is handy once you're inside the space.

Figure 6.20 *The Exterior Overview scene.*

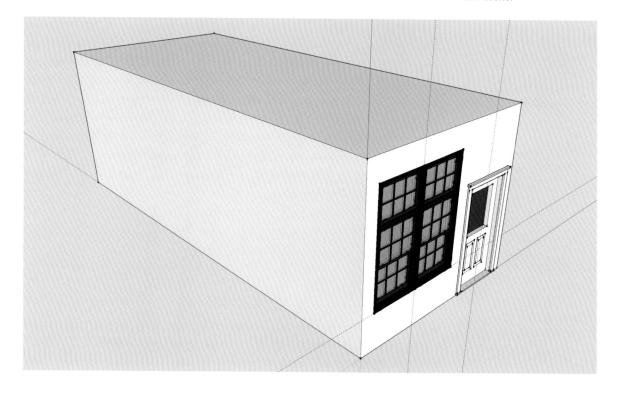

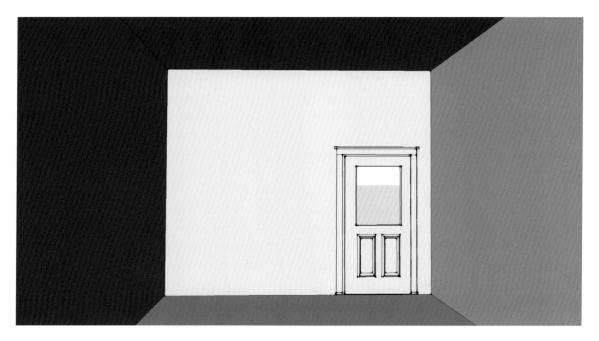

Figure 6.21 *Interior view.*

Just want to see what might be hidden in your model? Choose *View > Hidden Geometry,* and hidden objects will appear displayed with a gray grid on them.

Remember that these tabs are just views of your model, so resist the temptation to delete elements that don't seem well composed in the view—they will disappear entirely from the project.

Worried that you're going to accidentally change part of the existing conditions by mistake? Select the existing geometry, turn it into a group, and choose *Lock* from the *Entity Info* menu.

To save this new view of your model, go just to the right on the first tab, and from the context menu, choose *Add*. You will now see another tab pop up, with the clever name *Scene 2*. If you click on Scene 1, you'll return to the exterior view. Click on Scene 2, and you'll be back inside—very handy! These scenes will store all sorts of information, including the field of view, layer visibility, and other more advanced graphics settings.

Another strategy for entering the model, which can work better on more complex models, is to right-click on the roof surface and choose *Hide* from the context menu. You'll have to repeat this for the surface that represents the ceiling as well. I will often save a scene with these surfaces hidden, just for ease of navigation—scenes remember which elements are hidden and which are not. Once you have zoomed and panned inside the space, choose *Edit > Un-hide > Un-hide All* to display the ceiling and roof again, and then save the scene.

When starting a new project, it's a good idea to save several scenes around the existing conditions, to make it easier to place furniture, paint materials, and compose different spaces.

Try it out!

- Review a recent issue of a design magazine and sort the projects by wholly interior versus exterior architectural applications.
- Draw a 30' x 90' x 16'-high space with the long axis oriented north-south.

Figure 6.22 *Tabs visible at the top of the drawing area.*

- Go sit in a café. Generate an interior model of the space from simple shapes, estimating dimensions as best as you can. Try to finish before your coffee cools off.
- Search 3D Warehouse for completed café designs. Open one that looks interesting and create layers for existing walls and new furniture. Place objects on their appropriate layers.
- Search 3D Warehouse for your favorite furniture models, such as the Barcelona chair. Open the models and see how the components are divided into sub-groups or sub-components.
- Find the backup of the SketchUp component you modeled. Rename the component "recovery" and change the file extension so that you can open it in SketchUp.
- Take a design project from a magazine that you really like and scan the floor plan. Insert the scan into SketchUp, scale it, and then trace using simple shapes. Generate the three-dimensional volume based on whatever information you can find about the section or the RCP file.
- Model a two-level townhouse based on the section drawing.

Key terms

- FF&E
- Collections
- Field measurements
- Layer
- Origin
- Reference line

CHAPTER

7

Customizing the Interface

LEARNING OBJECTIVES

- Configure SketchUp Preferences for operational behaviors such as saving and backup.
- Define a unique keyboard shortcut for *Show/Hide Rest of Model* during component editing.
- Create a template for use in interior design presentations.

Once you've gotten to a certain skill level using SketchUp, it's nice to customize the interface to maximize productivity. Interior designers often have keyboard shortcuts assigned to tools they use frequently and for visibility settings that help see inside the model. You can also have easy access to special tools to manage nested groups and components, which are common in space planning types of projects. As we have seen in the section on adding the Large Tool Set in Chapter 3, it is possible to customize your interface by adding individual tools (typical of Mac) or whole toolbars (mainly on Windows). You can also control the size of the buttons. Now let's take a look at each of the SketchUp Preferences in greater detail, to help you configure your system for optimal performance and convenience.

> In Windows, the Preferences can be found under the *Window* pull-down menu.

SketchUp Preferences

Preferences is the catch-all term for the menu that collects together most of the default settings for different tools. In fact, most applications will have a Preferences menu hidden somewhere, although not all elements of an application can be configured. Choose *SketchUp > Preferences* (on Windows, choose *Window > Preferences*) to open up a dialog box with a series of panels, which are listed on the left side. Each panel has a set of options, gathered together more or less by what types of things they do. Any changes made in these menus will affect all sessions of SketchUp, although some may only activate after restarting the app.

APPLICATIONS

The first panel is for choosing the applications that SketchUp uses for editing image files. You only need this if you want to modify, say, a texture that is image based. Whichever editor is installed on your system, it will pop open when you double-click on the texture in the texture editor.

DRAWING

The *Drawing* panel is next, and allows you to change a number of features of how SketchUp operates. One that is handy to have on while working is the crosshairs—it helps me locate the cursor a little more easily on my giant monitor.

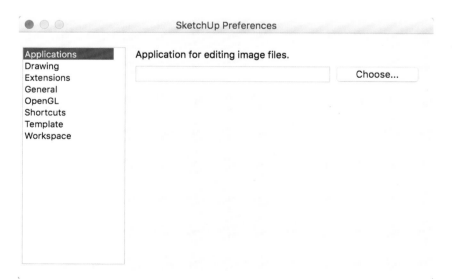

Figure 7.1 *The Applications panel of the SketchUp Preferences dialog box.*

Figure 7.2 *The* Drawing *panel.*

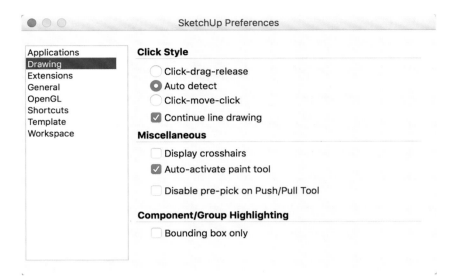

EXTENSIONS

The *Extensions* panel allows you to manage—wait for it—your Extensions. This is handy if your system is starting to slow down too much. Deactivate any of these that you're not currently using, and your start-up time should improve. On the *Policy* half of this panel, you can restrict the installation of Extensions to only those developers recognized by Trimble. There are some rogues out there who don't go through the Extension Warehouse, or whose installation is more complicated, and so need to be granted permission.

GENERAL

The *General* panel (which seems like it should go first, IMHO) controls behavior for saving and auto-saving models, and also self-checking

Figure 7.3 *The* Extensions *panel.*

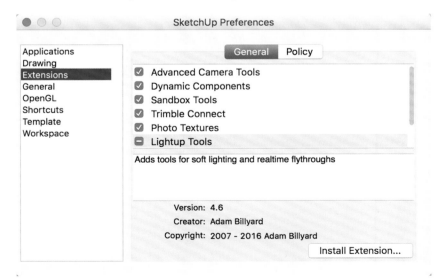

behavior. Not everyone likes to have a lot of warning messages popping up, but the one that warns about style changes is actually pretty handy when you're getting started with SketchUp. When using a template, however, it's not really needed, because most of the styles you need are pre-defined.

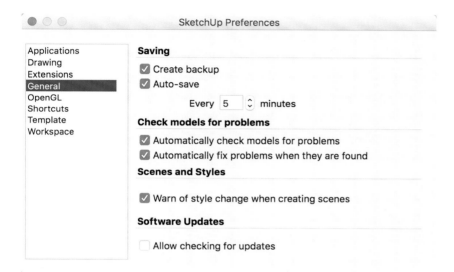

Figure 7.4 *The* General *panel.*

OPENGL

The **Open Graphics Library** (**OpenGL**) is one of those settings that can cause problems, but it can be something of a mystery why. OpenGL is a set of instructions telling different applications how to interact with each other, known as an **application programming interface** (**API**). In this case, it controls how the rendering 2D and 3D vector graphics are handled by the operating system. Basically, OpenGL sends Sketch-Up's graphical computing tasks (things like re-drawing what you see on the screen when orbiting around the model) either to your computer's **Central Processing Unit** (**CPU**), or, if you have one, to your dedicated **Graphics Processing Unit** (**GPU**).

If you haven't updated your graphics drivers in, like, forever, you could experience undue crashing when *Use Hardware Acceleration* is checked. You could also have a problem if your graphics card is not OpenGL compliant, which is probably not something you'd know off the bat, but is a good question to ask if you're buying a new system. The best thing to do is update your drivers, and hopefully the problem will go away. The expedient thing to do is just un-check *Use Hardware Acceleration* and hope for the best.

Figure 7.5 *The* OpenGL *panel.*

For the best appearance of colors and texture, set your screen to display colors with a 32-bit color depth; check in the control panel, under *Display Properties.*

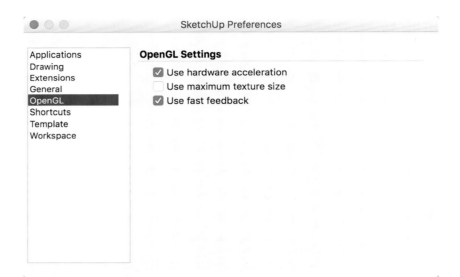

SHORTCUTS

The *Shortcuts* panel is where you can assign keys or keystroke combinations to different commands. The menu is organized alphabetically by the name of the pull-down menus, and within each pull-down, each tool is listed in the order in which it appears, with the full path. Let's assign the letter H to *View/Component Edit/Hide Rest of Model*. This will generate a warning message that the shortcut is already assigned—but go ahead and change it anyway, as it's such a common tool. Any extensions that you've installed will also show up here, under whichever menu they were placed, so you can assign keyboard shortcuts to those tools as well.

Figure 7.6 *The* Shortcuts *panel.*

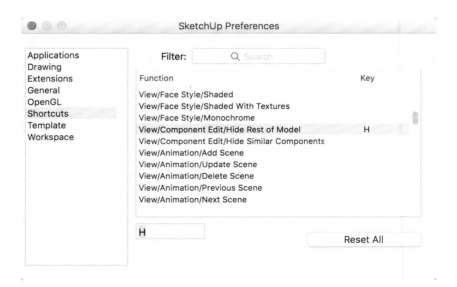

In Windows, you can save your custom keyboard shortcuts as an external file, which can then be loaded onto a new computer. On Mac, alas, there is no such option.

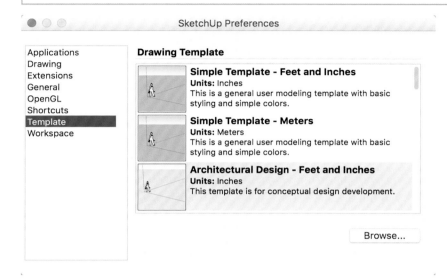

Figure 7.7 *The* Template *panel.*

TEMPLATE

The *Template* panel is where you choose the template you plan to use as the default.

WORKSPACE

The *Workspace* panel also just has a few options, including whether or not you would like to use the large tool buttons. As mentioned earlier, when working on a laptop, it's nice to use the smaller buttons, to save on screen real estate.

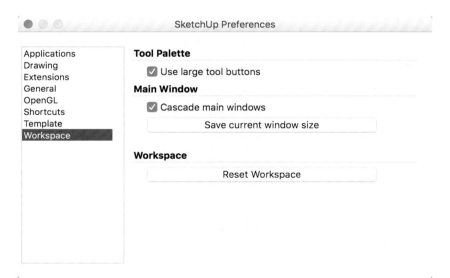

Figure 7.8 *The* Workspace *panel.*

If you started your model using the *Architectural Design—Feet and Inches* template, it already has the IFC 2 x 3 classification system loaded in. If not, you'll need to import one.

See the Online Resources for a list of the standard IFC classifications.

The *Model Info menu*

In addition to the global settings found in the Preferences, each individual schedule file also has its unique settings, which are collected together in the model info dialog box, which is found under the *Window* pulldown menu. These tend to be project specific, so many of them will be covered in the sections of this book that are more particularly relevant. For example, animation settings will be covered in that section, and statistics will be covered in the section on cleaning up your model.

ANIMATIONS

Creating and exporting animations is a complex subject, and will be treated in full in Chapter 18. For now, however, one thing to know about the animation settings is that they also affect the speed of transitions from one scene to the next. While working on a project, however, leave transitions turned off in this menu, so that the view changes from one scene to the next almost immediately.

CLASSIFICATIONS

With classifications, you can embed all sorts of data into SketchUp groups or components, which is basically a start to building information modeling (BIM). These details can then be tracked and managed, allowing you to count, measure, dimension, and generate reports. They rely on the *Classifier* tool, which is only available in SketchUp Pro, and also the *Generate Report* feature. With all this embedded data, you can create a model for energy performance or cost. This also allows a certain degree of **interoperability**, which is to say, the ability to import and export data of various sorts, with other BIM software, since you can export objects classified using the standard **Industry Foundation Classes** (**IFC**) system, which is a set of standard database formats for organizing a building project.

COMPONENTS

This panel controls the display of components during editing mode. Each component has its own internal axes, which are independent of the model axes, and are sometimes handy to see—their visibility can be turned on here.

CREDITS

Want everyone to know that you created your model? This is the place. Just click the *Claim Credit* button, and the model will embed your name, using the license information.

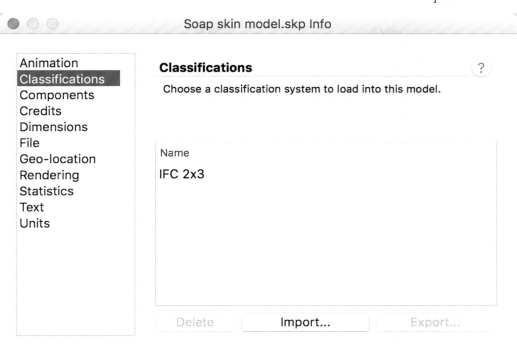

Figure 7.9 *The* Classifications *panel.*

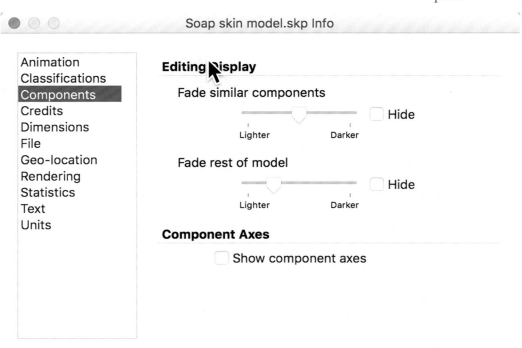

Figure 7.10 *The* Components *panel.*

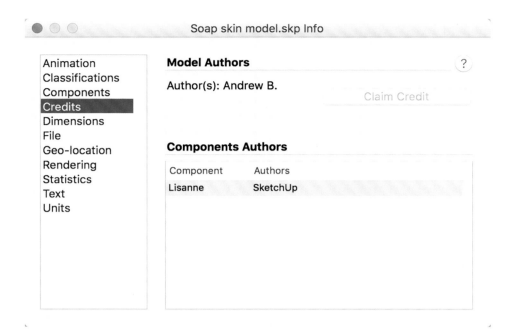

Figure 7.11 *The* Credits *panel.*

See the Online Resources for a demonstration of what changing many of the settings described will do to the SketchUp interface in general, and to your model in particular.

Want to show off for a client? Send your model to Google Earth by choosing *File > Export > 3D Model,* and then select the Google Earth file format (*.KMZ) from the drop-down list. You can then email this file, and if they have Google Earth, they will be able to see their project correctly located and scaled.

DIMENSIONS

This panel allows you to set the preferences for how dimensions will appear and behave in your model. Most design offices are going to be picky about the consistency of the graphical appearance of their drawings, so these are key settings to set when configuring a template. My personal pet peeve is that the text size and style for notes and dimensions should match. Click on the *Select All Dimensions* button to, you guessed it, select all the dimensions in the project. Once selected, any changes you make will apply to all dimensions in the model. This is especially handy if you've been importing content that may not comply with your office graphic standards.

FILE

There's not much to worry about here, since you've probably already named your file. You can, however, give the model some additional information, which could be handy in an office where there are several people collaborating on a project.

GEOLOCATION

This is where you can place your model at some precise location on the planet. Adding a location can be beneficial in several ways. For one, it will add a correctly scaled and oriented satellite image at the ground level of your model, which is certainly not easy to do otherwise. It also

Figure 7.12 *The* Dimensions *panel.*

If your file size is greater than about 50,000 KB (50 MB), you will probably start to see some significant slowing. See the chapter on cleaning up your model to address this issue.

Figure 7.13 *The* File *panel.*

means that the daylighting feature of SketchUp will be accurate for the longitude and latitude of your project. Finally, it will be possible to search for other geolocated models near the location of your project. This can be handy if you're trying to fill in some of the context quickly.

Type in your address, and tap *Search* to see your location on the map. You can zoom in and out to display the exact limits of your site, and move around the blue pins to change the area that will be selected.

Figure 7.14 *The* Geolocation *panel.*

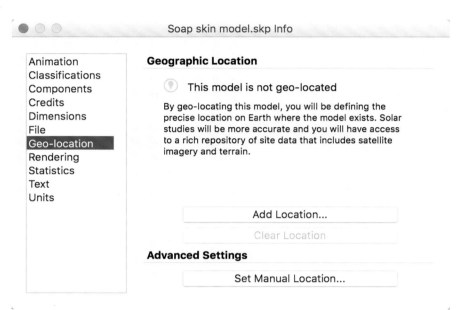

Figure 7.15 *The satellite map preview window.*

Tap *Grab* to capture that part of the satellite image and import it to scale into SketchUp. It's an image within your model, but because it's tied to metadata about your project, you can't manipulate it like other images—it's locked. It will also be visible on views outside the windows, and in plan view, which can be nice for giving some context to your project. Has your site changed? No problem—this information can be changed. Just go to *Window > Model Info* to open a dialog box with all sorts of settings that are specific to the project at hand. Click on the *Geolocation* tab and you can make any changes you want.

Looking for a great way to waste time? Install Google Earth on your computer and start exploring our planet. Any SketchUp model can be converted to a format readable by Google Earth—just choose *File > Export > 3D Model,* and then choose the Google Earth file format (*.KMZ) from the dialog box.

RENDERING

Textures in SketchUp, particularly those with lots of angles and curves, can sometimes appear pixilated, depending on the camera angle and the proximity of the objects. Anti-aliasing can smooth out this zig-zagging and make your view a lot sharper. So why not leave this on all the time? As with OpenGL and some other settings, if you're experiencing crashing, this can be one possible culprit, as it can add a significant load to your graphics processor.

You can actually unlock the image—just right-click on it, and choose *Unlock* from the context menu.

TEXT

Like the *Dimensions* panel, this is the place to apply any office standard that you might have. Most graphic standards use an arrow for leader lines, although of course you might have your own ideas. If you click on the *Select All Leader Text* button, this will select all leader lines in the model, which makes it easy to change them all to match—handy if you've been inserting content from outside sources. After making changes, click on the *Update Selected Text* button.

Figure 7.16 *The geolocating of the model.*

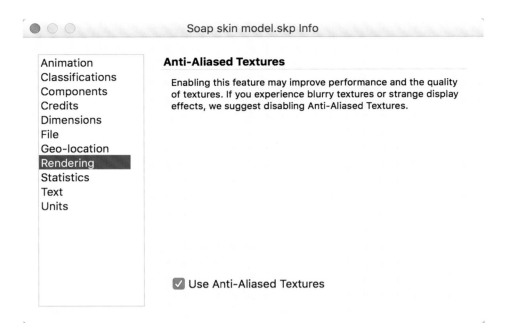

Figure 7.17 *The* Rendering *panel.*

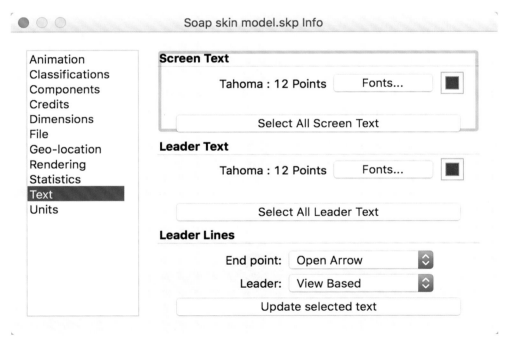

Figure 7.18 *The* Text *panel.*

For a special effect, such as projecting signage, use 3D text, which creates extruded letter shapes using whichever message and font you come up with. Choose *Tools > 3D Text* to call up the dialog box.

Click *Place* to insert the group into your project. The group can be modified using editing tools, as with any other geometry, but you can't go back and change the words once they are created.

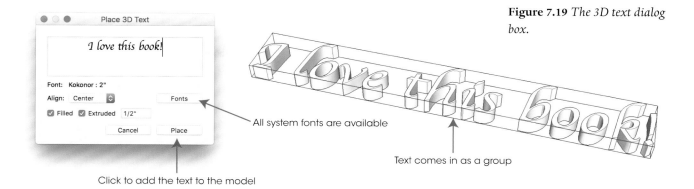

Figure 7.19 *The 3D text dialog box.*

All system fonts are available

Text comes in as a group

Click to add the text to the model

UNITS

Everything you create in SketchUp is actually drawn full size, without scaling. You can easily switch from metric to architectural units, and also control the precision at which objects are drawn. Unless you draw objects by typing in nice round numbers, they may end up having fractional dimensions. The precision setting allows you to round off these numbers in dimension strings, without changing the underlying geometry.

Notes and dimensions placed in a drawing model are generally only for simple annotation of design drawings. For construction drawings, the annotation is typically done in LayOut.

Create a template

If you have a long list of office graphic standards that you must comply with, it's probably a good idea to create a **template** for everyone to use,

A nice touch is to create your own font style using your hand lettering, for that old-school look.

Figure 7.20 *The* Units *panel.*

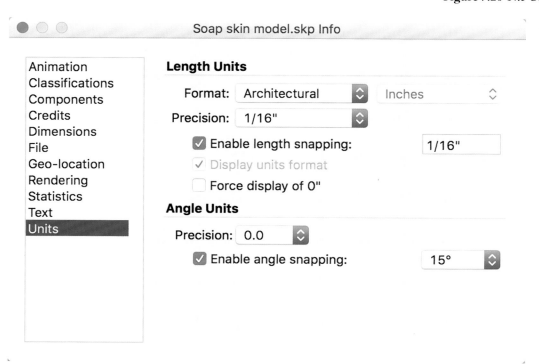

You should always back up your work, but what about your templates? SketchUp saves them in a particular location. On Mac, you need to make your library files visible in order to see them, first, and then navigate here: ~/Library/Application Support/SketchUp 2016 /SketchUp. In Windows, the folder is here: C:\Application Files\SketchUp\SketchUp Version\Resources\en-US \Templates.

for convenience and consistency. A template is basically a collection of settings and objects that can be used to start a new project more efficiently, so that things like special styles or scrapbooks don't have to be re-created each time. It's better to start from scratch—avoid the temptation to use a past project, as you will spend more time purging out unneeded geometry, components, views, and textures than you will save in having to add them.

You can't start drawing anything in SketchUp without using some sort of template. These instructions will take you through the basic settings that you should consider for an interior renovation type of template. This assumes that the project size will be somewhat less than 10,000 square feet total, that there will be a few design options, and that, ultimately, there will be construction drawings.

1. Open SketchUp and choose the *Architectural Design—Feet and Inches* template. This saves having to load in the IFC 2 x 3 classification system.
2. Choose *Window > Model Info*.
3. Click on the *Dimensions* panel and set up the style as per your office standard. Typically, a 12-point font is used, non-bold, with ticks for the leader lines.
4. Click on the *Text* panel and set up the style as per your office standard—make sure that it matches the dimensions.
5. On the *Credit* panel, assign any relevant information about you and your office.
6. Open up the layers dialog box and create the following layers: Existing Conditions, Site, Option 1, Option 2, Option 3, Annotation, Furniture, and Entourage. Make the first one the current layer.
7. Draw a 100' x 100' rectangle, starting at the origin.
8. Click the *Zoom* tool.
9. Type 55↵ to set the field of view.
10. Zoom out in *Orbit* to give yourself a perspective overview.
11. Save a scene from this angle and label it *Exterior Overview*.
12. Choose *Camera > Parallel Projection*.
13. Choose *Camera > Standard Views > Top View*.
14. Zoom and plan to place the rectangle in the middle of your view.
15. Open the *Styles* menu and click on the *Home* button to display the styles used in the model. There should just be the current one.
16. Verify that *Section Planes* and *Section Cuts* are not displayed in this style and update if needed.
17. Rename the style to be *Section Planes Off*.
18. Duplicate the style.

19. On the new style, turn on the display of *Section Cuts*.
20. Rename the style *Section Cuts On*.
21. Update the style.
22. Repeat steps to create the *Orthographic View Style* used earlier.
23. Create a style where everything is on, including hidden geometry and section planes.
24. Choose *File > Save As Template*.
25. Save the drawing somewhere that you'll be able to find it later—a templates folder is a good place.

Create a library folder for all of your templates from other programs.

Figure 7.21 *The save as template dialog box.*

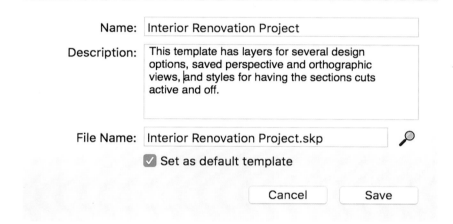

As you might imagine, there are many additional things that you could add, depending on your needs. Some offices may have particular styles that they have created for presentations, or specialize in stores in shopping malls, which are a good deal smaller. If you use the same furniture over and over again, you can add them to the template—the same for any materials collections that you might have. Finally, you may want to add your own custom classification system, which is especially handy if you need to generate specific types of purchase orders, such as for furnishings and equipment. This can be tied to the Construction Specifications Institute (CSI) numbering format, if needed. The whole process is very complicated, however.

Try it out!

- Set SketchUp to save automatically in a location that you back up.
- Memorize the keyboard shortcuts for all the tools in the Large Tool Set—you'll find a key to the standard Mac and Windows shortcuts in the Online Resources for this chapter.

- Configure a template to use your favorite font and graphic style.
- Create a template for the type of projects that you typically do and set it to be the default.
- Create an animated walkthrough of your project.
- Export animations configured for display on a computer and for distribution via email.
- Create a font using your hand lettering and set it as the default for text and dimensions in your template.
- Create an animation where you just look around a space without actually walking through it.
- If you're on a PC, export your keyboard shortcuts to a file and save it in a location that you will back up.

Key terms

- Application programming interface (API)
- Central processing unit (CPU)
- Graphics processing unit (GPU)
- Industry Foundation Classes (IFC)
- Interoperability
- Open Graphics Library (OpenGL)
- Preferences
- Template

Scene Management

LEARNING OBJECTIVES

- Identify different basic views needed to present an interior design project.
- Describe the different graphical settings that are saved in a scene.

As we saw in the last chapter, saving a few scenes is a great way to start a new project, as they allow you quick access to different views of your project. This is handy for both the creation of a design and evaluating it afterwards. Interior perspectives are particularly difficult to compose well, as possible vantage points need to show off both the spatial volume and the way in which the space is inhabited and used. As we saw in the last chapter, every scene can have a style applied to it, and this can be a very powerful feature for graphic control, especially when assembling presentation drawings. Details about each scene can be controlled and updated as you make changes, including when you create orthographic views.

Composing interior perspectives

To understand drawing composition, it helps to understand a bit about how we perceive the drawings and the spaces that they represent. It's actually a very impressive trick how we create and observe a three-dimensional world, re-create it on the computer, and then flatten that re-creation onto a two-dimensional piece of paper, or a screen. When another designer or a client looks at that two-dimensional representation

While 55° is certainly common for an interior field of view, it can still be hard to see some small spaces. Try hiding the wall or walls behind the camera—you should be able to move backwards in the space.

The *Advanced Camera* tool offers all sorts of controls: setting a virtual focal length, displaying the frustum, moving cameras directly, and more. For example, you can view and control the **frustum**, which is the point at which the camera crops the front and back of the view. These tools are more cinematic than architectural, though, and so will not be covered in this text.

See the Online Resources for a demonstration of creating a number of saved scenes in this project.

of an interior space, somehow they are able to re-build the original three-dimensional environment in their minds, or at least, that's the goal of our drawings. This neat trick relies on our ability to read a number of different perspectival cues within an image—the use of vanishing points, a horizon line, depth cues from different line weights, scaling elements, and so forth. These techniques have been used by artists, interior designers, and architects to help render three-dimensional space. The traditional architect's **Studio Method**, where perspectives are generated using a plan and section, dates back to the Renaissance, and is more or less what SketchUp builds views are meant to look like.

Interior views tend to be much more difficult to compose on the computer than exterior views, because the viewer needs to be inside the three-dimensional model, which is why there are so many specialized view tools. Most 3D modeling and viewing applications use the metaphor of a camera to explain how a 2D view of the model is generated. Compared to exterior views, interiors need a much wider **field of view**, which is how wide or narrow an area of the room the camera can see, in order to display enough of a room to describe its volume. The view tools in SketchUp are mostly designed to manipulate the virtual camera position and focus. Good interior perspectival composition has a balance of plan, ceiling, and walls, and there are a number of tools that will help us with view composition, all at the bottom of the Large Tool Set.

Let's first switch to a scene that shows the interior of the model. Click on the icon that looks like an androgynous little person standing on an "X." This is the *Position Camera* tool, and will allow you to set up your perspective. Now, click in the floor plan towards the back, and you should see your screen spin around to a partial view of your model. Your icon should also now look like an eyeball. You will probably notice that the eyeball tool is also highlighted in the Large Tool Set. Just click and drag from the left to the right in order to spin the model around so that

Figure 8.1 *Advanced view tools.*

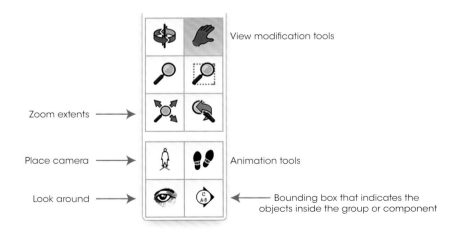

you can view the front of the project. At this stage, the section planes can be deactivated and their visibility turned off—see Chapter 4 to review how to do this. Let's save this view facing forward to the front, as another scene. Since the view settings have changed, you will be prompted with the option to create a new style for the new scene—create it, and rename the style Sections Off.

Each of these tools has different modifiers. As we have seen before, the *Zoom* tool also allows you to change the field of view, which shows up in the measurements box. Using the little androgynous person button, otherwise known as the *Place Camera* tool, and also the *Look Around* and *Walk* tools, you can change the eye height.

Where are your eyes, anyway? The average adult male in the U.S. is 5′8″, and the average adult female is 5′4″. But the eyes are probably about 4″ below that. Architectural photographers often use a slightly lower eye height—about 4′, and of course you could use a seated height.

Figure 8.2 *The saved views.*

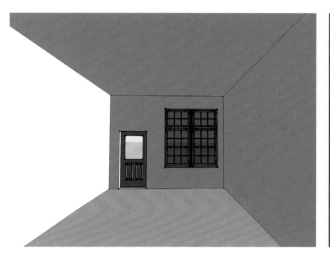
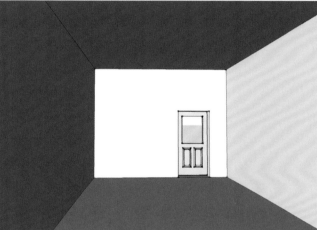

Saving these different views of a project is really the best way to start a new design problem. You can quickly navigate around the project, which will help for laying out furniture, but will also help you look at the project in perspective to better evaluate the effect of your design decisions.

Updating a scene

There are a number of different camera settings we can have in a scene. By default, the SketchUp interface is actually in three-point perspective, not two-point perspective, which can sometimes feel a little disorienting. This is especially true for older designers who were trained in the hand-generated Studio Method look, wherein the vertical lines are all parallel to each other, but all other lines conform to perspective composition rules about vanishing point or points. Let's modify the eye height and camera position of both of our interior perspectives.

1. Open your Existing Conditions model and navigate to your interior perspective looking toward the front of the project.
2. Click on the *Position Camera* tool.
   The *Height Offset* reading is probably some random value, because of all the zooming and orbiting that you had to do to get inside the model. Let's configure a view that's a bit more like an architectural photograph—type 3'⏎ and the camera should move down. There's no need to click inside the measurements box, as SketchUp knows that the text should go there automatically.
3. The default field of view is 35°, which is too narrow for an interior view. Type 55⏎ to change the value. This will cause some distortion, but this is typical of interior views.

Figure 8.3 *The effect of the field of view variable.*

4. Use the *Pan* tool to center the view.
5. Use the *Look Around* tool to see a balance of floors, walls, and the ceiling.

Choose *Camera > 2-Point Perspective* to give the view that Studio Method look. From this point on, be sure not to use any of the view tools, or you'll lose the two-point perspective configuration. Check before you save the scene that this feature is on.

6. Right-click on one of your scenes and choose Scene Manager from the context menu.
7. Select the View to Front scene and update.
8. Repeat these steps with the other saved scenes.
9. Save the model.

It's too bad that these settings are not part of the style properties—there's some deeply technical reason why not. In fact, it would be wonderful to be able to globally change a stack of scenes to all have a new field of view or some other camera feature, but as far as I know, that is not possible. If you ever find out, be sure to let me know.

Figure 8.4 *A normal perspective view and a two-point perspective.*

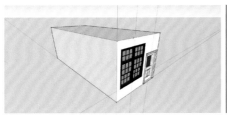  

Figure 8.5 *The updated scenes.*

Creating an orthographic view

Let's jump to the saved scene for interior overview. The difference between this view, which is sort of a bird's-eye, and a floor plan, is the perspective active in the drawing. We need to get rid of perspective and force the camera to be at a right angle to the floor plan. Fortunately, SketchUp is an architectural modeler, and so it is configured to allow you to set up many of the standard orthographic views that architects and interior designers tend to use.

1. Open your Existing Conditions model and navigate to the Interior Overview scene.
2. Choose *Camera > Parallel Projection* from the drop-down menu—this will turn off perspective.

   This is not a true plan, however—to create that, you need to force the camera to be perfectly perpendicular to the plane that the floor plan is drawn on. Choose *Camera > Standard Views > Top*, and the model is now perfectly flat. Note that north is toward the top of the screen, along the green axis, which is a graphic standard throughout the industry.

If you notice any extra lines inside the floor plan or the section view, they are probably from the way we used *Push/Pull* to generate the walls, floor, and ceiling thickness. This is the time to erase them. Just make sure you don't delete any surfaces that are on the inside of the project.

Note that the keyboard shortcuts for each of these standard views are visible in the drop-down menu. You can also add a toolbar to your SketchUp interface with buttons for all of the standard views on it. This is handy when you're setting up a set of construction drawings, as you'll make reference to the standard view a great deal.

You can also right-click on the section plane and choose *Align View* from the context menu.

3. **Poché**, which is the hatching or solid color that fills in the thickness of walls, floors, and ceilings in plan and section views, makes what is cut through and what is not much clearer. Click the *Paint Bucket* tool so that we can add some.

4. Choose a poché style that you like—there's no hard and fast graphic standard. Many designers will prefer the old-school look of diagonal lines, which you can find on the *Textures* panel, in the *Patterns* group.

5. Click on the inside of the walls to add the poché.

Figure 8.6 *The true, orthographic top view.*

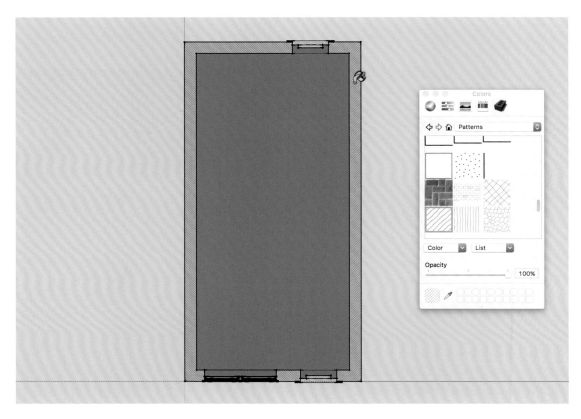

6. Right-click on one of your scene tabs and choose Scene Manager from the context menu.

7. Click the *Add* button to save a scene.

8. Rename the scene Floor Plan.

9. Save the model.

If you have a lot of scenes, the task of re-generating the thumbnails can be a drag on your computer. Select all the scenes, and then, from the fly-out menu, de-select *Use Scene Thumbnails.* This should speed things up a bit.

Creating a section view

The section as drawn is really just a cut-away perspective. The technical definition of an **orthographic** view is a drawing in which the projecting lines are at right angles to the plane of project. In other words, it is a drawing that has no vanishing points, and so no perspective depth. Such drawings can be difficult for non-designers to read, since the depth cues we are used to reading in three-dimensional drawings are not there, for the most part. But drawings such as plans and sections are the basic building blocks of any architectural set. Let's take the longitudinal section view created in the last chapter and convert it to an architectural section.

Skalp is a section tool extension that will make it easier to add poché to your view, although it is somewhat expensive.

1. Choose *Camera > Standard Views > Left* to see the inside of the project that you have exposed with your section plane.
2. This is not really an orthographic view, since there are vanishing points. Go to *Camera > Parallel Projection* to turn off perspective, creating a true orthographic view.

Note that when you have applied one of the standard camera views, SketchUp will indicate which view you are using in the upper left corner of the drawing window.

Is there a wall or other object in the view of your otherwise perfectly composed view? Hide it, or use an X-ray face style as an interesting effect. This is particularly true of furniture that gets chopped by a section plane.

Figure 8.7 *A true orthographic section.*

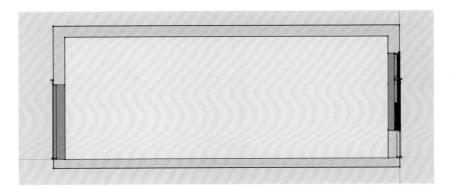

Poché is not always easy to create. Often the insides of walls have little subdivisions from components, side wall construction, or other modeling relics. This is also true when trying to draw poché in section and RCP view. Use LayOut techniques to create the poché instead.

Elevation drawings

Interior elevations are basically sections, but without showing the thickness of walls, floors, or ceilings. Within SketchUp, they are in fact exactly the same, because there isn't the ability to hide those elements within the SketchUp interface. It's only possible to create elevations by cropping away the wall, floor, and ceiling thickness of a section view in LayOut. We won't get to LayOut for a few more chapters, but let's set up the section/elevation view nonetheless.

1. Open your Existing Conditions model and navigate to the Exterior Overview scene.
2. Click on the section tool.
3. Orient the section plane perpendicular to the long axis of the space by tapping on the left arrow to lock the inference in that direction.

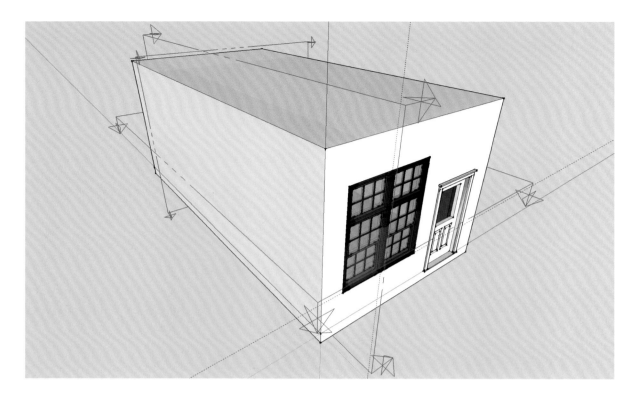

Figure 8.8 *Section planes visible in the Exterior Overview scene.*

4. Click to place the section about 1/4 of the way in from the back of the model.
5. Choose *Camera > Parallel Projection*.
6. Choose *Camera > Standard Views > Back*.
7. Apply the *Section Cuts Active* style.
8. Center the model on your screen.
9. Paint the insides of the walls with poché, just in case you decide to use this as a section drawing.
10. Save a new scene and call it Transverse Section.

Building sections do not typically show details about the wall, floor, and roof construction. Particularly for an interior renovation project, these details are not typically needed, unless of course you are trying to make ill-advised changes to the existing structure. We can add hatch patterns to the inside of the wall surface later, using LayOut.

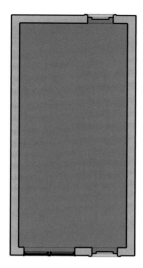

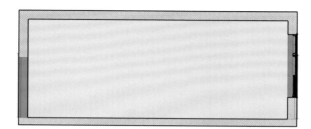

Figure 9.3 *The plan and section views with the orthographic style applied.*

aren't particularly useful when modeling, as they can obscure detail and texture. But they can make for some interesting presentation drawings.

Let's try a few, saving each test as different scene, to compare them easily. When exploring different graphic styles, it's best to work on a copy of the original model, as some styles can slow the model down. It's also a good idea to delete any section planes, since some styles can make them look quite peculiar. Start with your favorite perspective view—one which is most likely to be included in a presentation—and then choose *Window > Styles*.

 Some lovely, free custom styles can be found here: http://www.sketchupartists. org/sketchup-styles.

Figure 9.4 *Selected style collections.*

  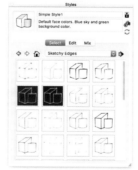 

Let's start with the *Blueprint* style, which has a nice white line on a dark blue background. Click on the icon to apply the style to your view, and then add a new scene—it will be saved with that particular style applied. Switch back to the original scene and see which one looks more interesting. Let's try a few more styles, *Brush Strokes* and *Whiteboard with Dry Erase Marker*, saving new scenes and comparing. The goal here is to find a graphical look that works with the aesthetics of the project and also makes for a compelling rendering.

 Some styles have a little green clock on their icon. This indicates that it is a fast style, which means that editing and navigating the model will be a little less taxing for your computer.

Mix and match style characteristics

The last tab on the *Styles* menu, *Mix*, is where you can really get into some trouble, but also begin to create a unique look for your drawings. If there are two different styles in your model, each with a feature that you want to use, you can literally drag features from one style into your current style, and those features will be applied to the current view. Let's make a copy of our current style, just to be sure we don't mess up the original. Click the home button to see icons representing the styles that you have used in this project. Right-click on the one that is active for this scene and choose copy.

Starting with the edge settings, let's browse for a sketchy edges style. Then just click and drag that style into your current style edge settings section. For example, you can take the pencil and paper background texture that was in one of your styles and drag it into this style. This is most useful for edge settings, which are the most difficult to configure.

Figure 9.5 *Mixing and matching styles.*

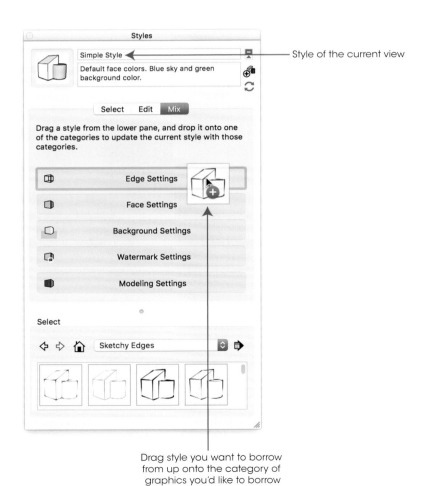

The Style Builder

The Style Builder is an external application that is only available with SketchUp Pro. With it, you can use custom-drawn lines, each with unique graphical characteristics such as **jitter**, which is how "shaky" the line looks, as well as line weight and color, to produce a unique effect. Custom lines, called **strokes**, are created using a template, wherein you draw lines at different lengths. In the Style Builder, these custom lines are applied to the model elements in a view based on how long the lines are when represented in the perspective composition, which can be previewed to make sure the effect is working well.

Figure 9.6 *The Style Builder stroke menu.*

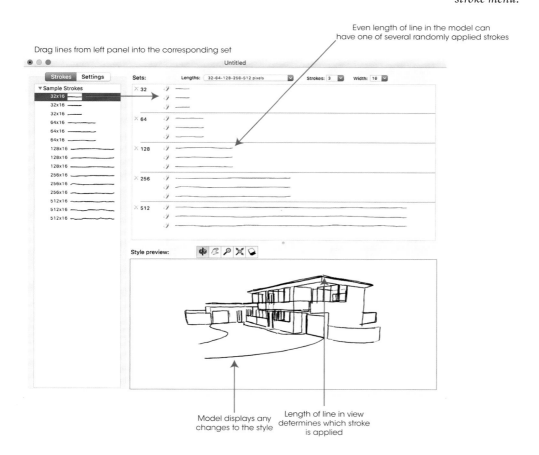

Some parts of the model will use a short stroke and others will use a long stroke. So, for example, a small piece of a window frame might only use a 32-pixel long line, whereas the edge of a building might need one that is 256 or 512 pixels long. Each length has at least three slots for different line weights or image strokes. The reason for this is that SketchUp will randomly pick one of those three every time it encounters a line that it needs to draw. This randomness helps the drawing have more of a hand-drawn look.

There are a number of simple sample strokes available with the default version of the software. To create a new style, find a sample stroke that you like and drag the stroke lengths from the left panel into the different gray box lots of the *Sets* panel. Be sure to match the length of the stroke, which is next to the preview image of it, with the size in the panel. Otherwise, the Style Builder will resize your image for you, and it probably won't look as good. The preview panel will give you an idea of what this is going to look like. The preview panel starts out as very fuzzy, which might be an interesting style on its own, but it's merely meant as a placeholder to give you an idea of what the line types you use are going to look like. As you drag lines from the strokes area into the sets area, you should see the elements of the building fill out using the different length lines that you have chosen.

You can also change a number of settings that affect the look of the drawing. The one that would seem to have the greatest hand-drawn look to it is the extensions aspect. This forces the lines to cross each other. As we saw when editing styles in the previous chapter, profiles and depth cues also add some variability to the line weights. The drop-out length determines when lines will not be drawn at all. Often, SketchUp will try to simplify a hand-drawn drawing so there aren't scribbles all over the place, but especially for interiors that have a lot of detail, it's nice to reduce that length to zero, so that you can see all those good things like crown molding and the edge details of furnishings. The fade factor is another thing that you can change. This is how much lines will begin to disappear as they get closer to the dropout length. This will give you some variation in the darkness of the line, but when you set the dropout length to zero, the fade factor, which is a multiple of the drop-out length, also effectively becomes zero.

To preview what this might look like on your own project, choose *Preview > Change Model* from the drop-down lists. Then, browse for your latest model—it will open up the preview of whatever you were looking at the last time you saved.

Once the style is loaded into a model, further changes, such as the display of section planes, section cut activation, the line weight multiplier, and other graphical characteristics can also be modified.

To share a style that is loaded into your project already, right-click on it in the *Styles* menu and choose *Save As* from the context menu. Put the style file (it actually has the file extension "Style") into a new folder on your computer, or, if your office has a networked library of custom styles, put it into that folder. In the model where you want to add the new style, choose *Add Collection to Favorites* from the *Styles* fly-out menu and browse for the folder you created. The collection will be added to the main drop-down list and will update as you add more custom styles.

Change the color of the lines

Examine the preview as you change parameters to get the best result

Figure 9.7 *Style Builder settings.*

Figure 9.8 *The custom style, applied to your view of the front of the model.*

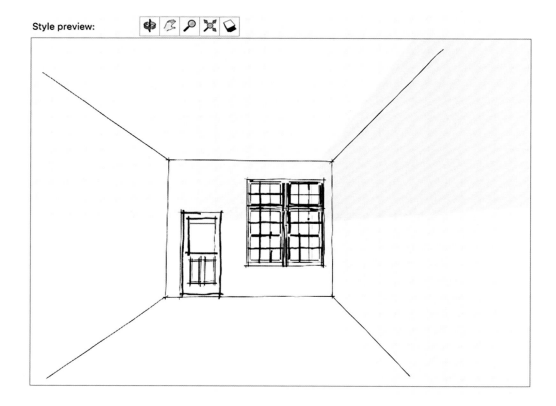

Create a style all your own

Wouldn't it be cool if you could create a custom style using your own hand-drawn lines? Yes, it would be cool, and it's actually easy to do. In the Style Builder, choose *File > Generate Template* and print out the blank form. You'll see a series of boxes of different lengths, each corresponding to a stroke length with the Style Builder. Take your favorite drawing implement and hand-draw the different length lines right onto the template. Then, scan this template back in as a high-resolution image. Save the scanned image as a BMP file and use Photoshop as needed to color correct, sharpen, or darken your line work. If you'd prefer, a drawing application such as Adobe Illustrator can be used to generate the lines.

Once you have created the template, choose *Strokes > Load from Template* and browse for the file you created. The Style Builder, hopefully, will recognize the lines you have drawn and load them into the *Strokes* panel. Of course, you can also go on to that little thing called the internet and try to search for custom styles to load directly, if this all sounds like too much work.

Figure 9.9 *The completed style template.*

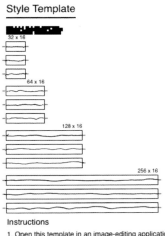

Insert the new style

Once you have created and saved your own custom style, it's fairly easy to load into SketchUp. Save any styles that you create into a folder, preferably named something clever, like *My Custom Styles*. Then, back in SketchUp, call up the styles dialog box. Click on the fly-out to the right and choose *Open or Create a Collection*. You can then browse for the folder where you have all of your styles saved. This will update every time you open the file up, so if you created new ones that you've dropped in there, they should be available in SketchUp right away. There are also styles available online from a variety of sources.

Apply styles to multiple scenes

Let's say you have decided to create an animation from several saved scenes, but you would like them all to have a sketchy line style applied to them. There is no direct way to apply a style to multiple scenes, but there is a workaround. It takes a few carefully orchestrated steps, however.

1. Save a copy of the model that you'd like to modify.
2. Open the Scene Manager.
3. While holding down ⌘, click on the name of each of the scenes that you'd like to modify to select them.
4. Click on the *Update* button.
5. A dialog box appears, wherein you can select which graphic elements are updated. Uncheck the box next to *Style and Fog*.
6. Click OK to update.
7. Apply the style that you would like to use to whichever scene you happen to be in.
8. Back in the scenes dialog box, make sure all of the scenes you would like to modify are selected.
9. Click on the *Update* button, but now, make sure that all radio buttons are unchecked except for *Style and Fog*.
10. Click OK to update, and the new style should be applied to all scenes.

Try it out!

- Apply three very different styles to your two interior views, saving a scene for each one as you go.
- Create your own style using the Style Builder that comes close to your hand-drawing style.
- Mix the blueprint style with different colors and edge characteristics to make it look more like an old-style sepia print.
- Print a sheet with four different styles applied to the same perspective view. Write a brief description of how each changes the perception of space and its aesthetics.

Key terms

- Jitter
- Strokes

Space Planning Tools

LEARNING OBJECTIVES

- Organize design options with layers.
- Locate and insert ready-made furniture models.
- Create rectangular and circular arrays.
- Annotate the drawing with dimensions.
- Describe a unique strategy for applying textures to components.
- Replace instances of a component with a different component.

Space planning is one of the most fundamental activities of an interior designer, and now that we've completed the existing conditions, it's time to come up with some design options. Let's call the project we'll be using *The Frozen Poetry Café*. The space has to accommodate serving coffee and pastries on a regular basis, and also occasional poetry slams, so the furniture will have to be moved around to form more of a stage.

Before filling the space to bursting with furnishings and equipment, some preparation is needed, especially when creating design options. For an interiors project, the existing building conditions will remain unchanged, so furnishings, fixtures, and equipment can be gathered together onto a single layer. It's best to configure the model first to handle multiple options, so that scene management is easier in the long run.

Analyze the program

It's important to analyze and understand the program when starting a new space planning project, and bubble diagrams are the typical way to do that. In this particular project, there really aren't any separate spaces, only the different areas created by furnishings.

- Main entry
- Café service, including a counter, register, and coffee prep area
- Adjustable seating
- Podium for speakers
- Rear door for access to storage and toilets

A **bubble diagram**, which is a graphical representation of the architectural program requirements, adjacencies, separations, circulation, and the like, is the traditional way to start the space planning process. This is typically done by creating circles (the "bubbly" part of a bubble diagram) that are roughly proportional to the required floor area, and then moving them around to experiment with different arrangements. In SketchUp, however, moving around objects means that you're always having to deal with sticky geometry, so drawing right on top of the floor plan is not going to work. We'll create circles and text for the different program areas, and then turn them into groups, to avoid the sticky geometry. Then it's just a matter of experimenting with different configurations.

1. Open the model from the last chapter and navigate to the interior overview scene.
2. Click on the *Circle* tool.
3. Off to the side of the plan, draw a circle that's roughly 3' in diameter.
4. Click just off the circle to start a piece of text without a leader line.
5. *Push/Pull* the circle up about 2".
6. Click on the *Text* tool.
7. Type in *Entry*.
8. Select the text, right-click on it, and choose *Entity Info* from the context menu.
9. Click on the *Font* button.
10. Choose a font that you like and make the font size 24.
11. Click the *Select* tool.
12. Click and drag a window around the circle and the piece of text.
13. Right-click on the selection and choose *Make Group* from the context menu.
14. Click the *Move* tool and tap the button to activate the *Copy* modifier.
15. Click on the group to establish a base point.

Fonts (Selected Text)

Q Search

Collection	+ −	Family	Typeface	Size
All Fonts		Didot	Regular	**24**
English		Futura	Light	9
Favorites		Geneva	Oblique	10
Recently Used		Georgia	Light Oblique	11
Fixed Width		Gill Sans	Bold	12
Fun		Helvetica	Bold Oblique	13
Modern		Helvetica Neue		14
PDF		Herculanum		18
Traditional		Hoefler Text		24
Web		Impact		36
		Iowan Old Style		

☐ Height [ ]

Figure 10.1 *The fonts dialog box.*

16. Click again off to the side to make a copy.
17. Type x3↵ to make three copies.
18. With the *Select* tool, double-click on the copy and then the piece of text.
19. Change the text to *Seating*.
20. Change the text in the other two components to *Service Counter* and *Rear Exit*.
21. Click on the *Paint Bucket* tool.
22. Paint each of the components a different solid color.
23. Choose *Window > Layer* from the drop-down list.
24. Click the + to add a new layer.
25. Name the layer *Bubble Diagram* and click OK.
26. Back in the model, select all four bubbles.
27. From the entity info dialog box, change the layer of the components.
28. Click on the *Move* tool.
29. Select the *Entry* bubble.
30. Click on the floor to establish a base point.
31. Click again on the floor plan to locate the bubble.

When moving the bubbles (or any three-dimensional object), don't use a base point that's on the component itself—it makes it too easy to accidentally move the component up or down, in addition to horizontally.

It's very easy to accidentally move a component up or down, instead of along the ground plane. To fix a wayward chair or table, move it using the part that sits on the ground (the bottom of the leg, for example) as the base point. Then, move your mouse over the floor until the tool tip reads *On Face*.

Figure 10.2 *The bubbles.*

 See the Online Resources for a video showing the creation of a bubble diagram, along with some ancillary graphics.

 If you have a good idea of how many options and bubble diagram alternatives you're going to need, create all of those layers now. Just turn all but the one you need now off.

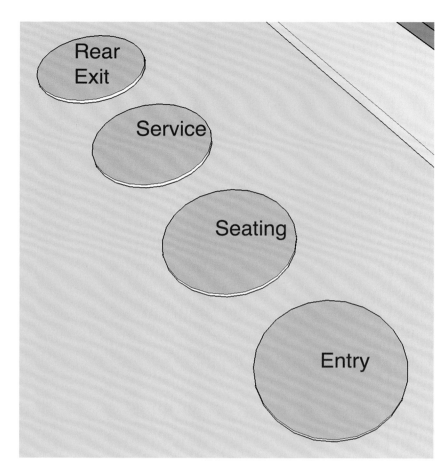

Figure 10.3 *Choosing the layer for the group.*

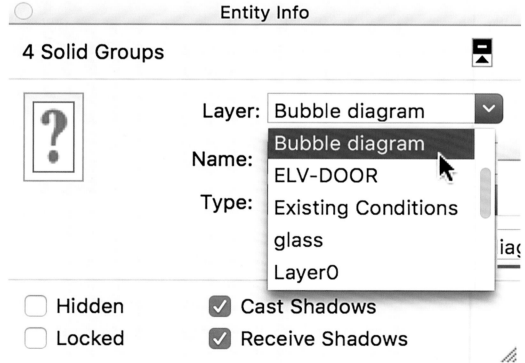

32. Repeat with the other bubbles and tweak their position until you're happy with the arrangement.
33. Click on the *Scale* tool.
34. Resize each of the bubbles to represent the amount of floor area that you think this part of the program will need.
35. Save a scene, so that it's easy to return back to this view.

It can be easy to accidentally move or delete these bubbles as you develop your project. To prevent that, make them into a group and go to the entity info dialog box. Make sure you expand the dialog to see the extra controls below, and check the box next to *Locked*. It's still possible to move a locked object, but not change the geometry.

There are quite a few handy extensions for space planning available from the good folks at the third-party website SketchUcation, although some are repeated in the Extension Warehouse. They also have textures, styles, and valuable tutorials.

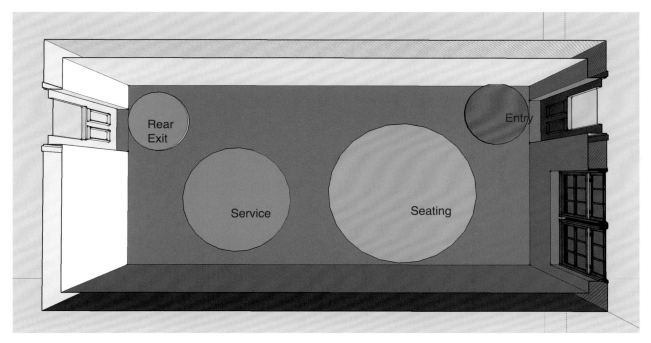

Figure 10.4 *The final diagram.*

Create design options

Often you want to present several different layouts for a client within the same space, in order to show off different concepts or strategies. It's ideal when you can have them visible within the same space, so that you can quickly switch from one to another. The easiest way to do that is to use layers, which we learned about in Chapter 6. Add a new layer for Option 1 and set it current—now anything that we draw will be placed on that layer. This is also true of components brought in from the Components Browser or from 3D Warehouse. Lay out your space for a lecture, with a podium and rows of seats.

Next, create a new layer for Option 2, set it current, and turn off the Option 1 layer. Now, add in new furniture for a seminar type of

Need to divide a space into three even sections? Draw a line across the whole length, right-click on it, and choose *Divide* from the context menu. Specify the number of divisions either by typing or moving your mouse and then clicking.

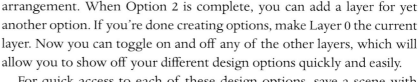

arrangement. When Option 2 is complete, you can add a layer for yet another option. If you're done creating options, make Layer 0 the current layer. Now you can toggle on and off any of the other layers, which will allow you to show off your different design options quickly and easily.

For quick access to each of these design options, save a scene with only one option visible. It is possible to have any number of design options represented this way. Note that if you add one more design option after setting up the first few scenes, the layer for that new design option will automatically be on in those original scenes. This is why it's a good idea to create a few extra layers, for different options, and then just leave them off until needed. If you have created a new layer after saving scenes, remember to hide those layers on the previously created scenes. Go to the existing scene and then turn off the new layer. Then, in the scenes dialog box, update the scene and verify that it is going to update the layer visibility status.

Populate the model

One of the most basic ways to lay out space is to start putting in furnishings to explore how the space will be used. We have already seen that there are a large number of resources available within the component collections. There are so many available online right there in the Components Browser, through SketchUp's own 3D Warehouse. Just type a word into the search bar of the browser—let's type in "stacking chair"—and you will see a list of chairs that are out there on 3D Warehouse. Many of these chairs are quite good and many of them are really awful, so you have to take a look at them carefully. Usually there's something in there that at least can get you started on your project, even if you will have to modify it later on.

Let's insert one instance of the "Inspire sled base stack" with arms. If you click on the little arrows at the bottom of the stack of components, you will see that there is page after page after page of results. There are over 33,000 different chairs! As you move each component around, you will probably notice the protractor that pops up as you mouse over each of the visible surfaces. Click and drag on the little plus signs to rotate the components around the center of that particular face.

There's another source for models, and some of you might have heard of it—it's called the *internet*. A quick search will reveal a number of different websites that have sources of SketchUp content. My favorite is a subscription service called www.FormFonts.com. The models are generally high quality, and they come in a number of different formats besides just SketchUp.

When you've got all of the basic elements created, turn off the bubbles layer to read just the furniture. Rotate the model so that it reads easily.

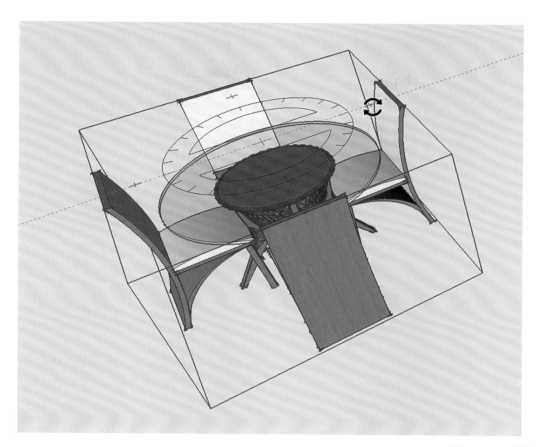

Figure 10.5 *Using the rotate inference of the Move tool.*

Figure 10.6 *The basic elements added.*

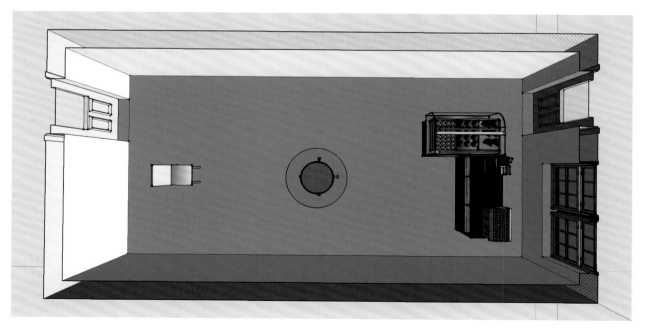

Want to create rows of components that aren't simple arcs? Use *CLF Component Stringer* from the Extension Warehouse to line up components along a chosen path, including circles and spirals.

Create a circular array

It's possible to use modifiers with the *Move* tool to create a **horizontal array**, which is a series of copies of an object spaced evenly in a row, with a user-defined dimension. A **circular array**, which is a series of copies arranged around a center point, and spaced a user-defined dimension or angle, can be created using the *Rotate* tool with a *Copy* modifier.

1. Select the object or objects you want to make an array out of.
2. Activate the *Rotate* command.
3. Click once to set the center point for the rotation command. If there is a particular spot in the plan, such as the center, be sure to draw in any reference lines first, to help select this point.
4. To activate the copy modifier, tap the ⌥ key and you will see a little + sign show up next to your cursor. That indicates that the command is now in copy mode.
5. Click once to define the base point—this can be either on the component itself or on some reference point, such as the back corner of the room.
6. Move your mouse to rotate around and click to define the second point where the copy will be dropped. As with the *Move* command, you can specify the exact distance, but this time it's in degrees.
7. And, as with the *Move* command, you can also use the / for + modifiers. Add as many chairs as you think will fit across your plan, while still leaving space for an aisle.

Figure 10.7 *A circular array.*

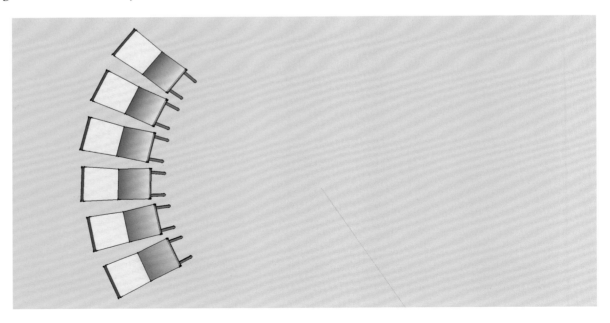

Arraying the array

Now let's imagine that this space is going to be used for a poetry slam event, so we'll need multiple rows of seating. Arrays in SketchUp are linear, which is to say, you can only do a row or a column, but not both at the same time, as in several other applications, such as our old friend AutoCAD. What you can do, however, is make an array of a row of seats that have already been grouped together. Let's try making a row of seating in an arc first, using a circular array. We will use the *Rotate* command to create a small arc of seating facing forward in the space. After the seating is placed and angled to the speaker, we can use a selection window to select all of the instances of this component.

Since we'll have several rows, let's make some copies of the arc of chairs we just created. If this was a larger project, such as a concert hall, it might be handy to create a component from my row of components, which would make it easier to create and modify exact copies. This is a very small space, however, and we will probably want to make changes to some of the rows for accessible spaces, so let's just create a group out of the chairs.

Select the row of chairs, right-click, and choose *Group* from the context menu. Now, invoke the *Move* tool and tap the ⌥ key to activate the *Copy* modifier. Then, make several rows of seats heading back into the space. Each of these behave similarly to a component, and you can move them all together, but it's also possible to edit them independently of each other. Let's make a change to the back row, though, to leave space for some patrons with accessibility concerns. Just activate the *Select* tool and double-click on the rear row of seats. You should see the screen become a sort of green, with only the back row of seats highlighted.

Need a mirror copy of a component? There is no mirror tool, but you can achieve the same effect by right-clicking on a group or component and choosing *Flip Along > Component's Red* (or green or blue, depending on the flipping you need to do). This will mirror only this one instance of the group or component.

Sub-components for arms, legs, and other parts are often **nested** inside complicated furniture components. This makes it easier to quickly create left and right sides that match, for example, but this can complicate painting. Keep double-clicking on the components to open up the part of the furniture that you want to paint, or break up the nested elements using the *Explode* tool.

Figure 10.8 *Editing the group of last rows of seats.*

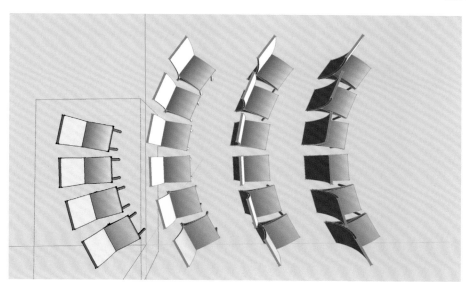

To help in space planning, use the 3D Grid Tool extension to place a grouped grid of reference lines on one or many planes.

Now you can select the interior two seats of each row on each side and delete them, in order to change the last row. Click outside of the gray bounding box that defines the limits of the block and you will exit block editing mode. Only that row is affected.

The difference between block and component behavior

A **group** is a unique collection of objects of any sort—copies of a group can be edited, and changes to one have no effect on the other instances of the group. A **component** is also a collection of objects of any sort, but is not unique—copies of a component are all linked, so that changes to one will affect them all. Let's apply paint to the chair to experiment with different materials. Doing so gives us an opportunity to see the difference between blocks and components.

If you invoke the *Paint Bucket* command, pick a color, and try to paint on the seat of one of the chairs, you will see that the organization within a group is going to give you some trouble—nothing at all happens. Let's double-click on that same row to edit the group, and then try to paint again. In all likelihood, nothing happens again! Okay, let's try double-clicking on one of the components to edit an individual chair. Now, click on the *Paint Bucket* command and try dumping a color onto the cushion.

Figure 10.9 *Painting the cushions.*

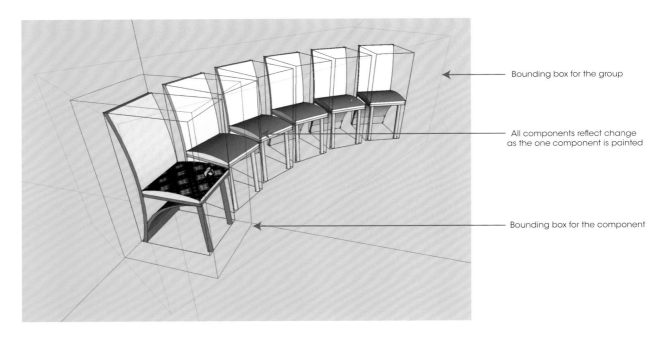

Bounding box for the group

All components reflect change as the one component is painted

Bounding box for the component

Dimensions

It is sometimes handy at this stage of the game to add dimensions in between the rows of furniture for reference. The *Dimension* tool is fairly straightforward in this way, and works in a similar manner to those found in other applications. Click on the tool, click once at the start of the dimension, and one more time at the finish. You can also select an object, such as a line or art or circle, and have an arrow leading off to describe the properties of that line.

Figure 10.10 *Different types of dimensions.*

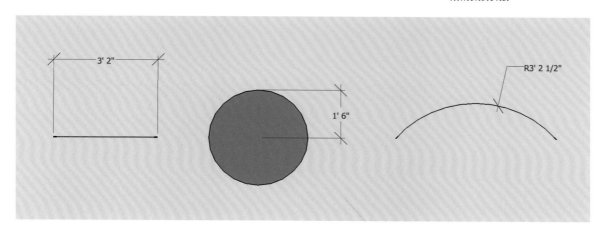

By default, dimensions are either on the ground plane or on a vertical plane. The text size will always remain the same relative to the screen, so as you zoom in, dimensions will stay the same size, but the drawing and the dimension's lines will get bigger. Try to place dimensions zoomed out to roughly the distance that you plan to print the view at, to avoid overlapping with objects.

See the Online Resources for a video showing different techniques for creating linear, rectangular, and circular arrays.

See the dimensions section in Chapter 7 for instructions on how to match dimensions and text styles.

Component management

There can be a lot of components in a larger project, especially if there are many design options. This can quickly get a bit complicated, as some components can have cryptic names or have nothing to do with a real product. As your design options become more concrete, use the Components Browser to rename everything to reflect the actual product or indicate if it's a custom piece. For a project like this, management won't be too hard. For an office systems type of project, however, great care should be taken in naming components.

Sometimes you want a slightly different version of a particular component. The easiest way to achieve this is to right-click on a copy of the component that you want to modify and choose *Make Unique* from the context menu. The component will have a different name and identity

Arrays can also have vertical offsets. This is handy if you're laying out furniture on risers, for example. See the section on creating a stair in Chapter 11 to see an array with both horizontal and vertical offsets.

If your model is geo-located using the Google Earth tool, you will be able to search for nearby models. In the Components Browser, from the *In Model* drop-down menu, select *Nearby Models*, which filters your search for other models in your geographic area.

than the original, and can be modified without fear of accidentally changing all of the other instances in the project. When should you create a unique component? When it would require a different ordering code is the best standard, as having a unique component will make it easier to create a purchase order. For example, in this project, we would do so if we wanted a chair with different upholstery.

Components, and especially groups or components made of other components, can sometimes be a little difficult to understand. This nesting of components and groups can be explained better using the *Outliner* tool, which shows the structure and sub-structure of your model. This is

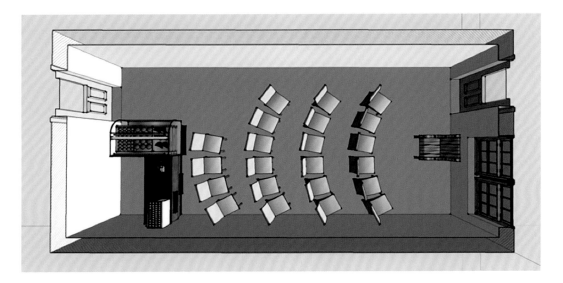

Figure 10.11 *The first design scheme.*

There is a quite robust (and also somewhat expensive) extension called BiMUp 5D, which can analyze your model and generate interactive reports and cost estimates in a flash.

particularly handy when you have a group made up of different components and other objects, and you want to swap out some of those components for a different option. For example, in my design for Option 1, there is a small coffee counter component we loaded in from the 3D Warehouse. Let's change the barstool to a different one, but we need to figure out what the name of the sub-component is first, so choose *Window > Outliner* (on Windows, edit the Default Tray and add the *Outliner* tool to display the dialog box).

Inserted images can be set to an exact dimension using the *Tape Measure* tool. Make the image into a group first and edit the group. Measure one side of the image, then type in the dimension that you want it to be and SketchUp will re-size it.

Place a painting on the wall

The last step in making a space look inhabited is to add those small-scale items, known as **entourage**, that add a sense of the human scale. Some items, like plants, place settings, or flower pots on the tabletops, can add a lot of extra information to the model, potentially slowing it down. Elements that are based on images are fairly light in terms of their impact

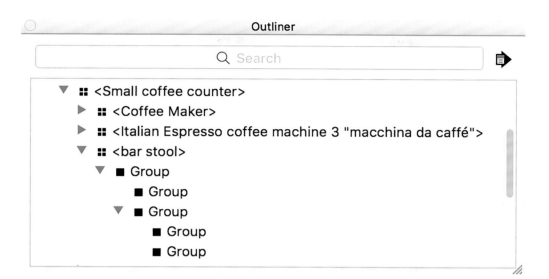

> Q Search

▼ ▦ <Small coffee counter>
  ▶ ▦ <Coffee Maker>
  ▶ ▦ <Italian Espresso coffee machine 3 "macchina da caffé">
  ▼ ▦ <bar stool>
    ▼ ■ Group
      ■ Group
    ▼ ■ Group
      ■ Group
      ■ Group

Figure 10.12 *The* Outliner, *breaking apart the coffee counter.*

on model performance and are easy to place and scale. An oriental type of carpet is a good example, but doesn't really work in our project. Let's add a photo to the wall instead.

1. Search for an image that you'd like to use, either on your computer or on the internet. Search engines can filter for image size, and in this case, approximately 1,000 pixels minimum in the largest dimension should give a good result. Save the image onto your computer.
2. Choose *File > Import* and browse for the image file you'd like to use. Make sure the *Use As Image* box is checked on the import menu, or you will end up with a texture to paint instead of an image that behaves like an object.
3. Click once on the wall where you'd like to plant the image and click a second time to define the size of the image.
4. Let's add a simple frame to give the photos some depth. Click on the *Rectangle* tool.
5. Draw a rectangle equally spaced from the edges of the photo.
6. Use *Push/Pull* to make the rectangle stick out from the wall—1/2" should produce a nice effect.

Moving the image away from the wall will produce a slight shadow if and when you render the view, which will also add an element of realism. Use this technique for oriental rugs, as well.

If you have added and deleted a large number of furnishings during the design process, you can purge unused components—just choose *Purge* from the fly-out menu in the Components Browser. There's a corresponding purge option in the *Layers* palette.

Images are co-planar with the face that they are placed on, which is to say, they are in the same geometric plane, and both have no thickness. This can cause a broken-glass look, known as z-fighting. Try moving the image away from the plane it's placed on.

Scenes will remember layer visibility, but not which is the current layer, so when preparing a presentation, set your current layer to one that is on in every saved scene.

Figure 10.13 *The photo on the wall.*

Resizing an image in this way will resize the entire model. If you already have parts of the drawing created, put the image inside a group, edit it, and use the tape measure to resize. It will only re-size the component.

An extension for filtering selected objects is called Selection Toys, by ThomThom. It allows you to add or remove objects from a selection using a large array of different criteria.

You can also use the Component Replacer, written by ThomThom. Insert new components into your model first, and then you can select old ones and replace them en masse.

Add another design option

Now we've got a nice furniture arrangement for a poetry reading—let's add two more schemes for what the space might look like when it's just a café. The idea would be to move tables and chairs around for these two types of functions, so you'd want to consider stacking and ganging of tables, for example, as you try out different types of furniture. Let's start another design option:

1. Consider whether or not you want to re-use the same furniture as your experiment. If so, select the furnishings components and make a copy.
2. Right-click on the copies and choose *Entity Info* from the context menu.
3. From the *Layers* drop-down list, choose Option 2. The copies will disappear from your view.
4. Open the *Layers* palette. You will probably see quite a few layers in there, and many components will have their own internal layering scheme.

5. Make the Option 2 layer the current layer.
6. Turn off the visibility of the Option 1 layer—you should see the furniture on your plan disappear, but, if you made copies of any furniture, those copies will now reappear.
7. Add furniture and equipment as before.
8. Add a scene and label it Option 2.
9. Repeat these steps for a third design option.

Figure 10.14 *Three furnishings layouts in one model.*

Having a few design options is great to compare and contrast, as sometimes you can come up with an interesting or unexpected use for a space.

Lose something?

Sometimes components or other objects disappear completely. This can be due to an odd placement of the model—it could be way off in outer space. Click on the *Zoom Extents* tool to see if there's anything lost in space. Objects can also be hidden, as sometimes happens when you bring in random components from the 3D Warehouse. To see what you might be missing, choose *View > Hidden Geometry*. If something was hidden that shouldn't have been, right-click on it and choose *Unhide* from the context menu.

Other times, objects are just on a layer that's turned off. To see what objects are on which layers, in the layer dialog box, turn on all the layers. Then, choose *Color by Layer* from the fly-out menu. This will cause all objects to display the color of the layer they happen to be on. In general, layers in SketchUp are used to control visibility, and not graphical characteristics, as in AutoCAD. Views like this are not terribly easy to understand, but it is sometimes handy to see different design options superimposed over each other.

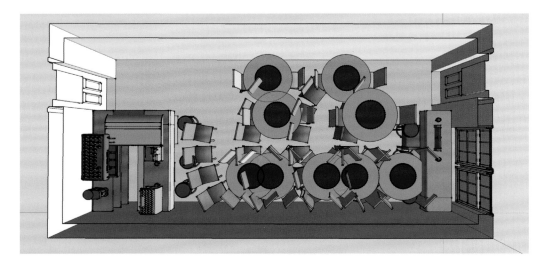

Figure 10.15 *Coloring by layer.*

Try it out!

- Create three different design options, each saved with its own scene. Add leader lines with notes describing each of the furnishings used, and also add dimensions indicating the spacing.
- Purge your model of unused components and layers.
- Create all custom furniture for your designs so that there is a unique aesthetic.
- Add scale figures and other entourage to your project, including place settings, window treatments, plants, etc.
- Create a riser for the seating and use an array to arrange the furnishings.

Key terms

- Bubble diagram
- Circular array
- Component
- Entourage
- Group
- Horizontal array
- Nested
- Space planning

Complex Building Elements

LEARNING OBJECTIVES

- Organize the elements of a two-story project for easy navigation.
- Construct a set of stairs and handrails.
- Produce design options using dynamic components.

Starting a multi-story project can be a little daunting, especially if you have to create highly complex yet dimensionally precise elements, such as stairs. Interiors projects often involve making these sorts of vertical connections, however, and a stair can be a great opportunity for a design statement. As with space planning, it's difficult to manage visibility of new elements on the inside of an already complex model. As we learned, existing conditions should be created and collected together onto a single layer. In multi-story projects, layers control the visibility of design options and also the visibility of each floor level, which leads to many more layers. We will use a simple two-level project, connected by a central stair, to illustrate this technique.

Organize with layering and grouping

The existing conditions of any project should be on their own layer as a rule. In the case of a multi-story project, however, it's best to have each level on its own layer. The furnishings for each level should also be on their own layer, that they can be turned on and off independently. Each of these layers will get multiplied as additional design options are added, so be sure to use names that are easy to understand. Let's also group

See the Online Resources for a copy of the model used in this chapter.

together the furnishings for each layer, as it makes it easier to quickly hide the rest of the model—handy for space planning. Most critical for navigating this type of project, however, is to save plenty of scenes with the different layer configurations, so that it's easy to navigate the model and view different design options as needed.

Model the existing interior

Let's create a simple two-story model to facilitate the design of a nice dramatic staircase—the building is 20' x 40', with 11'8" floor-to-floor height and 10' ceilings. This will give us an opportunity to learn to control multi-story geometry and also learn how to create a staircase. Because we only need this model for the creation of a stair, we only need to model the interior volumes. This will avoid the tendency of the smart cursor to infer snapping points on all the furnishings and other goodies that are in a full model. Once we've created the stair, we can load it into another file with all of the furnishings.

Figure 11.1 *Layers for a project with multiple levels and options.*

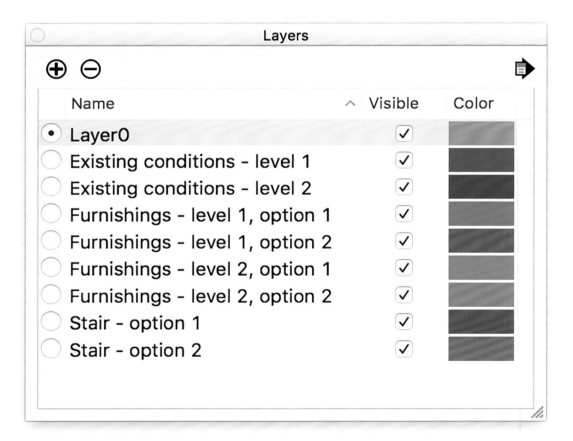

1. Let's start by creating the interior volume for each floor. Open a new blank file using the *Architectural—Feet and Inches* template.
2. We need to get the model organized first, so let's create a few layers. Open the *Layers* palette.
3. Create layers for *Existing Conditions—Level 1* and make this the current layer.
4. While the dialog box is open, create layers for the second level and for two design options for the stair and for furnishings on each level.
5. Click on the *Rectangle* tool.
6. Click on the origin to start the rectangle.
7. Type 20'x40'↵.
8. *Push/Pull* the rectangle up 10'.
9. Triple-click on the rectangle to select it.
10. Click the *Move* tool and tap ⌥ to activate the *Copy* modifier.
11. Use the lower corner as a base point and move your cursor until the tool tip reads *On Blue Axis*.
12. Type 11'10"↵ to make the copy.

Figure 11.2 *The levels for a multi-story project.*

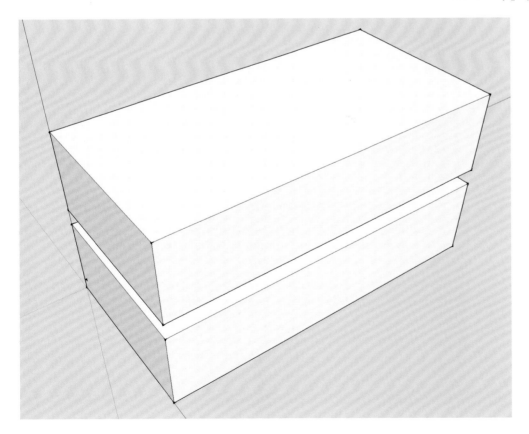

Creating a stair using standard units is a reminder that it makes a lot of sense for the United States to switch to metric, like the other 6 billion people on the planet. Base-12 and base-16 number systems are not terribly intuitive.

13. Select the copy, right-click on it, and choose *Entity Info*.
14. Change the object's layer to *Existing Conditions—Level 2*.
15. We need to save a few views of the model so that we can compose where the stair opening should be and draw the stair without any interference from the walls. Click on the *Section* tool.
16. Place a section plane on the long side of the model, a foot or so in from the edge of the wall.
17. Orient the model so that you can see inside clearly, and save a scene.
18. Now let's add sections to give views of the first level and the second level.
19. Add scenes for each view.

Figure 11.3 *The section and two plan views.*

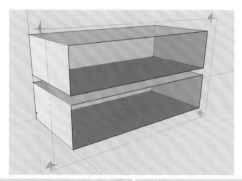

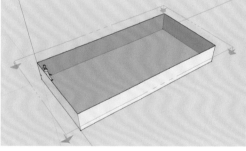

To draw the stairs, we need to know how big they need to be, for code compliance. To meet the building code, the risers can be a maximum of 7" and the thread can be a minimum of 11". This adds up to 20 risers and 19 treads, or a total length of 19 x 11 = 209" or 17'5". The last tread will be replaced by the second-floor level. This means we'll need a rectangular opening for the stair that's 4' wide by 17'5" long.

20. Click on the *Tape Measure* tool, so we can draw a reference line.
21. On the second level, click on the bottom front of the second-floor volume and then move your cursor toward the back of the model.
22. Type in 6'↵ to add a reference line for the start of the stair.
23. Click on a bottom edge of the long axis of the second floor.

24. Move your mouse over the middle of the short wall until the tool tip reads 10', which is the midpoint. Click to place the second reference line.
25. Click the *Rectangle* tool.
26. Click somewhere on the first reference line to start the rectangle.
27. Type in 17'-5,4'↵ to draw the rectangle the exact size of the opening.
28. Double-click on the rectangle to select it.
29. Click on the *Move* tool and use as a base point the midpoint of the short side of the rectangle.
30. Click at the intersection of the two reference lines to place the opening exactly in the middle of the second floor.

Figure 11.4 *Creating the stair opening.*

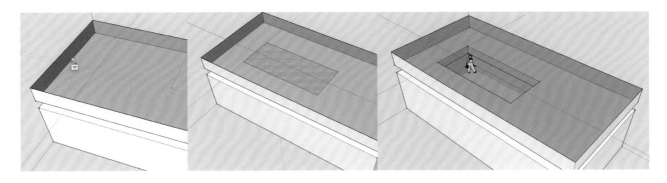

31. Click on the *Push/Pull* tool.
32. Click on the rectangle to define the base point.
33. Move your mouse over the upper corner of the first-floor volume until the tool tip reads *Endpoint*, then click to define the second point of displacement. A hole should be cut from the second floor to the first.

Most jurisdictions in the United States have switched to the International Building Code (IBC) as their base model code. Be sure to check for local modifications as well as fire codes and zoning laws that affect the dimension of egress components.

Create a stair the old-fashioned way, from scratch

Creating a stair is just a matter of creating an accurate component for the tread and riser and making the necessary number of copies. A landing can be created from a copy of one of the treads. It's more convenient to model the whole stair off to the side of the model first, because it's easier to see the exact configuration of the risers and treads without the walls getting in the way.

We'll make a component comprised of one tread and riser first and array it vertically to make the run of stairs. After some manipulation to create the landing, we'll collect all of the step and landing components into a single group and move that into the location that it belongs. From

Stair dimensions are governed by building codes and so must be drawn very carefully. See the section on units in Chapter 7 for instructions on how to change the scale and precision of your model.

It's possible to create a landing using one of the tread/riser components. Right-click on it and choose *Make Unique* from the context menu. Now that tread can be modified into a landing without affecting the other ones.

here on in, step-by-step descriptions will leave out some of the basic steps for creating simple objects like rectangles and moving objects, since we have gotten to the stage of the book where we are hoping that these operations will be fairly familiar.

1. Navigate off to the side of your two-story model so that you can start the stairs in an empty area.
2. Set your current layer as *Stairs—Option 1*.
3. Draw a rectangle that is 48" x 11", which is the size of our tread.
4. *Push/Pull* the tread up 7".
5. Select the tread, right-click on it, and choose *Make Component* from the context menu.
6. Click the *Move* tool and tap the ⌥ key to activate the *Copy* modifier.
7. Use the lower front endpoint of the component as the base point and the upper back endpoint as the second point of displacement.
8. Type in x20↵ to create a three-dimensional array with the total number of risers required.
9. It's hard to move around 20 individual tread/riser components, so let's group them together. Select all the steps, right-click on them, and choose *Make Group* from the context menu.

Figure 11.5 *Copying the stair tread component.*

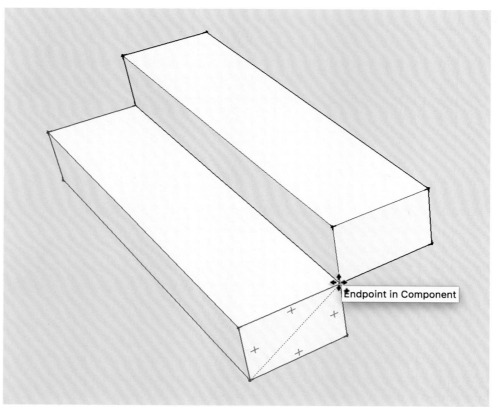

Endpoint in Component

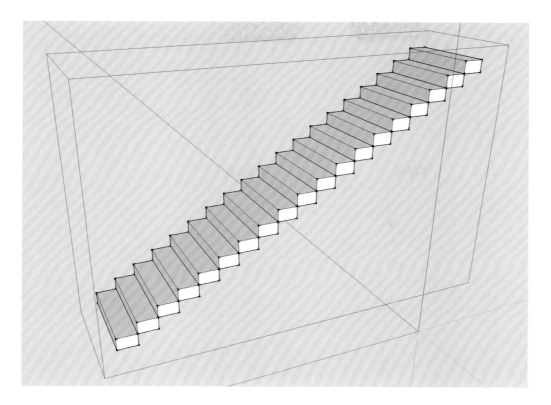

Figure 11.6 *The full run of steps, in a group.*

10. Move the stair into place. Make sure that the group actually fits and that the top tread lands right at the second level.
11. If everything fits, double-click on the stair group to edit it.
12. Delete the top tread and close the group.
13. To add a little realism, we can make the underside of the stair sloped. Double-click on the group and then the *Tread/Riser* component.
14. Click on the line at the top-back of the stair tread.
15. Move the line so that it lines up with the front of the next riser up. SketchUp will auto-fold the geometry to conform to the new boundary.
16. Close out of the component and they all should update.
17. Orbit the tread/riser to see the underside.
18. Click on the *Eraser* tool.
19. Hold down ⇧ while erasing the bottom rear edge line to hide it, making the underside of the run of stairs nice and smooth.
20. Save the model.

If you are planning to have some complex detailing of the tread/riser combination, it's a good idea to hold off creating the landing component until you've developed the final profile. Handrails can be added using extruded tubes, the *Follow Me* tool, or one or another extensions.

If you don't like the look of the lines between the risers, hide them: edit the tread/riser component, activate the *Eraser* tool, and hold down ⇧ while rubbing over the offending lines.

Are the fractions giving you a headache? Try this online construction calculator:http://www.mycarpentry.com/stair-calculator.html.

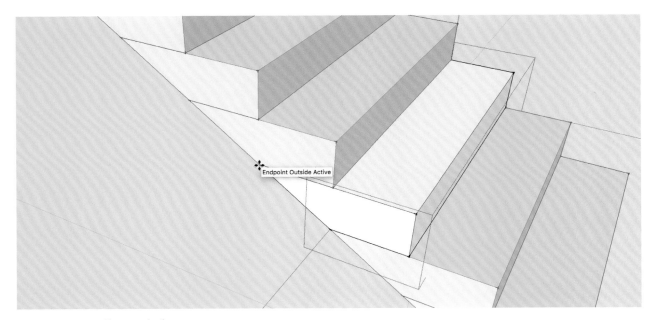

Figure 11.7 *Sloping the bottom of the stairs.*

Figure 11.8 *The finished stair.*

Helpful view tools

As you work on complex interior elements such as a stair, it can often be hard to see and select the pieces that you need to make objects fit in place. There are a number of viewing options that can help you look at the model by changing the way edge lines and faces are displayed, either with transparency or not. There are a number of view tools to explore to see which ones work best for your model—they are collected under the *View* pulldown menu, under the *Edge Style* and *Face Style* groups.

See the Online Resources for a video tutorial of how to make the existing conditions, these stairs, and add detail like a nosing. You could also just download the model and explore the finished product.

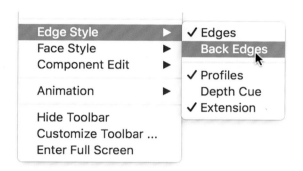

To see geometry that is hidden by faces between it and the camera, try *View > Edge Tools > Back Faces*. This will display the edge lines that are normally blocked out when there is a face in front of them. By default, back edges are displayed with a dashed, slightly lighter line. If you'd rather see a full representation of the hidden parts of your model, use the X-ray face style. This makes all faces semi-transparent, so that you can see all the way through the model.

Figure 11.9 *Options for view settings.*

Figure 11.10 *Display of back edges and X-ray faces.*

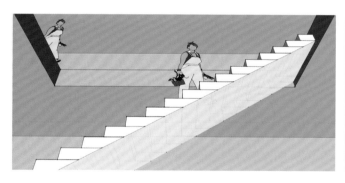

Extrude a handrail

It can be pretty hard to get up a set of stairs without a code-compliant handrail, but it can be pretty hard to draw a set of stairs *with* a code-compliant handrail. The trick is to get the angle and curvature of the handrail correct. For a simple stair, it is certainly possible to create a tube in the shape of the handrail and then move the end of the object into the correct position. For anything beyond a simple straight run of stairs, though, the easiest method is to draw a reference line and then use the *Follow Me* tool to extrude the handrail along that path. Here are the steps needed to draw a handrail.

1. Draw a run of stairs—let's use the one from the earlier exercise.
2. Draw a line from the front edge of the bottom step to the front edge of the top step. Move up to the desired height. Typically, by code, this is between 34" and 38" above the stair nosing.
3. Move the line in toward the middle of the front of the stairs. Again, by code, you'll want to leave at least 1 1/2" cleared space between the inside edge of the handrail and wall. My handrail will be 3/4" in diameter, so we need to add that distance onto the clear space, which gives me a total of 2.25" to move the line.
4. Start a circle at the end of the line. You'll probably need to mouse over a stair riser to orient the circle properly—just hold down ^ to lock the inference.
5. Type 1.5⏎ to draw the circle.
6. Choose Tools > Follow Me.

That is one long toolbar! Customize your toolbar to show just the tools you use frequently. In Windows, the toolbar has the option to be displayed in several pieces.

---

7. Click on the circle to select it as the profile to extrude.
8. Move your mouse along the line until you get to the end and then click to finish the handrail.
9. Click on the *Rotate* tool.
10. Select the railing. Tap ⌥ to activate the *Copy* modifier.
11. Click on the center of the landing.
12. Click along the red axis to make a mirrored copy of the railing.
13. Move the railing up to the same height above the stair nosing as before.

If you have multiple runs of the same configuration, place the stair components and the railing into a component, which makes it easier to repeat multiple times.

Hide/show components during editing

When editing a stair tread component, sometimes it's handy to be able to see the whole run as you edit. This is especially true when you are

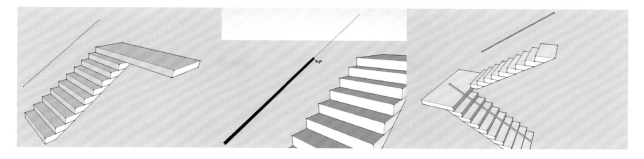

Figure 11.11 *The Follow Me tool in action.*

working on a staircase that is out in the open. If this stair is in a more enclosed space, however, you might want to hide the rest of the model while you are editing. To do this, choose the *Edit > Component Edit > Hide Rest of Model* option. You may want to make this a keyboard shortcut, because it can be handy to toggle on and off the rest of the model. See the section on shortcuts in Chapter 7 for more information on how to do this.

Create a stair the easy way, using an extension

There are quite a few extensions available to help you generate some of the complex geometry typical of architectural models. One that works well for creating interior elements of construction is called 1001bit Tools. It has a large number of handy tools that you can explore, but the one we're most interested in is for making stairs. This time around, let's make a stair with two runs and a landing, which would be quite time-consuming using the previous method.

1. Open SketchUp and go to the Extension Warehouse.
2. Search for "1001" and the tool should show up at the top of the list.
3. Sign up for the Warehouse if needed, and then install the tool.

Figure 11.12 *The 1001bit Tools toolbar.*

4. Install the tool as a single toolbar. Click on the *Straight Stair* tool.
5. Choose the dimensions and options we used to create the stair in the previous chapter (or, if you're working on a different project, enter your own). You'll also want to enter other parameters, such as the handrail heights and the left-to-right or right-to-left orientation.

Figure 11.13 *Stair dimensions.*

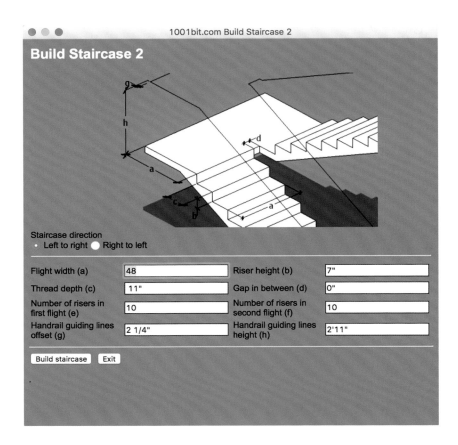

6. Click the *Create Stair* button.
7. Click once to define the base point for the stair.
8. Click again to define the rotation—the stair should appear, like magic.

Figure 11.14 *The finished stair, with railings.*

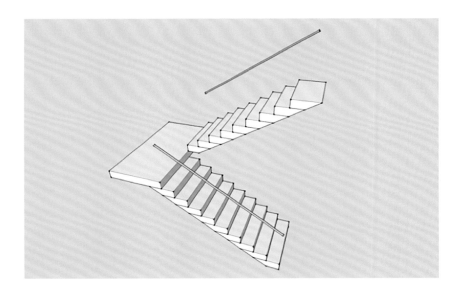

Once created, the stair cannot be dynamically modified by typing in values—the menu is only available when you are making the stair. The last settings you used will be saved in the tool, however, so it's possible to modify them the next time through. The stair is created as a group, so you can modify it using the usual editing tools. Note that this tool will leave a single line along the path where the handrail should go. You can use that series of lines, along with the *Follow Me* tool, to create the handrail.

How thick is a wall, really? 5″ is a nice round number for an interior partition. If finishes are critical, use the exact construction dimensions. For example, three 5/8″ metal studs with 5/8″ drywall on both sides add up to 4-7/8″ total.

Walls and openings

Once you have installed 1001bit Tools, you can also use one of my favorites: the *Wall* tool. This creates a single or string of walls, contained within a unique group, that keeps everything from getting sticky.

1. Click on the *Wall* tool.
2. Click the *Create Walls* button.
3. Click once to define the start of the wall.

Figure 11.15 *The* Create Walls *tool parameters.*

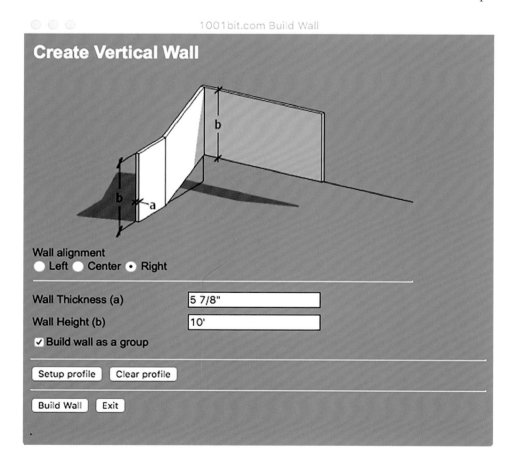

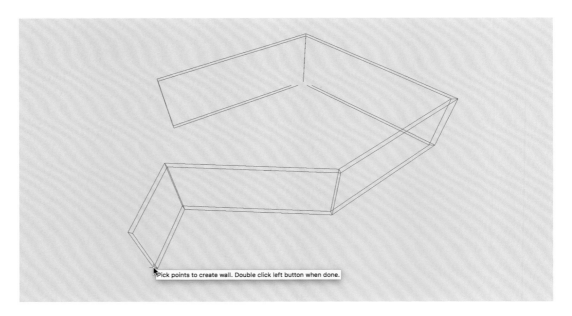

Figure 11.16 *Defining a chain of walls.*

Figure 11.17 *Opening parameters.*

As with SketchUp native tools, you can force lines along one of the axes by using the arrow keys and input dimensions into the measurements box.

4. Double-click to define the end of the wall or click a single time to define a corner.
5. Continue to click through to define a series of walls and double-click to complete the chain.
6. Click on the *Insert Opening* tool.

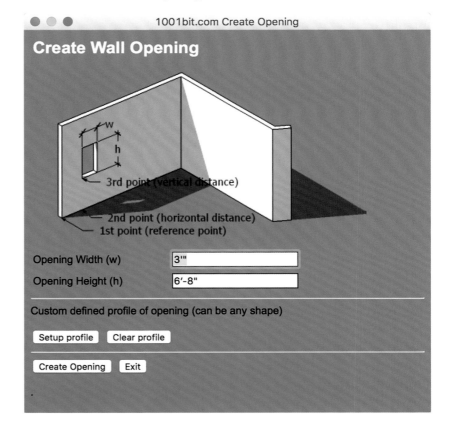

7. Click the *Insert Opening* button.
8. Click once to define the base measuring point for the opening.
9. Click again to define the distance along the wall.
10. Click a third time to define the height off the original point. The opening should appear, and it should cut through both sides of the wall.

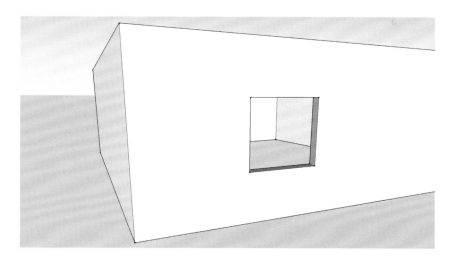

Figure 11.18 *The completed opening.*

While you can insert dynamic components into SketchUp Make, creating them is available in SketchUp Pro only.

Note that any part of the walls or inserted openings can be edited by double-clicking on the group. You should be aware that moving parts of walls can cause distortion in the wall geometry—they won't keep their original thickness.

Dynamic components

Regular garden-variety components in SketchUp are really just collections of edges and faces. If you edit one component's properties, you will change every instance of that component within the model. This is true for any number of **component properties**, including textures, scale, and number and arrangement of sub-elements. Components that are nested within the original—sub-components—are unaffected by changes to the parent. In fact, any SKP file can be inserted into another SketchUp file as a component.

Dynamic components behave in basically the same manner, but introduce **parameters**, which make it possible to edit certain types of dimensions on an **instance** level, so that two dynamic bookcase components can have different lengths. This might seem trivial, until you want to lay out, say, a restaurant with three different lengths of tables. You can quickly change these components, instead of having to make each one unique and edit the new one separately, or select them and swap out for different components. There are several dynamic components loaded

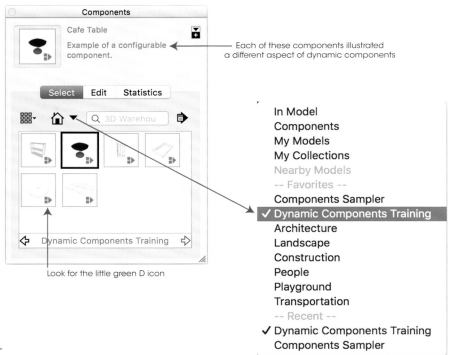

Figure 11.19 *Dynamic components training collection.*

into SketchUp automatically, in a collection called *Dynamic Components*—their icon has a special green D symbol next to them.

Insert the café table and let's take a look at it. Then, we'll take our table model and modify it to have some simple dynamic parameters. Note that your installation of SketchUp may not have the ability to manipulate dynamic components right off the bat, which seems to be the case mainly on Mac. If that is the case, you'll need to activate it in the same way you need to activate sandbox tools. Go to *SketchUp > Preferences > Extensions* and then check the box next to *Dynamic Component Tools*. The tools should become available right away.

1. Right-click on the café table component and choose *Dynamic Components > Component Options* from the context menu. The menu allows you to choose from whatever options have been created already for the dynamic component. For example, the base and tabletop style can be round or square and there are a number of pre-defined colors.

2. This is the menu where you actually get to define parameters. In this case, it's possible to see that the author has set a cost, material, and a number of dimensional options.

3. Now that we have a sense of how dynamic components work, let's create our own from the table created in Chapter 5. Open the original coffee table file.

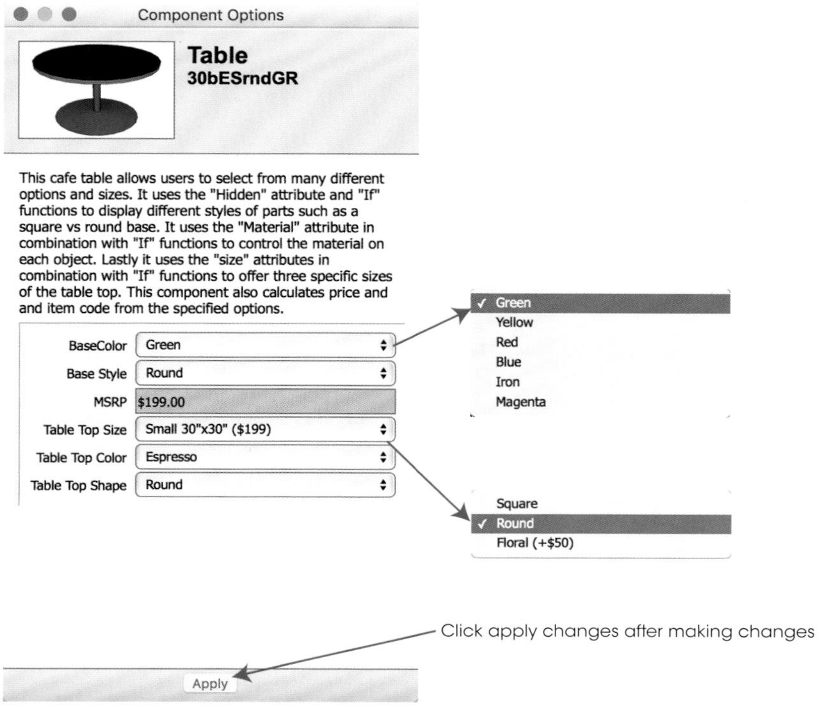

Figure 11.20 Dynamic Component Options *menu*.

4. Select all of the table geometry, right-click on it, and choose *Make Component* from the context menu. Give it a clever name, such as *Custom Coffee Table*.

5. Right-click on the table and choose *Dynamic Components > Component Attributes* from the context menu.

6. Click on the little + sign next to *Add Attribute* and a menu will appear off to the right with a list of possible dynamic attributes.

There are several ways you can configure dimensions in a dynamic component. You can constrain values, such as the width of a particular element within the component. A window frame might remain two inches wide, even if the height and width change. There can be animated features, where the dynamic component moves when you click it with the *Interact* tool. This is good for things like having doors and windows that open. Evenly spaced sub-elements, such as cubbies in a wall unit, can be configured to automatically add additional instances as you scale the overall component to be longer or shorter. Other examples might be things like pickets in a fence or studs in a wall. Finally, you can have configurable values, such as a bookcase length or the picket spacing in a fence component.

7. Look for the *Size* group and click on *LenX* to add it as an attribute— this will allow us to input values for the length along the component's red axis.

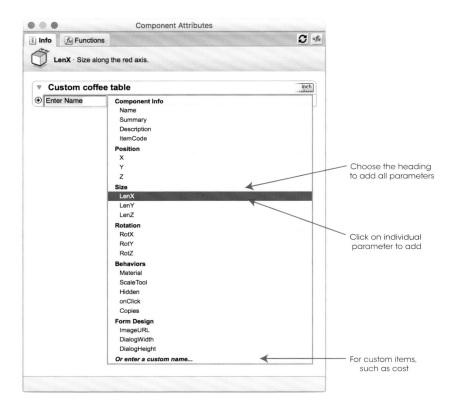

Choose the heading
to add all parameters

Click on individual
parameter to add

For custom items,
such as cost

Figure 11.21 *Adding a parameter.*

Note that the dimensions in these menus do not round, but instead are accurate to three decimal places. This is a bit more precise than we need, but our dimension strings and schedules will round as needed.

It would be cool if you could add parameters to sub-objects, such as the legs, but this causes the attributes to go haywire.

8. Click on the little arrow to the right of the *LenX* value to open up the *Attributes Selection* menu for choosing how users will interact with this particular variable.

9. Click *Apply* to make the selection permanent and then close the *Attributes Selection* menu.

10. To test out your newly flexible component, let's check the *Component Attributes*. There will be a dialog box where you can enter whatever value you'd like for the coffee table. Enter a new length and click *Apply*.

Locking the position of the component would probably be good for something like a shared structural grid from a consultant, so updates will show up in exactly the same position. Even if you choose to let the user alter these attributes, it will be possible to extract them later on, when you produce schedules. All this business about the definition of components and instances of components is important, because when you edit entities within a component instance, you edit the definition, too. Change the door's glass, and the glass in all component instances changes. Change the double panel into a single panel, and all the doors in your model have a single panel, too. You can scale, rotate, and flip an instance of a component without changing the other instances, using editing tools and the context menu items.

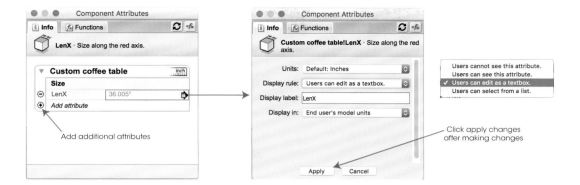

Figure 11.22 *Specifying dynamic behavior.*

Dynamic components can easily be swapped with each other, too. Just right-click on the one you want to change and choose *Dynamic Component > Swap Component* from the context menu. Another technique, which works with any component, is to select the component that you want to change in the model. Then, in the Components Browser, right-click on the component you'd rather use and choose *Replace Selected* from the context menu.

It is possible to create options within a dynamic component to easily change certain features, such as paint color. Activate the *Interact* tool and then click on a dynamic component within your model. If there are options available, you might see a door open or the color of a scale figure's shirt change.

This technique works well for certain actions, but changing the overall component dimensions will warp any sub-objects. Use alternative geometry for things such as leg height.

Try it out!

- Create a model representing the interior volumes of a two-story project. Design and build a stair that will fit within the two levels and that is also code-compliant for a non-residential project.
- Create a second option for the design of the stair. Furnish the two different options to be a retail project.
- Create a custom dynamic component for a display rack, where it's possible to change the length of the rack easily. Model the infamous open-riser winding glass stairs that are at the center of most Apple stores.

Key terms

- Component properties
- Instance
- Parameters

Advanced Geometry

LEARNING OBJECTIVES

- Modify standard objects to create complicated shapes.
- Create shapes by adding and subtracting simple solids.
- Develop organic geometry using the sandbox tools.
- Construct a spiral and a soap bubble using extensions.

The basic modeling tools of SketchUp are certainly adequate for most tasks, including generating a base model of a building, interior partitions, furnishings, and the like. Sometimes an interior designer will want to create something more dramatic, though, such as an organic light fixture, furnishing, or an unusual ceiling or wall shape. To do this, simple geometry can be modified in special ways to create a number of different types of shapes. The basic editing tools can change parts of objects in unpredictable and interesting ways, or you can use one piece of geometry to cut off or add to other pieces of geometry. If that's not enough for you, there are additional tools, some integral with SketchUp and others that are extensions, which allow the creation of ever more complex geometry.

Auto-fold

Let's start with a simple box and manipulate it using standard editing tools. Click on the *Move* tool, but be sure not to select any objects first. Then, mouse over the endpoint of one corner of the box—you should see the endpoint tool tip pop up. Click and drag that on the point, and

Intersecting objects

If you have a model element that you want to slice through, you can use the *Intersect Faces* option to create a similar effect to the solids tools, which only works with individual, non-nested groups and components. If we wanted the coffee counter component to conform to an angled wall, for example, we could do the following: rotate the model into the desired orientation, right-click on the surface of the wall, and choose *Intersect > With Model* from the context menu. The component will have new divisions wherever it intersects the adjacent wall.

Figure 12.7 *Trimming away a counter.*

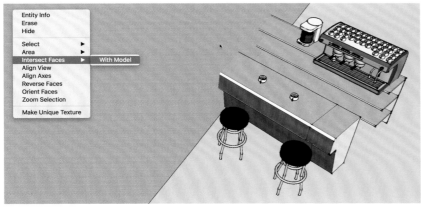
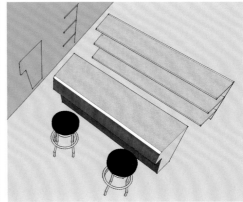

If you select the wall instead of the coffee counter component, you will end up with a section of the cut of the counter, which can be handy when creating, say, casework drawings of a very organic shape.

You can also use sandbox tools to slump a grid over a shape or shapes and to create terrain.

Sandbox tools

Sometimes you just need to break free of the orthogonal grid and create something organic. The sandbox tools allow you to do just that, using either a blank grid or creating contours from a collection of objects. Using a blank grid is actually the easiest and can be scaled for various types of uses.

1. Activate the sandbox toolbar by choosing *View > Toolbars > Sandbox*.
2. Click on the *From Scratch* button.
3. Click once to start drawing the grid.
4. Click again to define the width of the grid—10 or 12 grid cells will do.

Figure 12.8 *The sandbox toolbar.*

From Scratch tool for drawing a base grid

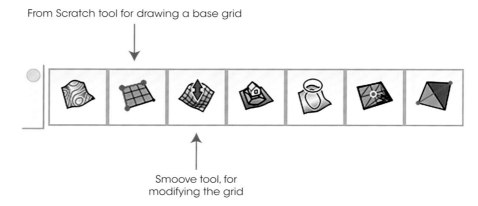

Smoove tool, for
modifying the grid

 Round Corner 2 is a great
extension for creating
curved geometry to soften
the edges of faces meeting
at right angles. It's one of
many useful tools by author
fredo6.

 Need to make a curving
ramp? Try CLF Shape Bender
to extrude a component
along any path, no matter
how curvy.

5. Click one last time to define the length of the grid.
6. Click on the *Select* tool.
7. Double-click on the grid to edit it.
8. Click on the *Smoove* tool.
9. Click and drag on the center of the grid—it should expand up with your cursor, in a similar manner to the *Push/Pull* tool.
10. Click and drag again in a different area.
11. Click outside of the grid area to finish editing.
12. Right-click on the group and choose *Soften/Smooth Edges* from the context menu.
13. Drag the slider to the right until the object appears as smooth as you'd like.
14. Check both the *Soften Edges* and *Smooth Coplanar* buttons.
15. Hit *Apply*.

Figure 12.9 *The* Smoove *tool in action.*

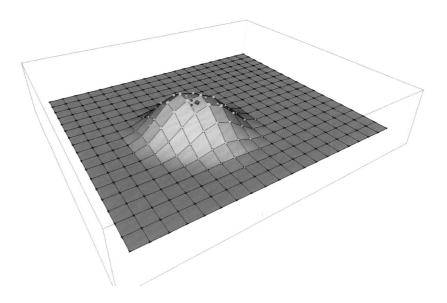

Soften/Smooth Edges

Angle Between Normals   180 Degrees

☑ Smooth Normals
☑ Soften coplanar

Figure 12.10 *The soften/smooth edges dialog box.*

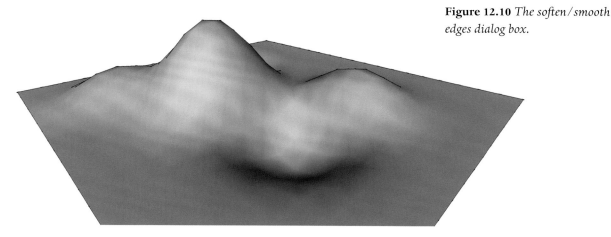

Figure 12.11 *The final shape.*

The grid can be rotated and edited again for different effects. This is because the *Smoove* tool only extrudes along the blue axis. These objects can also be saved as components or scaled to be larger (e.g., a mountain) or smaller (e.g., a lampshade) objects.

Complex curves

The default curves in SketchUp are basically simple three-point arcs. To get more interesting curves, such as a spiral, you will need to add an extension—my favorite is called Curve Maker. As with a lot of extensions, there are quite a few interesting tools here, but let's just use the spiral for now.

1. Open SketchUp and go to the Extension Warehouse.
2. Search for Curve Maker and the tool should show up at the top of the list.

Just need to make splines that are smoother than the *Freehand* tool allows? Take a look at the Bezier Curve extension—it only does one thing, but it does it very well.

Use this tool in conjunction with the *Follow Me* tool to create some interesting extruded objects.

3. Sign up for the Warehouse, if needed, and then install the tool.
4. If you receive a warning, be sure that your system is secure, with updated antivirus and a reliable backup system. This extension appears to be safe, though.
5. Click *Yes* and the toolbar should be installed. Most extensions install immediately, with a new toolbar showing up on your SketchUp interface. Others will need you to re-start the program.
6. Click on the *Spiral* tool.
7. Click on your screen to start the spiral.
8. Click again (or type in a value) for the second radius and the tool will create a spiral.

Once created, you can't really change any points along the spiral, but you can draw additional lines and arcs to make it fill in with faces. These can be extruded using the *Push/Pull* tool. Once created, the spiral can be modified using any of the editing tools, just like a freehand line. There

Figure 12.12 *Warning message.*

Figure 12.13 *Successful installation of the extension.*

Figure 12.14 *The curve maker toolbar.*

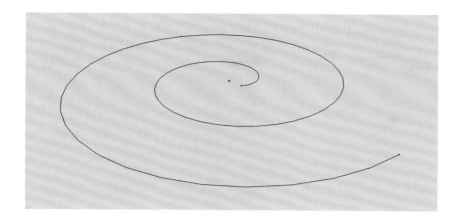

Figure 12.15 *The complete spiral.*

Surfaces created with this tool can make your model very large, depending on the number of grid divisions. Keep this in mind and avoid slowing down your model too much. If you plan to render, however, you might need those extra cells.

Most extensions install both toolbars and commands in the pull-down menus. Under which pull-down will vary based on the OS, but it is typically either under the *Tools* menu or the *Extensions* menu.

are many, many extensions like this for creating complicated geometry. A good rule of thumb is that if you're trying to create a recognizable form or object, there's probably an extension somewhere that will do it.

This tool is free, but seems to come with a time limit, which is usually the following year.

Warped surfaces

Sometimes you need to create an **organic** surface, which is to say, one that is not rectilinear, that has to fit within a proscribed boundary, such as you might see on a tensile type of canopy. The sandbox tools can create the right shape, but it would be a pain to have to trim away the extra parts using the solids tools. Instead, let's turn to one more extension, the *Soap Skin & Bubble* tool. You can connect almost any random lines with a skin-like surface, no matter what plane any of them are in. You can also "inflate" that skin, to make the surface more or less bulge-y.

1. Open SketchUp and go to the Extension Warehouse.
2. Search for *Soap Skin & Bubble* and the tool should show up at the top of the list.
3. Sign up for the Extension Warehouse if needed, and then install the tool.

Figure 12.16 *The Soap Skin &*
Bubble toolbar.

 Having trouble rotating arcs
to be off the ground? Draw
a cube next to the arc. Now,
when you rotate the arc,
move the protractor icon
over one face of the cube,
so that it flips up in that
direction. Then, hold down ⇧
to lock the inference, and go
ahead and rotate the arc.

4. Draw a series of lines and arcs—let's create a vaulted base of a dome shape.
5. Select all the edges.
6. Click on the *Skin* tool.
7. Type in a value from 1 to 30 for the grid divisions—you'll want enough to give you a fairly smooth surface. Let's type in 20↵.
8. Hit ↵ again to start the tool and watch the skin being created.
9. Select the newly created skin—it's a group.
10. Click on the *Bubble* tool.
11. Type in 50 ↵ and watch the bubble expand.
12. Type in -50 ↵ and watch the bubble deflate. Find a value that looks good for the boundary that you've created.

These bubbles can also be edited using the sandbox tools, although there is a tendency to crash the computer. The nice part of this tool is

Figure 12.17 *The outline for the*
bubble.

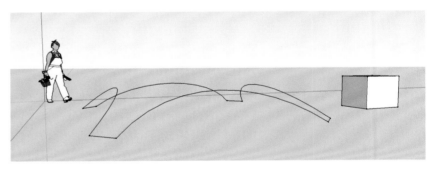

Figure 12.18 *The basic skin.*

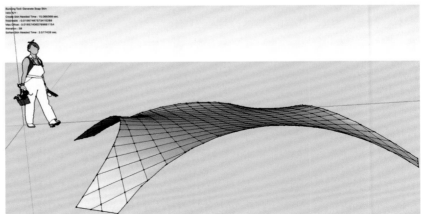

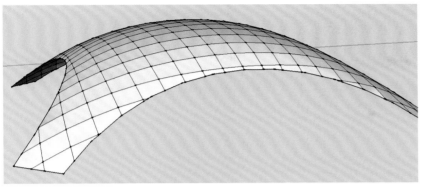

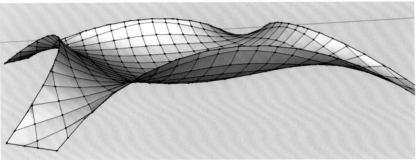

Figure 12.19 *The skin with a pressure of 50 and -50.*

The SketchUcation (www.sketchucation.com) website is a great place to find additional extensions that might not be in the main Extensions Warehouse.

that you can experiment with different pressure values to get just the look you want. Also, the outline remains, so you can always delete or hide the skin group if needed.

Managing extensions

Sometimes extensions are available from places other than the Extension Warehouse. To install those, download them onto the computer, and then open the *Extension* panel of the SketchUp Preferences. Click on the *Policy* panel, and then check the *Unrestricted* button to allow installation of extensions from all sources. Now proceed with the installation, as with other extensions.

Too many extensions can make booting up SketchUp slow and clutter up the interface once it's up and running. To uninstall an extension from SketchUp, you'll have to go to the Extension Warehouse and navigate to *My Extensions*. From there, it's possible to uninstall anything that originated from within the warehouse. This is also the way to re-install extensions if you had to re-install SketchUp for some reason.

Extensions that came from rogue sites are harder to uninstall—they need to be deleted from the extensions folder that SketchUp creates, and this can be hidden, depending on your system configuration. It's best to try searching your computer for any files with the RB file extension and see if you can find them.

Figure 12.20 *Allowing all extensions.*

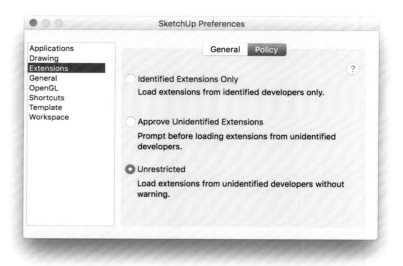

There is even an extension to manage other extensions, called On-Demand Plugin/Extension Loader. This will load only those extensions that you need for a given session of SketchUp, and leave the rest out of the interface.

Try it out!

- Create a "crown" by moving the endpoints of a hexagonal volume.
- Create a bulging shape, scale it to the size of a bean bag, and then cut out a rectilinear seat using the solids tools.
- Create a human face using the sandbox tools.
- Create a tensile canopy inside a large atrium space.
- Create a groin vault in a 100' x 100' x 40' shape.
- Create a bubble structure for parking cars.
- Create a parabolic arch.
- Create a Guastavino-style tiled vault, with a round opening cut in the center.

Key terms

- Auto-fold
- Organic

Simple Design Presentations Using LayOut

CHAPTER 13

LEARNING OBJECTIVES

- Prepare a SketchUp model for use in LayOut.
- Identify an appropriate LayOut template for a design presentation.
- Modify model viewport graphics, including scale.
- Explain the layer structure of LayOut.
- Organize sheets of drawings using pages.
- Illustrate your drawings with external images.

Sooner or later, it's necessary to exit the electronic world and put together a presentation of your masterpiece for your clients and colleagues. Most printed presentations will have a combination of orthographic drawings such as plans, reflected ceiling plans, and interior elevations, and perspective drawings. Interiors projects in particular will have a lot of images of the materials proposed, along with specification information and endless schedules and legends. All projects, no matter the type, are likely to have a nicely designed title block, stylish text, and other ancillary graphics to keep the whole thing organized.

LayOut is a handy application for arranging different views of SketchUp models onto a single sheet for printing and presentation. It's somewhat akin to paper space in the AutoCAD world, or, in Revit, sheets of drawings. Note that it's perfectly possible to put together presentation drawings in Photoshop or some other application. To get LayOut, you have to pay for the Pro version of SketchUp—it will download automatically when you sign up, along with the Style Builder. The

See the Online Resources for a demonstration of these techniques and the files used in their creation.

See Chapter 9 for instructions on how to set up orthographic views.

SketchUp model can continue to be updated, and the sheets drawn in LayOut will update to reflect those changes. It's not as tightly integrated as you might find with BIM applications, but for small projects, it is quite adequate for page layout. The sheets of drawings that you create can include any type of view within SketchUp, and include any of the styles you created. Most annotation, however, is done in the LayOut interface, and not in SketchUp.

Let's take our café project from earlier in the text and set up a pair of presentation boards, one with perspective drawings and the other with plans and sections.

Prepare the SketchUp model

The best way to prepare a SketchUp model for use in LayOut is to have ready-made scenes created for the views that you would like to include in your construction drawings or presentation. The basic strategy here is to have saved scenes for each of the different types of drawings you'd like to include. These are typically going to be a mix of orthographic and perspective views. Let's use the Frozen Poetry Café from our space planning project to create a set of schematic design presentation drawings. As you might remember, we set up several design options in that exercise, so let's make a presentation where each of those options is shown on a different sheet, for our clients to compare and evaluate.

Here's a list of drawings that we should include for each option, which conveniently will also give a nice introduction to the range of tasks you would typically need to do in LayOut.

- Floor plan @ 1/4" = 1'0"
- Transverse and longitudinal sections @ 1/4" = 1'0"
- Bird's-eye perspective
- Interior perspective looking forward
- Interior perspective looking toward the back

Open the model from Chapter 10, or, if you'd prefer, use any project that you'd like to set up for presentation.

1. Set a true plan view, if you didn't have one already.
2. In the *Layers* palette, leave on the layer for Option 1, but turn off the layers for the other options.
3. Apply the style for orthographic views, which hides the visibility of the section planes and makes the drawings black and white, and save

the scene. It's important to give the scenes names that indicate which option they are, so that they can be easily differentiated in LayOut.

4. Repeat steps 1–3 for both the transverse and longitudinal sections.

5. Save scenes for your two favorite perspective views, with whichever style you'd like to use for the presentation board. If you're not sure, save several versions of the scene with different styles for each. As with the plans and sections, make sure Option 1 is visible and the others are hidden.

6. Now we need to set up scenes for Option 2.

7. Open the plan scene again.

8. Back in the *Layers* palette, turn off Option 1 and turn on Option 2.

9. Save a new scene, labeled *Option 2 Plan*.

10. Repeat steps 6–9 for each of the other drawings.

11. Save the file.

Figure 13.1 *Tab for scene labels.*

An alternative to this method is to save separate files for the three options, which is handy if you are collaborating with other people to generate ideas for the project. Each of those files can be linked to a single LayOut file, so a single board comparing options is possible.

Send to LayOut

Save the model one last time (SketchUp will give you a reminder if you haven't anyway), and then click the *Send to LayOut* button. LayOut will launch automatically, and you'll be presented with the splash screen with a Tip of the Day, with hints on how to use the application. If you're feeling confident, you can un-check the button so that this menu doesn't pop up again.

Close the Tip of the Day pop-up and you will be prompted to choose a template for the project. As in a lot of page composition applications,

The Windows version of both SketchUp and LayOut allow only one document open at a time. In the Mac version, however, you can have multiple windows open. This can be handy, but can also start to tax your system resources. Be sure to close unused documents.

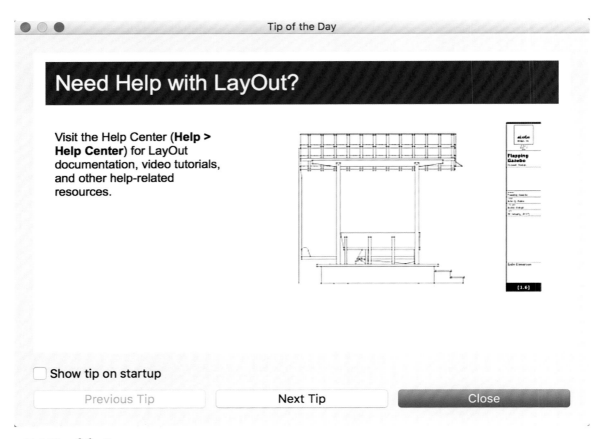

Figure 13.2 *Tip of the Day.*

 Refer to Table 18.1 for the exact dimensions of standard architectural paper sizes.

the page size can be changed later, but in this case, the template you choose typically comes with a sheet border, title block and drawing titles, and all sorts of other graphics meant to match the look and feel of the template, and those are more of a problem to load in later. LayOut has a few templates to offer, arranged by the purpose of the drawing set: a blank drawing, a presentation drawing, or CDs. Also, the typical office will have its own template, with the office logo, project numbering system, and so on, so be sure to use that template, if available—check in the *My Templates* folder.

The icons should give you a good idea of what the sheets will look like, and there are really just a few things you need to decide: the overall size of the printed drawing and where you'll want to use any of the standard architectural drawing sizes. It's always a good idea to check which sizes your printer can actually produce. You'll also want to choose landscape and the type of title blocks, if any. Some are more oriented toward construction drawings, which are typically aligned vertically on the right side of the sheet, and others are more oriented toward presentations. If this is a renovation of a very tall atrium space, then portrait might be the way to go. Otherwise, landscape is a bit more typical. Let's use the *A4 Landscape* lay-

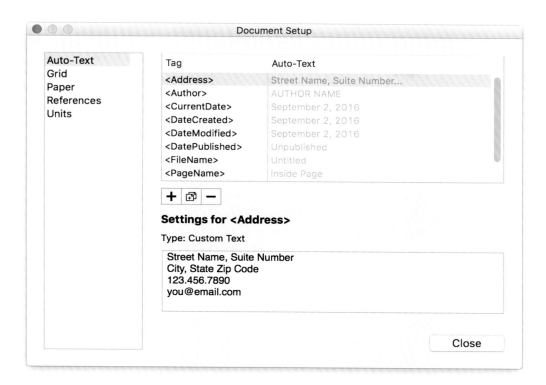

Figure 13.8 *The* Document Setup *menu.*

Figure 13.9 *Grid settings.*

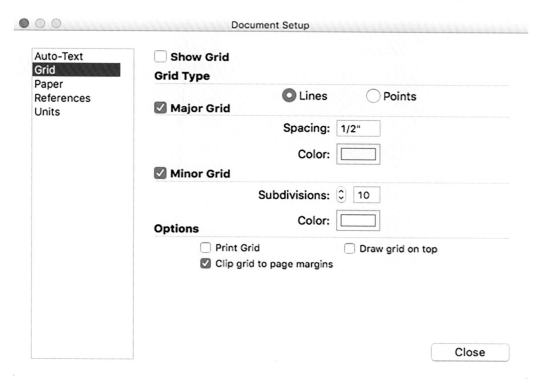

it easier to align titles and notes. Most objects, such as image files, can also be made to snap to one another or to a grid. Grid lines don't print by default, although that is an option. You can also make objects snap to that grid, using *Arrange > Grid Snap*, and snap to each other, using *Arrange > Object Snap*.

The color of the paper can be controlled here, along with its size and the dimensions of the margins. For presentation drawings, there is often either a base color to the sheet or a background image. This can make the presentation dramatic, so long as the background doesn't distract from the actual drawings. Construction drawings, on the other hand, are almost always black lines on a white background. Note that the display resolution can be set to low, while the output resolution can be set to high, which is handy if your LayOut file is starting to slow down.

The *References* panel is where you'll be able to see the status of any documents that you've inserted in LayOut. These can be multiple SketchUp files, but also images. You can collaborate with other people in your office this way, assigning, say, a detail drawing to someone else. You'll be able to insert the drawing and then update it as changes are made. This template comes with a logo embedded in it already—let's change it to use an image file on our computer. Select the logo reference and then click on the *Relink* button. Browse for your image file and click *Open* to apply the image. Resize on the title block as needed.

Figure 13.10 *Paper settings.*

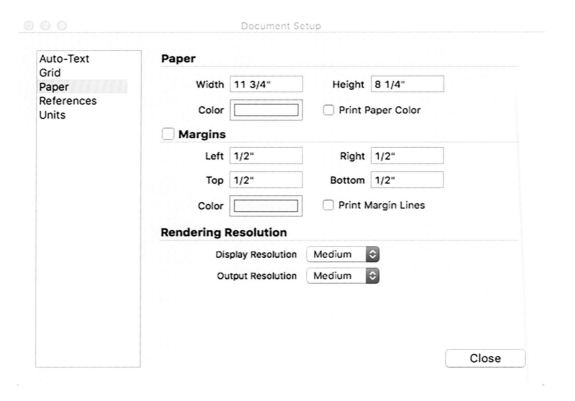

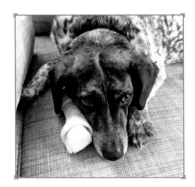

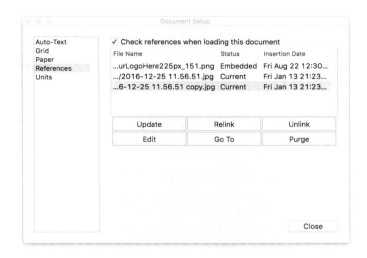

Figure 13.11 *The* References *panel.*

Figure 13.12 *The* Units *panel.*

Just like in SketchUp, it's possible to switch your LayOut file to metric in the *Units* tab. It's also possible to control the precision of drawn elements. These changes will not affect the original model in any way, but will change the behavior of dimensions drawn in LayOut.

LayOut drawing and editing tools

As with SketchUp, related tools are stacked together in LayOut, to keep a clean interface. The two tools at the end of the main toolbar, however, are unique to LayOut. *Split* allows you to cut viewports and shapes, while *Join* will add shapes and viewports. These are handy when you have an irregular section of plan or interior elevation, such as with a vaulted ceiling. Several of the keyboard shortcuts are the same, too—the space bar for select, and L for starting the line tool. These can be customized in the LayOut Preferences.

Editing objects is slightly different in LayOut when compared to SketchUp. Once selected, you need only click on and drag an object to move it. For the most part, however, objects have different handles that are used to resize, stretch, rotate, or crop shapes. Clicking and dragging on corner handles resizes the object proportionally, while clicking and dragging on the side handles distorts the object along that axis. There is also a rotate handle in the middle of the object. Click and drag on the X to rotate or the box to move the axis.

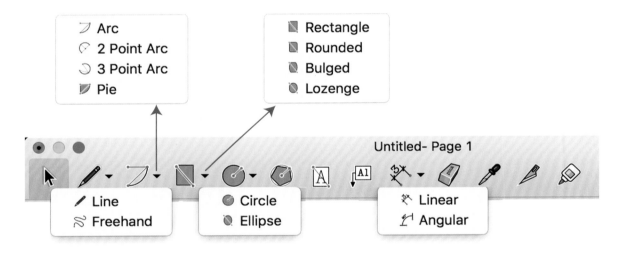

Figure 13.13 *LayOut drawing tools.*

It is possible to control both the stroke (line weight and line type) of an object and its fill color. Available colors and fill patterns are exactly the same as in SketchUp.

Layers

In SketchUp, layers are mainly used for organization. In LayOut, a particular layer can be isolated and then given unique graphic properties, such as being dashed or red. The *Default* layer is the one on which pretty much every new object gets placed, and this will show up only on individual

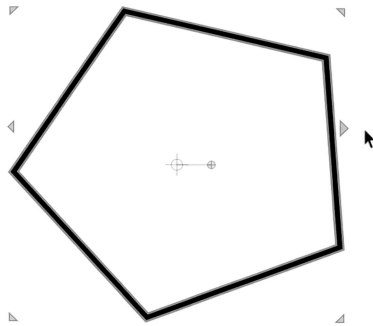

Figure 13.14 *Object editing handles.*

Figure 13.15 *The Shape Style menu.*

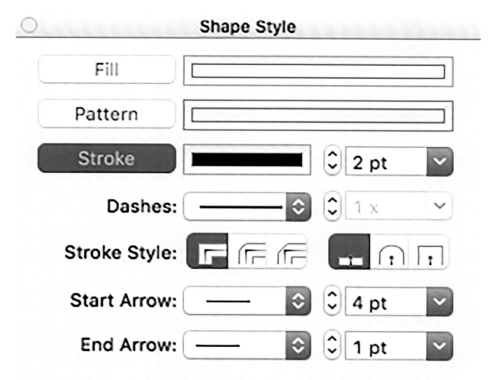

sheets. Objects drawing on the layer labeled *On Every Inside Page* will show up on every sheet that's not the title page. This is good for the title page on those inside sheets, which is usually different than the cover of a set of drawings. The *Cover Page* layer is for elements that only show up on the title page or pages. Make sure that *Default* is set as the current layer.

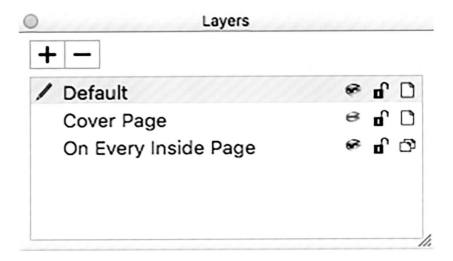

Figure 13.16 *The Layers Inspector.*

To create a new layer, click the + sign in the dialog box, just like in SketchUp. Why would you need additional layers? Sometimes it's nice to add a layer for markups and comments, or for notes and dimensions.

Text and titles

Using text in LayOut is very similar to other software applications, wherein you click and drag a rectangle that you want to fill with text. Then, type away, and the box will force the text to automatically scroll to fit. Resizing the box will re-scroll the text. To change the size and font of a selection, right-click on it and choose *Text > Font* (or CMD + T) from the context menu. From there, you can make any changes that you want. Selections with blocks of text can be changed using the standard system keyboard shortcuts: ⌘B for bold, ⌘I for italics, ⌘U for underlining, ⌘+ for increasing size, and ⌘– for decreasing size.

Add a title below each drawing describing what it is, and a big piece of text to the title block that says Option 1. Note that text boxes, and actually almost any drawing in LayOut, can be moved in front of or in back of other objects merely by right-clicking on them and choosing *Drawing Order* from the context menu.

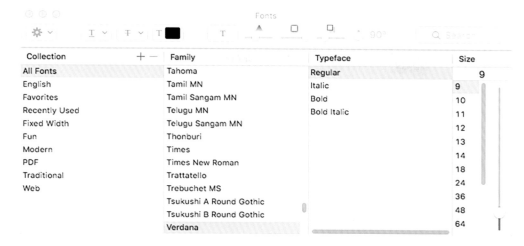

Figure 13.17 *The* Font *menu.*

Edit the title block

The default title block in this particular template has a couple of different text boxes, each of which typically shows up on the layer labeled *All Inside Sheets*. So, anything you create on this layer will show up in exactly the same way on any other sheets. The discipline letter and sheet number can be changed independently from one sheet to another. As before, just use the select commands to double-click on the text, and you can edit it. The parts of the title block for the date, project location, and project title are actually special kinds of text called auto-text. You can double-click on these to edit the text, but you can also control what they say globally by changing the auto-text values in the document setup menu. You can also add new auto-text values if you find that you are using a lot of repeated terminology.

Insert images

There will be instances where you want to include pictures of the furnishings, finishes, or other elements in a project that do not occur in the model. This is especially handy if you have a complex piece of furniture that would really be a waste of time to model in all its glorious detail. Instead, model a simplified version, but include a high-quality photograph to show your client what the object really looks like. Just choose *File > Insert*, browse for an image file, including JPG, BMP, PNG, and even PDF, and click to place. These objects can be resized just like other elements, and, because they are linked to original files, they can be updated or changed. As with any page layout application, be careful with image resolution, so that your prints will not appear pixilated. Small images copied from manufacturers' websites will not print well unless they are small on the sheet layout.

LayOut uses the system font, so if you want to add a new font, you'll have to add it to the system font folder. On either Mac or Windows, search for "font," and hopefully you will find the folder where you can drag the font file to.

LayOut will link back to the original images and SketchUp files inserted into the project, so you need to make sure that the files are saved in a consistent location—don't move files around.

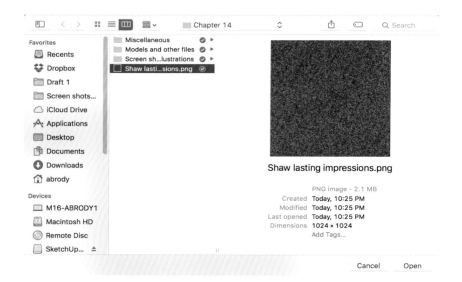

Figure 13.18 *Insert image dialog box.*

Pages

Most LayOut templates open up onto the page layout that's meant to be repeated on sets of multiple pages. There are usually two different designs, though, one for the title page, and another for all the inside pages. Typical printed design presentations, as opposed to pamphlets or handouts, have several instances of the same board layout. Open the Pages Inspector to switch to the other pages already in the project and to add or subtract new ones.

We are not really going to have a cover page for this project, so let's delete that page by selecting it on the Pages Inspector and clicking on the little - sign. Now we've already set up my sheet perfectly for Option 1, so it'd be easiest to just make a copy of that sheet and change all the views to reflect the next option. Select the remaining sheet in the Pages Inspector and click on the *Duplicate* button to create sheets for Option 2 and Option 3.

Figure 13.19 *The Pages Inspector.*

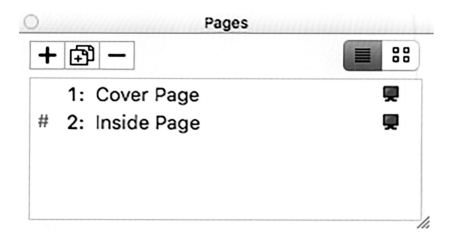

Switch to the Option 2 page and you should see that it looks exactly the same as the one for Option 1. Click on the viewport for the plan, and then, in the SketchUp Model Inspector, change the scene to the one saved for Option 2. While you're at it, change the other views to be for Option 2. Finally, change the title to read Option 2, and you've got your finished sheet. Do these same steps one more time for the Option 3 sheet, and you've got a pretty quick and pretty good looking set of drawings.

Present your masterpiece using LayOut

Presenting these sheets is pretty straightforward in LayOut—just click on the *Present* button on the upper-right of the LayOut interface and you'll enter a full-screen view of your current sheet. You can switch pages using the arrow keys on your keyboard, and you can even draw on the screen with a bright red line using your cursor. Those annotations can be saved, too, and will become free-floating linear objects when you are done presenting.

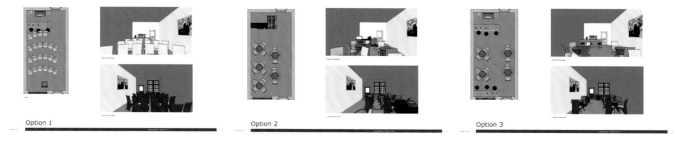

Figure 13.20 *The finished pages.*

Export file to print

Sheets are not typically printed directly from LayOut, but instead are converted to a PDF file. This also gives us a chance to do one last preview, without any reference lines or the grid visible. Choose *File > Export* and then browse for the file location where you'd like to save. Make sure to choose the multi-page PDF format and then click on the *Options* button.

It's a good idea to choose high quality, although it does make the file size a little bit larger. This multi-page document can be printed or distributed via email. If you are not completely satisfied with the graphics of the final boards, you can convert them to image files and open those files in a photo editor. From the same export menu, choose either JPG or PNG as the file format. This method allows a much higher resolution,

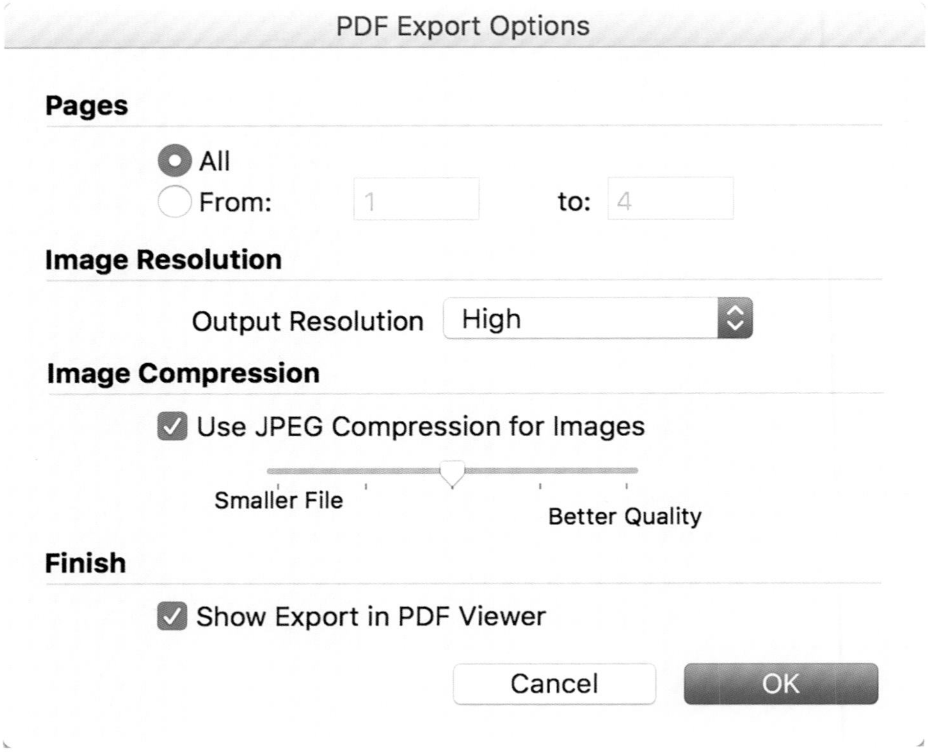

PDF Export Options

Pages

○ All

○ From: [1]   to: [4]

Image Resolution

Output Resolution [High ⌄]

Image Compression

☑ Use JPEG Compression for Images

Smaller File ——————○—————— Better Quality

Finish

☑ Show Export in PDF Viewer

[Cancel]   [OK]

Figure 13.21 *The PDF export options dialog box.*

which is useful for post-processing in Photoshop. You can also export your sheet as a DWG file, which can be read by AutoCAD, but also can be imported into Adobe Illustrator or similar vector editing programs for further touch up. If your computer is connected directly to a large format printer, or you just want a check-print, the usual print dialog menu applies.

Note that LayOut gives options for printing all pages or not, and also to print in black and white. If you have Adobe Acrobat on your computer, a press-quality PDF file can be created with the print menu, which will give a better result than exporting directly from LayOut. Mac users will also have a PDF option in this menu, but this will not be as high quality as with Adobe.

Try it out!

- Prepare your café project for use in LayOut by setting up scenes for plans and perspectives of three different design options.
- Open your model in LayOut using any of the 24 x 36 sheets. Customize the title block for your project and set up sheets for model views for each of the three design options.

Figure 13.22 *Print preview.*

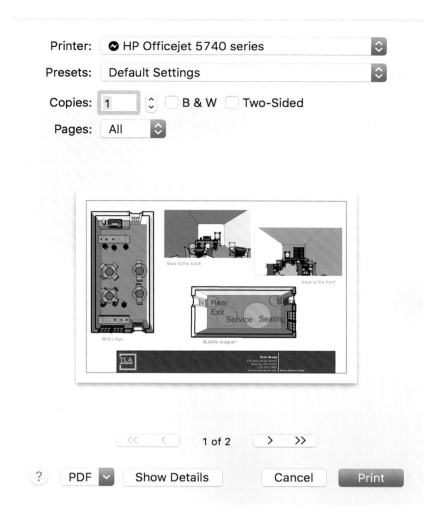

- Annotate each of the drawings with titles and notes indicating the primary features of the design option.
- Illustrate the materials used in each of the design options with JPG swatches arranged near where they'll be used.
- Use an irregular boundary, such as an oval, for the perspective viewports.
- Load your hand-lettered font into LayOut and use it for notes.

Key terms

- Grips
- Tray
- Viewport

Construction Drawings Using LayOut

LEARNING OBJECTIVES

- Compose a floor plan for construction documents.
- Compose a reflected ceiling plan and section drawing for construction documents.
- Create interior elevations for construction documents.
- Apply dimensions and notes at different scales.

At some point in the design process, we have to move from a rough scheme to a set of drawings that will explain to a contractor and a building official what exactly you want to build. LayOut is the best place to put together a set of construction drawings for your SketchUp project, as it can leverage model information, as well as create new detail drawings, using internal drawing and annotation tools. If you plan to use SketchUp for construction drawings of any sort, you'll need LayOut, so you'll need to purchase the Pro version of SketchUp.

It's possible to produce drawings from scratch or using legacy formats, and to add dimensions, notes, and other graphics typical of this type of drawing. Let's take design Option 3 again and turn it into a set of design development-level construction documents. We will first prepare the model in SketchUp, and then go ahead and add annotation in LayOut.

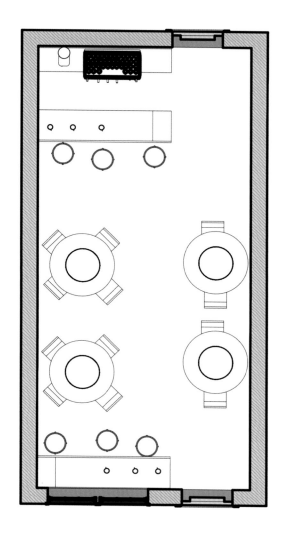

Figure 14.5 *The composite plan view.*

If you're like me, and have a little trouble following direction precisely, you might find that the overlays are out of order. Move them apart and right-click on the one that needs to be adjusted. Right-click on the viewport and choose *Drawing Order > Move to Front,* or whichever direction it needs to go.

Copy and paste works for most objects in LayOut. For a new viewport, you can also choose *File > Import* and then browse for your model. Just make sure that you use the same version!

16. Select all three viewports.
17. Right-click on the selection and choose *Group* from the context menu.
18. Repeat these steps with the reflected ceiling plan.
    The graphic standard for an RCP is that it has the same orientation as the floor plan. To accomplish this, right-click on the group and choose *Flip > Left to Right* from the context menu.
19. For the elevations and sections, we'll need another interior sheet. Go to the Pages Inspector and add a new sheet.
20. Repeat these steps with each of the section views.
21. We also need to create elevations. These are much simpler than sections, because we don't need to worry about poché and wall thickness. Insert a new viewport and set it to the north view of your model.
22. Save your LayOut file.

Figure 14.6 *The RCP.*

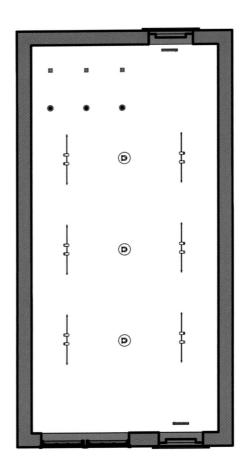

Figure 14.7 *The south and east sections.*

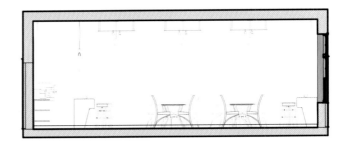

Figure 14.8 *North and west interior elevations.*

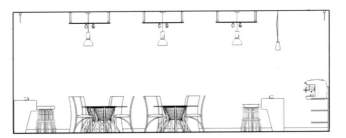

Typically, a floor plan is cut at approximately four feet above the floor. Reflected ceiling plans are typically cut at about six feet, so that you can show the door head. Interior designers tend to think a lot about lighting, so it's a good idea to cut the reflected ceiling plan a bit lower, to show any sconces or projecting switches. Those are items that are likely to get labeled and scheduled in the reflected ceiling plan, too. Interior elevations and section drawings for construction drawings do not usually show movable furniture, so the section planes can be placed close to the walls. If there are features in the ceiling that you want to show, however, such as soffits, you will want to place the section plane accordingly. In either case, it may be handy to have your furniture on a separate layer, which can be turned on and off as needed.

Just like plans, reflected ceiling plans are cut at a more or less standard height. Make the cut height low enough to show the door and window heads, to make placing exit signs, recessed blinds, and the like easier.

A finishes plan

Any specialty plan is going to have the same basic configuration as a floor plan in terms of graphics. Since you've already created the floor plan, along with the additional views needed to use poché and line weight enhancement, just make a copy of one of those groupings. For a finishes plan, however, you'll want to hide all of the furniture, so that only the floor finishes, thresholds, and other transitions are visible. This can be done easily enough by turning off the furniture layer. If there are any material transitions that need to be called out, this can be done here with a note. Use a heavy line in LayOut to call attention to these transitions or any other flooring details, as needed.

Add dimensions of model elements

Adding dimensions in LayOut is very similar to adding dimensions in SketchUp, except that the size of the dimension stays fixed to the size of the sheet, and does not rotate around with the model. Simply click the *Linear Dimension* tool and then click on the first corner of a room to start the dimension string, and then the opposite corner to define the end. Finally, click one last time to place the dimension string some distance from the wall. It will run parallel to the two points that you clicked on.

If you have any two points that are at an angle to one another, the dimension will also reflect that angle, although if you move your mouse along the orthogonal, LayOut will infer that you want the dimension orthogonally drawn also. If you double-click at the end of the last dimension, LayOut will start a new string at the same snapping point and string offset.

Figure 14.9 *The finishes plan.*

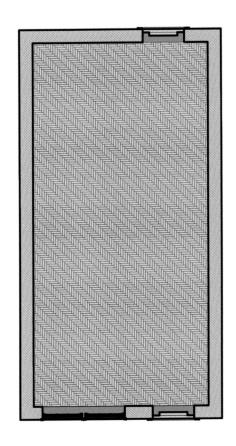

 Are your dimensions reading 4" instead of 16'? Both ends of an angled dimension must snap to an object in model space in order for the string to work. Otherwise, you will be measuring paper space.

 Change these settings before placing dimensions and all new ones will have that setting. You can also change each one individually. You can even have a free-floating dimension, not referencing any object in LayOut or a viewport.

 SketchUp and LayOut both use a lot of palettes, menus, and dialog boxes. If you have the space and money, use two monitors: one for all of the menus and the other for the drawing area.

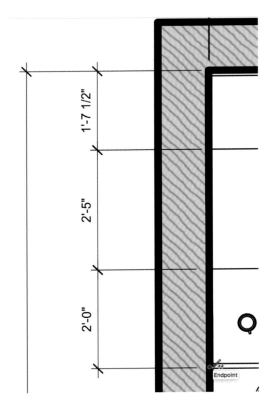

Figure 14.10 *Dimension strings.*

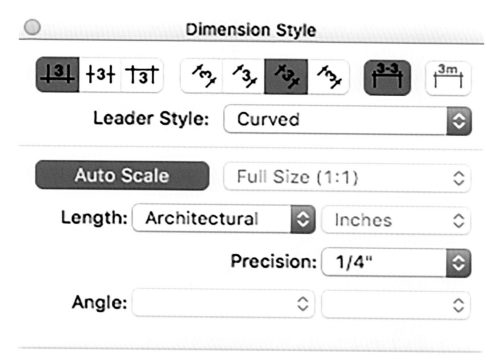

Dimension Style

Leader Style: Curved

Auto Scale   Full Size (1:1)

Length: Architectural   Inches

Precision: 1/4"

Angle:

Figure 14.11 *The different types of dimensions.*

Angular dimensions are the other option within LayOut. They are a bit more complicated than linear dimensions, in that they require four clicks, two each to define each side of the angle to be measured.

Tools in LayOut also have modifiers, although not as frequently as in SketchUp. With the dimension tool, you can hold down ⌥ in order to draw a dimension string that is not constrained to the orthogonal grid, which is handy for angled walls or furniture.

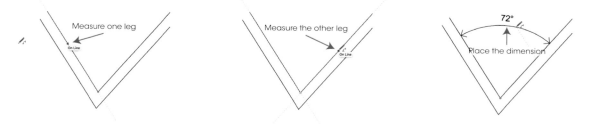

Figure 14.12 *Annotated image of the steps needed to draw an angular dimension. Image courtesy of Mike Beganyi.*

Dimensions are actually somewhat complicated in their parameters. They utilize both parameters set in the Dimension Style Inspector, but also parameters set in the *Fonts* panel. They also take their line weight and color parameters from the Shape Style Inspector.

Mike Beganyi is a timber frame house designer and builder in Burlington, Vermont. He uses SketchUp for client presentations, as working through a design in 3D is the best way to help clients get a good understanding of a design. He also uses SketchUp to develop working drawings, including designing the complicated timber framing details typical of his work. See more at www.MikeBeganyi.com.

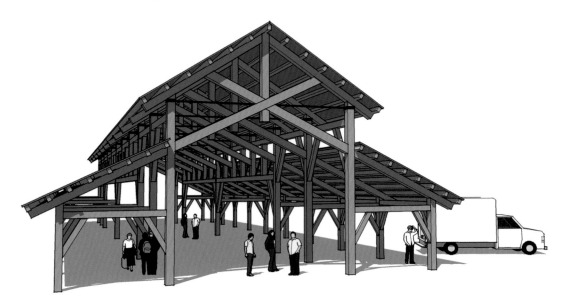

Case Study 14.1 Framing exploration by Mike Beganyi.

Figure 14.13 *How the three menus work together.*

Note that dimensions depend on a view being to scale, so always make sure that you have set the drawing to scale.

Add room names

Text notes also operate in a similar way to those in SketchUp. There are two options: the text tool and the label tool. The former is for a single piece of text, such as a title, and the latter is for an annotation where an arrow points at a particular element in the drawing. Activate the *Text* tool and click once to plant the cursor on your screen. Note that you can also click and drag a window in which to fill with text. Then, just type away, and click outside of this box, or on any other tool, to finish typing.

Putting in all the room names is fairly simple. Just click on the text tool, configure it to be center justified, and of course choose a font that you find invigorating. Then just click to place the text and type out the room names. Since these names might show up multiple times, on different drawings, it's a good idea to group them together. Just use the *Select* command, along with the *Shift* button, to select each of the room names individually. Then, right-click on them and choose *Group* from the context menu. This particular project really doesn't have separate rooms, but just areas.

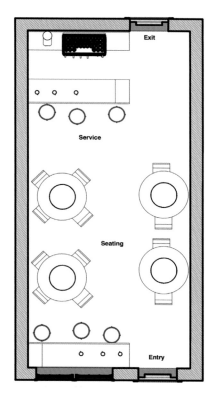

Figure 14.14 *The plan with room names.*

Add notes

Notes typically have a leader line, an arrow head, and a piece of text at the other end. All the notes should line up with each other, and the leader lines should never cross. The *Label* tool also works in a very similar manner to the corresponding tool in SketchUp. Click once to plant the arrowhead, again to define the leader line end, and once more for the "tail" of the leader line, which is also the start of the text box. LayOut will automatically change the justification of the text based on the direction that your arrow is facing. Labels can be selected and adjusted by dragging their grip handles, which adjusts the text and arrow direction, or moved in their entirety.

LayOut will fill the note with auto-text based on whatever it is that you are pointing out. Typically, this ends up being either an area, if you are pointing out a face, or a linear dimension. Parameters for note styles are also controlled in multiple places. In this case, it is the same as dimensions in that you need to look at both the font menu and the Shape Style Inspector to control all aspects of the note. As with any text editor, you can fiddle around with fonts, font size, and other features such as justification.

To set the default text style, make sure you have nothing selected and then choose the font parameters that you prefer. This only seems to work for the text tool and not the label tool.

Figure 14.15 *The fonts dialog box.*

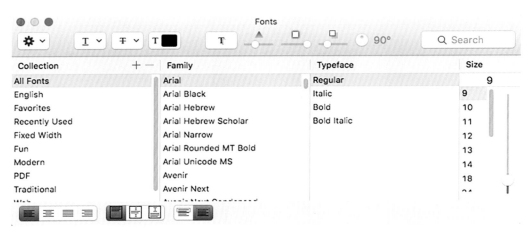

Try it out!

- Set up a new LayOut file for construction documents and configure the floor plan for poché and enhanced line weights. Be sure to add room names, dimensions, and notes.
- Add titles, a north arrow, and other ancillary graphics from the Scrapbook.
- Create a **legend** for the different elements and graphic standards in the floor plan.
- Create transverse and longitudinal sections with the same graphic standards as the floor plan.

Key terms

- Legend
- Poché

Advanced Orthographic Drawings

CHAPTER 15

LEARNING OBJECTIVES

- Organize the details of your drawings using the Scrapbook.
- Develop a legend for the plan.
- Prepare a finishes plan with a legend.
- Coordinate detail numbering.
- Design the title page.

As mentioned in the previous chapter, producing construction drawings with SketchUp really requires purchasing the Pro version to get access to the LayOut tool. If you prefer AutoCAD or some other drawing system for these types of drawings, you can export orthographic views to the DWG file format, but once again, that is a feature of the Pro version of SketchUp.

The base drawing for most sets of construction drawings is the floor plan, where keys to a number of other drawings are found, such as enlarged sections of the floor plan, building and wall sections, interior elevations, and other details. Interiors projects often have specialized plans for finishes, furnishings, equipment, and a robust reflected ceiling plan. Each can be accompanied by a key to graphical elements, and often a large schedule tabulating product specifications, quantities, and ordering information. As with the floor plans, those other views need to be configured in SketchUp first. They can then be referenced in LayOut, given appropriate line weights, poché, and annotation.

 See the Online Resources for a demonstration of these techniques and the files used in their creation.

The Scrapbook

Creating construction documents is often an exercise in trying to be as consistent as possible with your graphic standards. Most modern CAD and BIM applications give you the tools to have consistent graphical symbols through the use of components and libraries. Within LayOut, the library of graphical symbols is called the Scrapbook, which is actually just another LayOut file with a number of different pages in it. Each page has different drawings on it, and they are grouped thematically, such as floor plan symbols, arrows, people, etc. These mini-drawings are, in turn, typically made up of a combination of shapes and text, and occasionally images. You can even create your own or download them from any number of sources.

Most of the templates have a small library of the standard architectural symbols that you will need to set up a set of construction drawings. We began this project by choosing the *TB—Contemporary* title block. If you open the Scrapbook Inspector, you will see that there are already quite a few different options under the drop-down list of available groups.

Figure 15.1 *Scrapbook folders and sub-folders.*

▼ Arrows
   ✓   arrows | 3D | curved
        arrows | 3D | straight up & down
        arrows | 3D | straight left & right
        arrows | 3D | curved, flat
        arrows | 3D | curved, tilted
        arrows | 2D | north
        arrows | 2D | straight
        arrows | 2D | crazy
  ▶ Cars
  ▶ Colors
  ▶ People
  ▶ Signs
  ▶ TB-Contemporary
  ▶ TB-Elegant
  ▶ TB-Plain
  ▶ TB-Simple Serif
  ▶ TB-Simple
  ▶ TB-Traditional
  ▶ Trees (Elev)
  ▶ Trees (Plan)

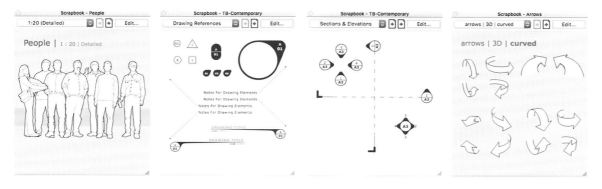

Figure 15.2 *Greatest hits from the Scrapbook.*

Let's start right at the top with the arrows grouping. When you click on the group selection arrows, you will see a long list of what are basically different folders with different types of arrows in them. Let's go to the *Arrows | 2D | Crazy* grouping, just to see what could possibly be in there. Lo and behold, there are actually just a bunch of squiggly-looking arrows in there. To use them in your drawing, use the *Select* command and click and drag on one of the arrows. Drag it into the drawing area and you should be able to drop it right onto your drawing. It then becomes an object within the drawing, which is a group, so you can double-click on it to edit it if you need to. You can also use the basic editing commands, such as rotate and stretch.

Okay, some of these are better for design presentation than they are for construction documents, but it was certainly fun. Let's take a look at the *TB—Contemporary* grouping in the drawing references sub-category. There, you will find a number of different things that you can drag into your drawing, including both left- and right-justified drawing titles, detail call-outs, and door and window tags. As with the arrows, just use the *Select* command to click and drag these different elements into your project. To edit the groups, double-click on them with the *Select* command. You can then double-click on individual pieces of text to change their number.

Once you've got the drawing titles the way you like them, just copy and paste under each of the individual drawings, numbering them as you go. Remember that construction drawing conventions are typically that you start numbering from the bottom right, moving across to the left, and then from the bottom to the top of the sheet.

If you have a project that has a complicated finish system, in which you might need separate furniture and floor finish plans, put the furniture on a separate layer within SketchUp so that you can turn it on and off in different views.

Section and elevation symbols

We have already decided to have sections and interior elevations in this particular project. There are standard symbols that are used to represent where the sections are cut in your drawings. These can be found under the *Sections and Elevations* grouping in the *TB—Contemporary* section of the Scrapbook. You can always create your own symbol, but it's most efficient to learn using the standard items first, before you customize them with funky fonts and wacky graphics. Click and drag the section symbol into your sheet as before. Then double-click on the Scrapbook elements to edit them and to change the numbering for the sheet where they have been placed.

Often, early on in the creation of a construction document set, it's easier to leave these symbols blank, filling them in later when all of the sheets have been laid out and you know what the detail and sheet numbers will be. One of the processes in which BIM applications have a major advantage over SketchUp is the coordination of these detail references, which will typically update automatically as drawings are added to sheets or moved from one sheet to another. SketchUp and LayOut don't have the capability to track coordinate detail numbering from one sheet to another.

Figure 15.3 *Editing a section icon.*

The section icon, like most things in the Scrapbook, is composed of groups of different types of drawing elements. Double-click on the group to edit the sub-elements, and you'll find that some parts, like the bar that spans the drawing, are just lines. Other elements, such as the tail at the end, are sub-sub-groups in their own right. Double-click on those to drill down the elements that you want to modify. Keep clicking outside of the groups until you have returned to the sheet level.

Floor plan legend

Legends are simple diagrams that explain the graphic vocabulary used in a drawing, and are commonly used with floor plans and reflected ceiling plans. For example, a floor plan legend would show how existing,

On Mac, use ⌘⇧4 to take a screenshot of the entire screen. In Windows, there is no default keystroke combination to take a screenshot, which makes me a bit snippy. CTRL+PrtScn will take a screenshot, if you have a full keyboard. If not, you'll have to open the *Snipping* tool.

new, and demolished partitions are drawn—they are really just lines, arrows, or symbols from the project with bit of text explaining what each is. In the case of a floor plan legend, you'll need to indicate the difference between new walls and existing walls. It would certainly be possible to use a copy of the floor plan layers, but this might slow down the LayOut file quite a bit. In this case, let's use a screenshot of the floor plan, which is easier to crop and rotate for my legend.

Individual viewports can be easily converted to an image file. Right-click on the viewport and choose *Explode* from the context menu. Note that you'll lose the reference back to the original model this way, so make a copy of viewports that you need.

1. Zoom in on the floor plan so that sections of both existing and new construction are visible.
2. Type ⌘⇧3 to take a screenshot of just a portion of the screen. An image file will be saved to your desktop.
3. Insert the image you created into LayOut. Crop and rotate so that a single length of existing wall remains, which is all we need for the legend.

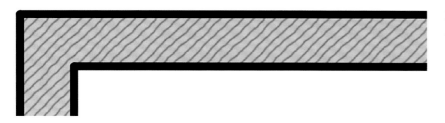

Figure 15.4 *Cropping the image of the floor plan.*

4. Create another single length of new construction wall.
5. If you have used half-height walls, storefront systems, or any other type of partition, create sections of those too.
6. Create a piece of text next to the first piece of wall and label it *Existing Construction to Remain*.
7. Activate the *Move* command and, while holding down ⌥ and ⇧, click and drag directly down to place a copy below and aligned with the first piece of text.
8. Change the text to *New Construction*.
9. Continue with any other wall types that you might have. Other elements, such as icons used for casework or furniture, can also be included.
10. Create a larger piece of text for the title of the floor plan legend—it's typically called *Key to Symbols* or something similar.
11. Draw a dark rectangle around the entire legend, including the title and all of the elements.

Now where did that file go? Some screenshot apps will save directly to the desktop or to their own directory. Automatic backup systems, such as Dropbox, will harvest screenshots into their own folder structure.

The scope of every project that you work on will probably be a little different, so you might need to add or subtract from this legend. This is

Figure 15.5 *A simple floor plan legend.*

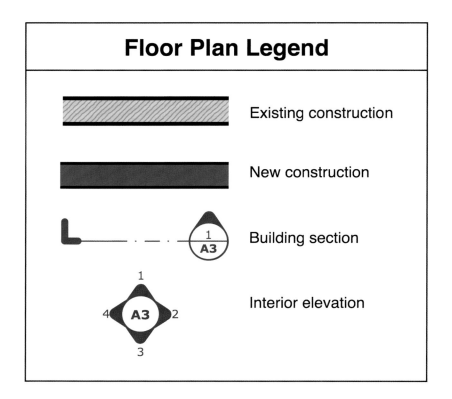

particularly true when you're working on a historic renovation, where only portions of existing interior or exterior wall might be demolished, while others might be salvaged for reuse. In this case, a more complex drawing might be needed, or better yet, annotated photographs to accompany the floor plan.

Drawing call-outs

It's easiest to start with the floor plan in LayOut to place all the major **call-outs**, which are graphical icons that link to an enlarged drawing somewhere else in the drawing set. This helps to avoid things like hidden elevations, which do not always show up unless you are looking at the floor plan. As we learned in the last chapter, the Scrapbook has a lot of handy dandy annotations that we can use. The *Sections and Elevations* grouping has components for all the drawings that we will need. Just click and drag the components into your plan and rotate them into the correct orientation.

Let's also insert a call-out for an enlarged section of the plan where the built-in custom podium will sit. Let's use the *Drawing Title* scrapbook group with the detail number on the left side. While we're in the neighborhood, let's put in some annotation indicating transitions be-

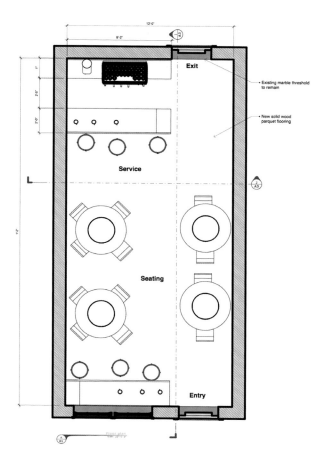

Figure 15.6 *Floor plan with all the references.*

tween different flooring materials. These can sometimes be tricky if you have materials of significantly different thicknesses, but they are a very typical interior detail.

Creating a clipping mask

What if the model view, such as an interior elevation, has an irregular boundary, such as you might have when there is a soffit around the perimeter of the ceiling? It is possible in LayOut to draw an irregular boundary using any of the line, arc, or shape tools. Just draw the shape you want and then select both the shape you just drew and the viewport that you want to crop. Right-click on them and select *Create Clipping Mask* from the context menu. LayOut will find the center part of whatever shape you created and use that as the clipping mask. Your model will show through that portion of the shape.

Want to edit the shape? Just double-click on it and you will be able to select the clipping mask—you should have access to endpoint grips and other editing tools. Double-click outside of the shape to finish editing the clipping mask. If you want to undo the clipping mask entirely, just right-click on it and choose *Release Clipping Mask* from the context menu. So long as the lines and arcs you draw form a continuous loop, you can use that shape as a clipping mask. You can also apply a clipping mask to images.

Figure 15.7 *A highly cropped section.*

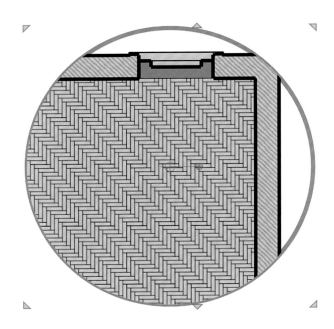

See the Online Resources for a custom scrapbook you can download, with a variety of goodies in it for use in construction drawings.

Adding your own scrapbook

There are certain graphic symbols that show up frequently and can be a little hard to track down in the menus. You can create your own scrapbook, as it is really just a blank LayOut file with a lot of objects on different pages. Let's create blank LayOut file and copy my favorite drafting symbols. These will make it easier to save and find everything in the future.

On the main page that opens up in the new document, let's copy and paste the floor plan legend created in the last chapter. Now that it's on the blank Scrapbook page, we can make a group out of it—just select all the objects in the key legend, right-click on them, and choose *Create Group* from the context menu. Let's go to the *TB—Simple Serif* group in the Scrapbook and on the *Drafting Symbols 2* page, drag the break line into our drawing. Select the break line we just dragged in, which is not quite dark enough for my taste, and under the *Shape Style* menu, increase the stroke value from 0.5 point to 2.0 point.

Now, choose *File > Save a Scrapbook* to save the file you just created into the LayOut default scrapbooks location. Let's name it *Handy*

Dandy. Now, when you close the Handy Dandy LayOut file, you will still be able to access the elements in it, in the Scrapbook. These new scrapbooks tend to show up down at the bottom of the list. If you get into making scrapbooks, you might want to make multiple pages in your scrapbook. Each of those pages will show up as subpages in the *Scrapbooks* menu. You can edit the pages by just selecting them in the Scrapbook Inspector and clicking on the *Edit* button. It will then open up that original file.

If you have created a library folder for templates and other resources within your backup system, add that file under *LayOut Preferences > Folders > Scrapbooks* section. Any new scrapbooks that you add to this folder will show up in the same menu with all of the default ones.

Creating the cover page

LayOut has actually already created a cover page for you—the main difference being that it has a slightly different title block from the so-called inside pages. If you don't like having the front of a drawing set using a different title block, by all means, delete it, and add another inside page. Whichever style you choose, just go to the first page in your set of drawings. Let's go with a different first page, just to be difficult.

Figure 15.8 *LayOut Preferences with the* Folders *panel open.*

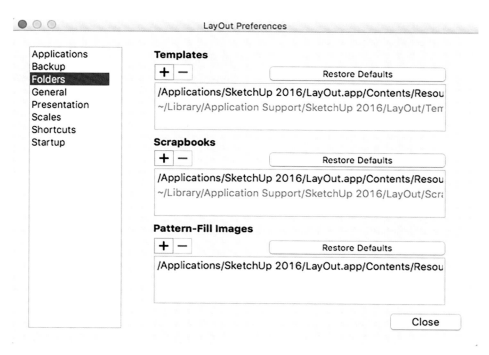

Egress plans are unique to each project. Add all dimensions and notes to make the drawing crystal clear. To change the text dimension, right-click on the string and choose *Explode*. The text will be available for editing.

The boundaries of viewports are generally not visible. If you're using a line drawing perspective, go to the *Shape Style* menu and turn on *Stroke*. Adjust the weight as needed.

There are a number of things that typically go on a title page, and of course every office will already have a look that they like. Since we are creating a whole new set, here's a list of the things that typically go on the title page.

- Cool perspective image of the project
- List of drawings
- Code analysis
- Life safety plan
- General construction notes
- List of abbreviations
- Key to symbols

Let's start with an easy drawing—the perspective view. Because LayOut, for some reason, does not give us a viewport on the title page, you'll need to insert one. Choose *File > Insert* and browse for the model of your project. You can then set the model to be any of your saved views, or double-click on the viewport and modify the view from within LayOut. Then, just double-click outside of the viewport to set the changes. Use a piece of text to give the drawing a title, such as *View to the Back*.

Several of the other elements typically found on the title page are probably things that your office already has typed up somewhere, even if it's in AutoCAD or just a Word document. LayOut allows you to insert a number of different file types, including PDF files, but also blocks of text—they just need to be saved in the correct file format. If you have them already typed up somewhere else, you can also just select the text in that other document, copy it to the system clipboard using ⌘C, and then paste it right into the document using ⌘V—there is no need to create a text box for it to go into first. There may be issues with formatting on occasion, but generally, this will work fairly well, as LayOut will apply the default text style to whatever you paste in.

Next, we need to create a **key** to the symbols you're using in this project, which is a chart showing each icon and describing what it signifies. If this is not your first time around the construction documents block, you may already have created one of these for another project. If so, you might want to add it to your construction drawings scrapbook for easy access in the future. If not, create it now, using the appropriate symbols and text, make a group out of it, and then add it to your scrapbook. Make sure to include each symbol that you are using in this particular drawing.

The last part is to create a **life safety plan**, which is a reduced-size floor plan indicating compliance with the major egress requirements of a particular project. It is typically at 1/32" = 1'0", with graphical depictions of the egress components and a key to the symbols used. It also typically includes exits and exit access corridor locations, minimum and actual exit separation, the path of egress, the maximum length of travel, exit signs, and even fire extinguishers, as the specifics of the project require. For more complex projects, there will be a code analysis along with the plan, describing any occupant loading and egress component dimension calculations, and other code issues pertinent to the particular project.

Our project has a simple floor plan, so the egress plan can be created from a copy of the main plan, with the furniture and any materials turned off, for a clean, empty view. We need to have two exits at a minimum for this non-residential project, and they need to be separated by at least one-third the diagonal of the floor plan. You can identify these requirements using a dimension showing the overall diagonal of the plan, and then determine what the actual separation of those exits should be. Let's indicate a few other goodies, such as a fire extinguisher location in my commercial kitchen, and the exit signs. These can all be done using graphic notations on a small-scale floor plan.

Figure 15.9 *The completed title page.*

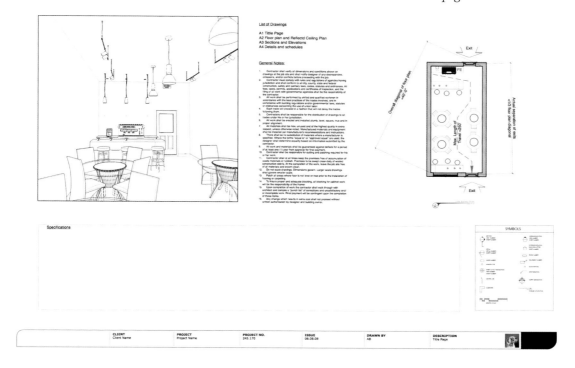

On a small interiors project, the title sheet can also be a place to collect a number of project-wide parameters, such as general construction notes and product specifications. Much depends on the complexity of the overall set: an FF&E type of project may only need a few sheets of drawings, and so the elements needed will be jumbled together. Larger projects tend to have more divisions between the different parts of the drawing set, so that there may be whole sheets devoted to details or interior elevations, for example.

Try it out!

- Configure the reflected ceiling plan and section drawings with poché and enhanced line weights. Be sure to add room names, dimensions, notes, and a legend.
- Create interior elevations for the entire project. Arrange on a sheet with titles and annotation, including notes as dimensions where needed.
- Create a finishes plan, along with a legend.
- Create a title page with a perspective view, list of drawings, general notes, and a code analysis.
- Create the life safety diagram for your project, using the building and accessibility codes applicable in your region.
- Create a custom title page, including your own logo and fonts.
- Draw a custom tile pattern for the toilet room, at large scale. Include color and size information and the section view indicating the base and top transition tiles.

Key terms

- Call-out
- Key
- Legend
- Life safety plan

Schedules, Take-Offs, and Charts

CHAPTER 16

LEARNING OBJECTIVES

- Organize components using IFC definitions.
- Extract schedules from component metadata.
- Prepare materials quantity take-offs.
- Create and import blocks of text.

It's inevitable in the life of both interior designers and architects that they will have to complete the tedious job of scheduling building components. Something like a door schedule for a large project can be vast and time-consuming. Interior designers often create the most elaborate schedules, since they are responsible for all finishes (e.g., the room finish schedule), furnishings (e.g., office systems, seating, etc.), and equipment (e.g., lighting, kitchen cabinets, etc.).

For SketchUp users, there are a couple of possible routes for these complex elements, most of which use brute force to count up and/or measure the elements in your model. Options include creating a schedule using graphical components from within LayOut; creating a schedule using a spreadsheet application like Excel, and then inserting an image of that sheet; or, for advanced users, using different extensions to capture metadata embedded in components, to help compile schedules automatically, which is worthwhile if you work with projects that require a lot of furniture layouts. For these tasks, we'll return to the SketchUp model to develop our schedules and take-offs.

If you're organized when you're creating a component, you can assign it an IFC type by selecting from the *Type* drop-down list in the create component dialog box.

Counting components

The Components Browser has a number of features that make it very easy to get information about elements in the model. Click the *Home* button on the *Components* menu and scroll down the list to find a particular component that you're interested in. Then, right-click on it and choose *Select Instances* from the context menu.

Figure 16.1 *The* Statistics *panel of the Components Browser.*

The statistic that is typically most important is the total number of instances of a particular component. You can count all of the components in your model this way fairly quickly. You cannot do the same thing with groups, however, so be absolutely sure that you use components consistently. Also, if you have used the *Make Unique* feature a good deal, you will end up with components with different names, making counting the total a little more difficult, so be sure to check all objects in your model. A knowledge of how these particular elements are ordered would be helpful here: if a chair, for example, requires a separate **purchase order** for each different type of upholstery, or if they can be grouped together.

Creating components with embedded metadata

To take advantage of metadata, you need to start with components for all the elements that you want to show up in your schedules. These can then have IFC classifications applied to them, and any definitions you give the component will apply to all instances in the model. You can assign different classification systems to your model, IFC 2 x 3 being the most common. This is what we'll use here. If you have more than two or three different components, this whole process will be a lot easier if you have the dynamic components toolbar active, rather than having to hunt through context menus for each component.

On Mac, you'll need to call up the dynamic components toolbar and add the Classifications Selector to your main toolbar. In Windows, you can add everything all at once with the classifications toolbar.

1. If you're on Mac, add the Classifications Selector to the standard toolbar (or the classifications toolbar in Windows). This will allow you to easily apply a classification to a selected object.
2. Select a chair component.
3. From the drop-down menu in the Classifications Selector, click the arrow next to IFC 2 x 3 and select an object type.
4. Let's try a slightly different method to apply an IFC definition. Select a different chair component.
5. Right-click on the component and choose *Entity Info* from the context menu.
6. Choose the type from the *Type* drop-down list.

That's all there is to it. For interior designers, the most common use of this feature is for tracking quantities of things like furniture and lighting equipment, but really anything with metadata can be tracked.

Reports are available in SketchUp Pro only. Note that components with IFC classifications will be unaffected by using either the Make or Pro versions.

See the Online Resources for a full list of the IFC classifications.

Figure 16.2 *The classification toolbars.*

Figure 16.3 *Assigning an IFC type.*

Materials applied directly to an instance of a component will show up in the report, but materials applied to elements inside of a component will not.

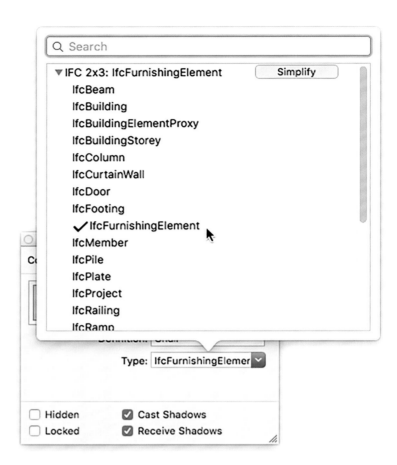

Generating a report

Now comes the reward for meticulously adding classifications to components—a report with data about components that have had IFC data applied. A **report** in SketchUp parlance is an analysis of the model that generates totals for instance counts, area, and any other data that has been applied.

1. Choose *File > Generate Report*.
2. The first time you run this feature, you'll need to run the default report, which will list every instance of different objects in your model.
3. Choose the fields shown in Figure 16.5 for our furniture report.
4. Click OK to exit back to the generate report menu.
5. Click on the report you just made and click *Run*. This should display a summary of the components in your model.

Figure 16.4 *The generate report dialog box.*

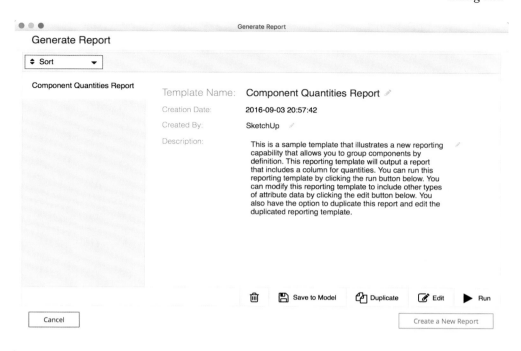

Figure 16.5 *Choosing which fields to calculate.*

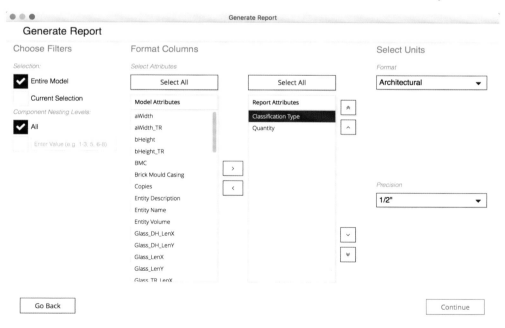

Generate Report

Definition Name	Classification Type	Quantity
Chair	IFC 2x3:IfcFurnishingElement	12
Coffee Maker		1
Component#12		42
Component#13		42
Component#14		42
Component#9		12
Conjunto Rústico Saccaro com tampo de 90cm	IFC 2x3:IfcFurnishingElement	2
Conjunto Rústico Saccaro com tampo de 90cm#1		1
Cup#1		42
DH		2
DH#1		2
DaveLite Slim Metal Green Exit Sign		2
DaveLite Slim Metal Green Exit Sign#1		2
Downlight square		3
FJSCO1SN		6
FJSCO1SN with SCOA		6
Framed half door with double panel		2

Figure 16.6 *The summary report.*

Sometimes you may accidentally move or copy components off into outer space. Use *Zoom Extents* to check for random components. You also might want to choose *View > Hidden Geometry* too, just in case, before creating the report.

6. Click *Download* to save the file to your computer in CSV file format, which can be imported into Microsoft Excel or any spreadsheet program.
7. Click *Save Changes* to go back to the main menu.
8. Exit the *Generate Reports* menu.
9. Open Microsoft Excel and choose *File > Import*.
10. Browse for the CSV file that you just saved and click OK.
11. Format the file to use the same font and graphics of your project. This is also the chance to add notes, additional product data, etc.
12. Excel files can't be exported directly as images, so you'll have to go through the *Print* menu. Choose *File > Print*.
13. Choose *Save as PDF* and save the model onto your computer. If you're in Windows, you'll need to install some sort of virtual printer, such as the one from Adobe Creative Suite, in order to save the document as a PDF.

	A	B	C
1	Chair	IFC 2x3:IfcFurnishingElement	12
2	Conjunto Rⱱ∫stico Saccaro com tampo de 90cm	IFC 2x3:IfcFurnishingElement	2
3	Conjunto Rⱱ∫stico Saccaro com tampo de 90cm#1	IFC 2x3:IfcFurnishingElement	1
4	Cup#1		42
5	DaveLite Slim Metal Green Exit Sign		2
6	DaveLite Slim Metal Green Exit Sign#1		2
7	Downlight square		3
8	bar stool	IFC 2x3:IfcFurnishingElement	6
9	bulb holder#1		3
10	coffee cup		6
11	exit_g#1		2
12	exit_g#2		2
13	light		3

Figure 16.7 *The spreadsheet in Excel.*

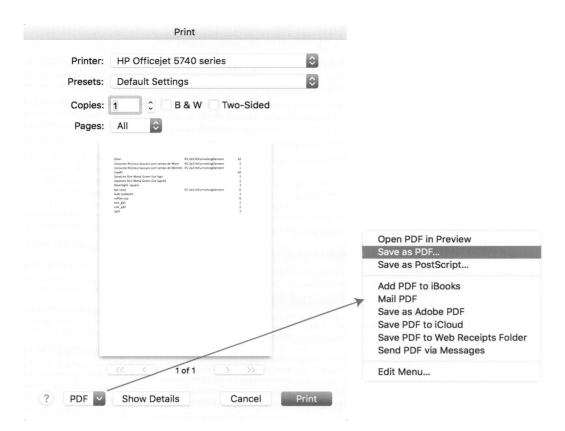

Figure 16.8 *Saving a PDF from the print dialog box.*

14. Back in the LayOut project, choose *File > Insert* and then browse for the PDF you just created.

15. Click OK to insert.

16. Made a change to the original spreadsheet file? Re-create the PDF file with the same name.

17. In LayOut, right-click on the image and choose *Update Image Reference*. This should update the image to reflect the newer version.

You can copy and paste text and image files directly into LayOut. Just not at the same time—image files must be handled on their own.

Schedules created in this manner will not automatically update in your LayOut project—you'll need to revise the PDF file each time. The image file is a reference, however, just like inserted SketchUp models, and so changes to the PDF will be updated automatically when you re-open the LayOut file.

Measuring the surface area

Interior designers will frequently have to make a **material take-off**, which is basically a measurement of the area covered by a particular material in the project. Every line and surface has properties that can be measured.

If you right-click on a face and choose *Entity Info* from the context menu, you will see the square footage of that particular object. You can hold down ⇧ to select more than one face at a time, and in this way, count up the square footage for things like flooring and wall coverings.

Another method is to use a note and leader line. Activate the *Text* tool and then click on the surface that you want to measure. Move your mouse off to the side and click again to plant the text box. It will display the area of the surface that you clicked on by default, unless the surface happens to be part of a group or component. In that case, you'll have to edit the group or component first to find the area.

Figure 16.9 *Measuring the area of a face.*

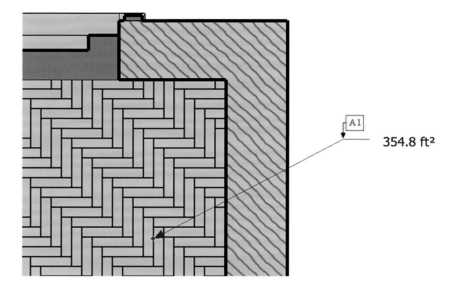

Creating a schedule within LayOut

Within LayOut, simple gridded schedules can be created using the *Text* tool. They don't have very many formatting options or any ability to have formulas such as what you'd find in Excel, but they do have the benefit of being expedient, which for smaller projects is just what's needed.

1. Click on the *Text* tool.
2. Draw a text box the size of the schedule that you'd like.
3. Type in the title of the schedule and select the text you just typed.

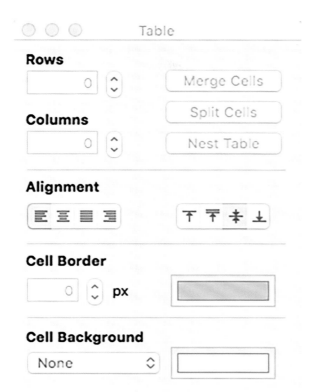

Figure 16.10 *The tables dialog box.*

If you create a lot of furniture schedules, take a look at BiMUp 5D for SketchUp (http://www.bimup.co.uk/buy). It takes information within the model, and, so long as you follow its guidelines, generates all sorts of schedules.

LayOut needs to have a piece of text defined first in order to start the chart. The rows and columns will fit within the text box that you draw, so give yourself plenty of space.

4. Choose *Text > Table* from the pull-down menu.
5. Choose the number of rows and columns you'd like. Be sure to leave the top row for a title. This is also a good time to assign borders and a border color.
6. Close the tables dialog box.
7. To make a title, you'll want to merge the top row of cells into one big cell. Click and drag across the top row of cells to select them.
8. From the drop-down menu, choose *Text > Table*.
9. Lower the number of columns to 1, and change to a larger font size and a darker border.
10. Close out of the *Tables* menu.

Furnishings Schedule		
Item	Manufacturer	Quantity
Chair	Ikea	12
Table	Ikea	4
Espresso machine	Gaggia	1
Bar stool	Ikea	6

Figure 16.11 *The completed schedule.*

This simple table can be edited at any point, and also copied from one project to another. It would also be a good one to have in your construction documents template, if you do that type of drawing frequently.

Try it out!

- Add IFC definitions to your furniture components and generate a report indicating quantities of each. Place the schedule of quantities on the sheet with the finishes plan.
- Find the relevant accessibility code standards that apply to this project. Copy the text and images of regulations relevant to this project onto your title page.
- Create a door schedule using the text tool method. Specify dimension, quantity, manufacturer, material, and finish.
- Create a room finish schedule indicating the exact areas of all materials used in the project.
- Create an entire room finish schedule, with manufacturer and product information.
- Generate a cost estimate using the quantities listed in the room finish schedule above, accounting for industry-standard dimensions and overages.

Key terms

- Material take-off
- Purchase order
- Report

Construction Details

LEARNING OBJECTIVES

- Prepare enlarged floor plan and section details.
- Create casework drawings.
- Organize drawing content from other software.

Construction details are where an interior designer's big design ideas meet the human scale of architecture. It is where your broad concept and space planning meet the ergonometric and social reality of the people inhabiting your spaces. These drawings are large-scale studies of exactly how a part of your project is assembled and finished, typically referenced from one of the smaller-scale drawings. The most typical details that you're going to see in an interiors project are for things like casework and finish construction, such as flooring or tile transition details. These are often created just using lines and other 2D elements from the outline of the 3D model.

Enlarged floor plan

It is common to create enlarged plans, for detailing complicated patterns and transitions, for example. Let's create an enlarged plan of the toilet room in this project, so that we can show the tile pattern. The first step is to insert a call-out for the enlarged view. Then, on your sheet of details, make a copy of the floor plan, but set it to a much larger scale. In this case, 1" = 1'0" is probably fine. Then, draw the tile pattern, either by using lines and the paint bucket, or using a photo editor to create the pattern wish. Be sure to annotate the different parts of your drawing to indicate the different materials being used.

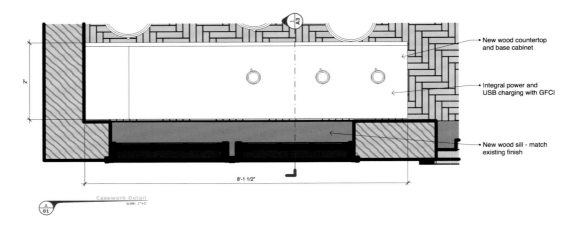

Figure 17.1 *The enlarged floor plan with annotation.*

See the Online Resources for a demonstration of these techniques and the files used in their creation.

There is an extension for creating tile patterns with depth, which is nice for tiles and wood paneling. Oob Layouts creates 3D tiles, although it costs $29, as of this writing.

The most typical sort of annotation is for things like tile patterns and other situations where the finishes are complex. Often it will be too complex and time consuming to model these conditions completely, so drawing with a few extra lines and patterns in LayOut, along with plenty of notes and dimensions, will explain the design better and faster than modeling every single tile in three dimensions.

Enlarged section

A common occurrence is to enlarge a section drawing to indicate the construction of a lighting soffit. Let's go to our sheet with the section drawing and insert a call-out for the detailed drawing, as before. Now, go to the sheet where you intend to have details and insert that same section, but scale it up as needed.

Rather than trying to model complex construction systems, it's easier to use drawing elements in LayOut to create 2D representations of things like drywall, metal studs, wood blocking, and of course light fixtures. All of this can then be annotated, as we learned in the text section of Chapter 13, and even saved to a scrapbook. Having the underlay of the section drawing is very helpful for getting the dimension correct, but be aware that as you draw the details, you may find that the measurements need to be adjusted to fit your equipment or the specifics of trim and other elements. If the details of construction indicate that there needs to be a larger dimensional change, you'll have to go back and modify the SketchUp model to reflect the new dimensions.

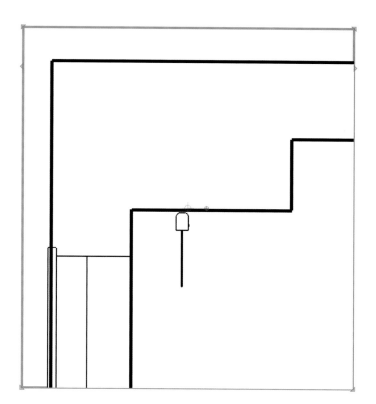

Figure 17.2 *The raw section, with no detail.*

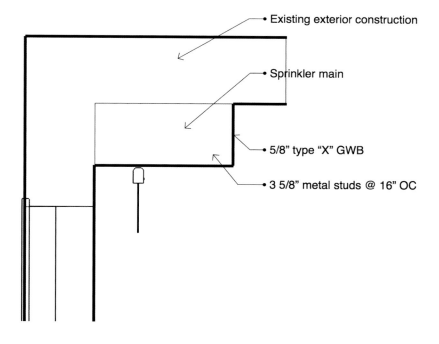

Existing exterior construction

Sprinkler main

5/8" type "X" GWB

3 5/8" metal studs @ 16" OC

Soffit Detail
scale: 1"=1'

A
01

Figure 17.3 *The complete soffit detail.*

Casework drawings

The podium is a nice simple piece of custom furniture that we can draw. It's very difficult to produce decent casework drawings while the component is inside the main model, and elevations are especially challenging. For that reason, we should save the casework that we plan to detail into its own SketchUp file. In an empty model, we can study it from all angles without the interference of all the other elements in the project. In terms of workflow, this strategy allows someone else to complete the model, such as a casework specialist. Right-click on the component in your SketchUp model and choose *Save As* from the context menu.

Open up that saved drawing in a separate SketchUp window and make sure you study it very carefully from all angles. Now you can save elevation and section views from all sorts of different angles. Be aware that, unless you have a lot of spare time on your hands, you will not be modeling every element of the casework, such as drawer slides and internal blocking. But you do want to save things that are section views where you will insert those elements when you get the drawing into LayOut.

Speaking of which, open up your LayOut file and go to a sheet you have reserved for casework drawings. Then, choose *File > Insert* and browse to find your casework file. This becomes yet another reference in your LayOut file. You can now create viewports with each of the dif-

Figure 17.4 *Casework design.*

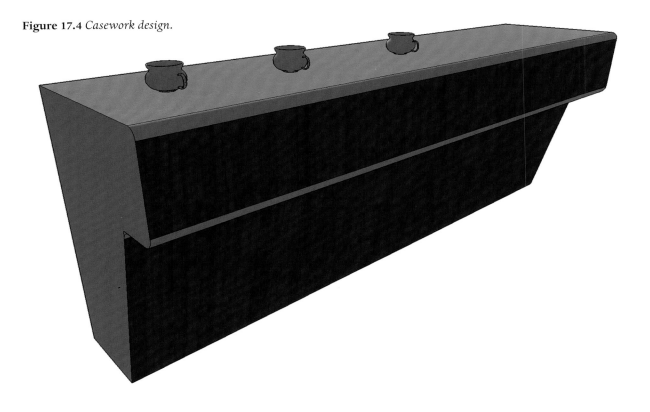

ferent views that you have saved. As we saw in the section drawing, you can add detail items as needed to represent the construction of the casework. And of course, you can never have enough annotation! It would be handy to build up a library of frequently used drawing elements and details that can be quickly accessed in your scrapbook.

See Chapter 14 for more information on importing and exporting different file formats.

Importing drawings

There are plenty of times when you need to import a drawing from Auto-CAD, or at least a 2D drawing that is in DWG format—most BIM software can produce scaled drawings in this format. You can't import it directly into LayOut, but what you can do is create a new blank file in SketchUp, and then import the drawing into that. Be sure to check that the dimension of the imported file is correct for what is depicted, and save it into your project folder. You'll also want to prepare the file with line weights and remove any text and dimensions. That file, in turn, can be imported into LayOut, and you can set the scale and the standard top view.

Let's add a crown molding to our project. Details for molding profiles are readily available at most manufacturers' websites and can be configured easily. They are typically made up of lines, which can be placed on different layers, if need be. Those layers can be used as individual overlay in LayOut, for line weights.

Figure 17.5 *Completed casework plan and elevations.*

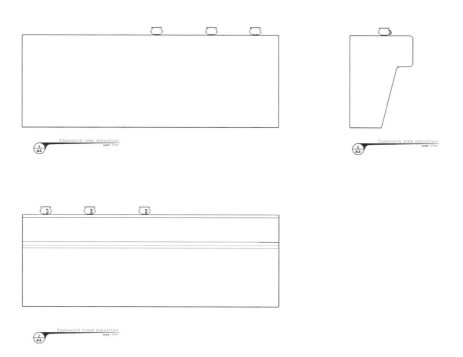

These 2D profiles can be used to model 3D crown moldings in SketchUp using *Follow Me* or *Push/Pull*. See the Online Resources for a video showing how to do this.

Depending on how the drawing was created, there may already be a number of layers for defining the graphics of different elements, such as line weights, leader lines, and dimensions.

1. Locate the detail that you want to import.
2. Open a blank SketchUp file and delete the default scale figure.
3. Choose *File > Import*.
4. Set the format to AutoCAD files (*DWG, *DXF).
5. Under *Options*, make sure you check inches (or millimeters, if you're in metric).
6. Click OK twice to import.
7. Create a layer called *Cut Through* for lines that you want to be heavier.
8. Right-click on the drawing and choose *Explode* from the context menu—this should break it into individual lines.
9. Place lines for elements that are cut through on the cut-through layer.
10. Place all other objects on another layer.
11. Delete any text and dimensions.
12. Save the file into your project folder.
13. Open your LayOut project and import the detail that you just edited onto the appropriate page.
14. Set the viewport to scale.
15. Make a copy of the viewport in the exact same location.
16. Turn off the layer that has all the other objects on it in the copy of the viewport.
17. Set the line weight for the new viewport to a heavier value.
18. Add notes and dimensions to explain the detail.

The trick here is to massage the line weight, as with the floor plan, to create a drawing that's easier to read. Once the graphical elements of the drawing are created, notes and dimensions can be added, as with other drawings.

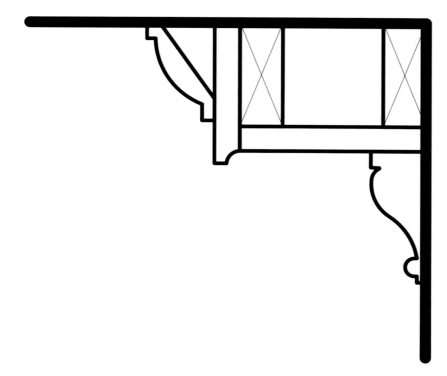

Figure 17.6 *A standard detail created in AutoCAD.*

Try it out!

- Create a floor plan detail for the tile pattern in the toilet room. Annotate all relevant information, including materials, application, and dimension of the pattern.
- Create a section detail of a gypsum board soffit.
- Import the threshold detail from the Online Resources. Configure with line weights and annotation.
- Create a template for configuring imported details. It will probably be in the top view, with parallel projection. It should also hide axes and have a white background color and a few layers for poché and different line weights.

Key term

- Construction details

CHAPTER

18

External Media

LEARNING OBJECTIVES

- Arrange a view to print using different media.
- Prepare a view to print at scale.
- Understand 2D export settings.
- Organize the scenes needed to create an animation.
- Set up a model for 3D printing.
- Set up a view for use with a laser cutter.

Sooner or later, you have to leave the virtual modeling world of SketchUp and make some sort of physical representation of the model geometry you've created. This can be a simple as a check-print of whatever you're working on or as complex as laser-cut pieces to assemble a physical model. Interior designers creating, say, a custom light fixture, furnishing, or piece of cabinetry may want to create a large drawing or physical model for presentation and evaluation. Each of these types of output needs to be configured for the exact hardware on hand, but there are certain general settings that will apply to most situations.

Print a perspective view

The first thing to consider when printing is what size paper you plan to use. We have a printer that takes 8.5 x 11 paper, and we could certainly squeeze our perspective view onto that. That's too small, however, for presenting to a group, so we need to make it larger. SketchUp allows us to choose a paper size independently of choosing a printer, which means that we can configure a view to print on a paper size that we don't actually have.

See the Online Resources for a demonstration of these techniques.

Let's configure our view to print on a 36" wide x 24" high sheet and allow SketchUp to figure out how to tile the smaller prints, so they can be assembled into a mosaic of the final drawing at the larger size.

1. Open a perspective view of your project that you want to print.
2. Choose *File > Page Setup*.
3. From the page size selector, choose *Manage Custom Sizes*.
4. Click + to add a new sheet size and name it Arch D.
5. Make the dimensions 36" wide and 24" high. There are several systems for measuring standard architectural drawings, using both imperial and metric measurements (see Table 18.1).
6. Save, and close the dialog box.
7. Choose Arch D as your page size and close the page setup dialog box.
8. Choose *File > Document Setup*.

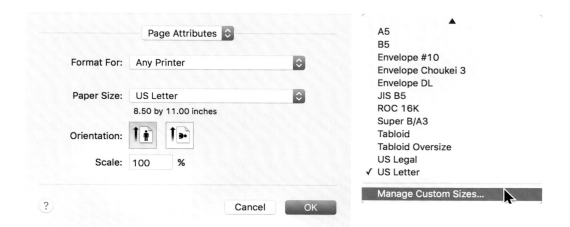

Figure 18.1 *The* page setup *dialog box.*

TABLE 18.1 STANDARD ARCHITECTURAL PAGE SIZES		
Designation	Width	Length
Arch A	9 in.	12 in.
Arch B	12 in.	18 in.
Arch C	18 in.	24 in.
Arch D	24 in.	36 in.
Arch E	36 in.	48 in.
A0	841 mm	1189 mm
A1	594 mm	841 mm
A2	420 mm	594 mm
A3	297 mm	420 mm
A4	148 mm	297 mm

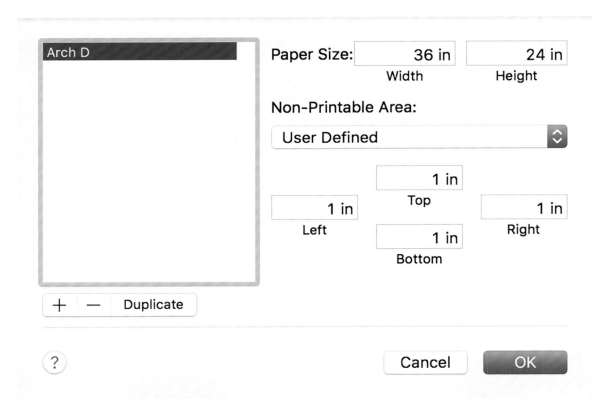

Figure 18.2 *The manage custom sizes dialog box.*

9. Be sure to choose the *Fit View to Page* option, unless you have a specific dimension for the view that you need. Note that print scale is gray, because this is a perspective view.
10. Click OK to exit the dialog box.
11. Choose *File > Print* or type ⌘P.
12. From the Preferences Selector in SketchUp, choose *Layout*.
13. Pick an arrangement for the sheets to be tiled, so that you'll be able to assemble the final version.
14. Click OK to print and SketchUp will divide up the image into the correct number of pages.

You could also just print a small image, or connect to a printer that handles oversized sheets of paper, but what fun would that be?

Print a scaled view

The only thing you need to know about printing to scale is that the model must be in an orthographic view. The view needs to be in parallel projection in order to have any hope of being set to scale, and it should be set to one of the standard architectural views. Printing a floor plan

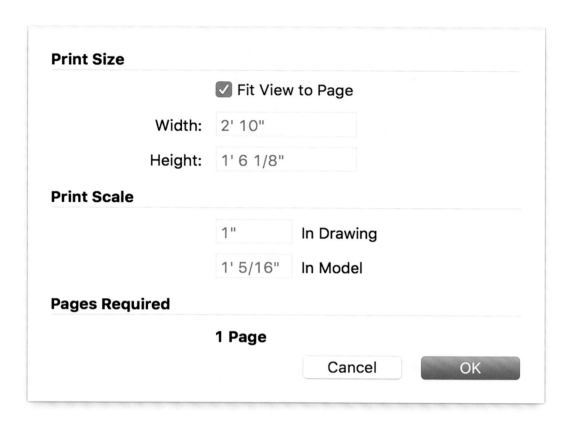

Figure 18.3 *The document setup dialog box.*

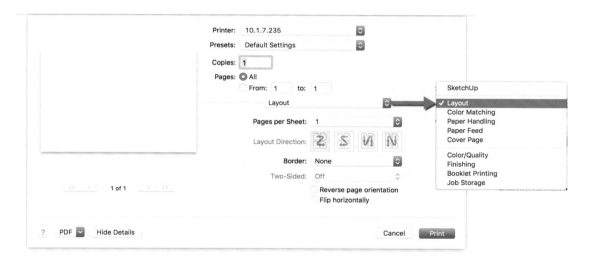

Figure 18.4 *Layout options for a multi-page print.*

or section directly from SketchUp is great for a check plot or making a markup, but not for whole sets of drawings.

1. Cut away the top of your model if needed with a section plane to create a floor plan.
2. Choose *Camera > Parallel Projection*.
3. Choose *Camera > Standard Views > Top View*.
4. Choose *File > Document Setup*.
5. Un-check the *Fit View to Page* option.
6. Under *Print Scale*, type in 1/4" for the measurement in the drawing (this is the size an object will be in the print), and 1' for the measurement in the model (this is the size that the object was modeled at).
7. SketchUp will adjust the print size to match your scale settings. Click OK to exit the dialog box.
8. Now, complete your page setup and then print, as before.

While it's not ideal to print a large drawing this way, there are a number of things you can do to make assembling it easier, including adding a border with thin lines, which is found under the layout section of the

Figure 18.5 *Document setup for an orthographic view.*

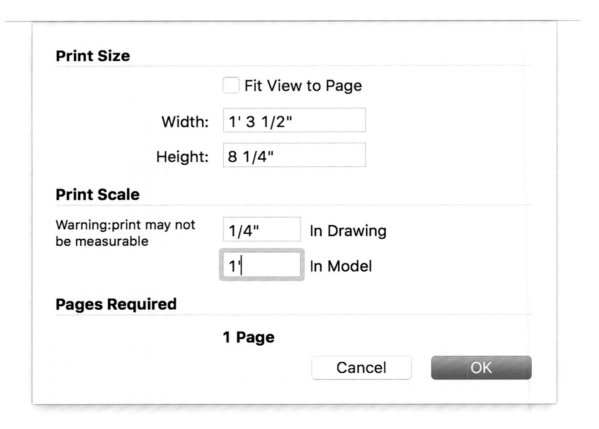

page setup dialog box. This will leave some space for tape or trimming, which is especially handy if your printer can't print all the way to the edge of the paper, in what is known as a full bleed. You can even print double sided or make a little booklet.

Export images

It is common to apply some **post-processing** to SketchUp images, which is to say, manipulate different views to make them more expressive of the design aesthetic or more artistic. Post-processing is typically done in a photo editor, such as Photoshop. But first you need to get images out of SketchUp that can be read by the graphics application you intend to use and that are of a resolution adequate for the different types of operations typically done. We will revisit this topic later on, in the section on preparing the ingredients for a composite rendering in Chapter 21. For now, the basic decision you have to make when exporting a 2D graphic is the type of file: a **raster** file, which is typically an image made up of little dots called pixels, or a **vector** file, which is a file type that describes what you see with mathematics.

Raster files will capture what you see on the screen, and so are a sort of snapshot of what you are working on, which can be handy if you just want to apply some photographic effects or filters. Vector files do not capture materials or lighting, but have the advantage of being scalable without any loss of fidelity. So, if you want to render a floor plan in a third-party drawing application such as Adobe Illustrator, a vector file will be most useful. Whichever you choose, the options are all found in *File > Export > 2D Graphic*. In the menu that pops up, click on the down arrow next to *File Type* to see your options.

Each of these file types has a large number of options, depending on the parameters available. In general, PNG, JPG, and PDF file formats are equivalent in terms of file size. TIFF has only mild compression losses,

Figure 18.6 *Export 2D graphic menu.*

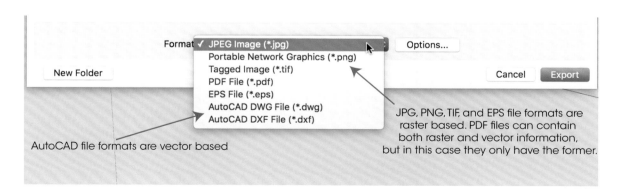

AutoCAD file formats are vector based

JPG, PNG, TIF, and EPS file formats are raster based. PDF files can contain both raster and vector information, but in this case they only have the former.

Why would you want to use the alpha channel? If you're planning to Photoshop in an image of a cityscape or sunset, for example.

which in a JPG file can sometimes lead to graininess, and this leads to much larger files. Some file types, such as TIFF and PNG, support a **transparency**, otherwise known as the **alpha channel**. With this feature, any part of the view that doesn't have objects visible—outside a window, for example—will not show up at all in the image file. There will be no pixel information at all in those locations. We are more concerned about image quality here, so TIFF is the best option for post-processing.

Create an animation

The first thing you want to do is map out exactly what sort of animation you want to create. A long animated presentation will have a storyboard, where you can plan out titles, subtitles, scene transitions, and any other special features, such as timed pauses during the presentation.

Figure 18.7 *A cartoon set for an animated presentation. Image courtesy of Laurie Foustoukis.*

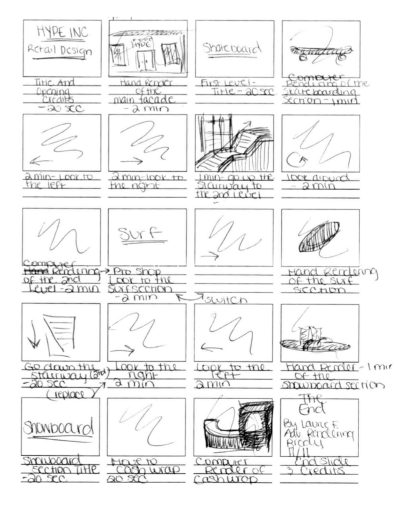

Be sure to click the *Options* button to open the options dialog box. Choosing a standard resolution crops the export to be a standard computer or cinematic aspect ratio, such as 4:3 or 16:9, so the final product will not look exactly like you see on your screen. You can also choose a custom size, which will keep the same proportion as on your screen. You can preview the size of the animation before exporting to make sure that your perspective views don't look peculiar. For use as a stand-alone presentation in, say, a kiosk, be sure to check the actual resolution of the device first.

Choosing "custom" for both the resolution and the aspect ratio allows you to type in a larger frame size, which might be needed for higher resolution devices. The largest dimension is 4096 x 2160.

One thing you can do to use up all the hard drive space on your computer is to increase the frame rate. The default value is 24 frames per second, and your typical movie is 24 or 30 frames per second. Some films, such as those in super high definition, will have a frame rate up to 48 frames per second. This is extremely smooth, although this setting will increase the size of your file exponentially. If your exports are a little shaky, changing this value will help you out. Be sure to check the option for *Anti-Alias Rendering*, which will smooth edge lines. If the animation will run continuously, check *Loop to Starting Scene* and the animation will

Figure 18.13 *Advanced export settings.*

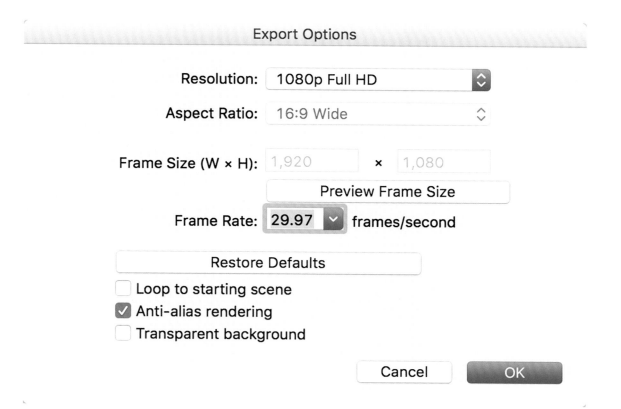

Fixing a model that isn't watertight can be tough, and missing facets can be very small. Models can be checked and even fixed by third-party applications, such as MeshLab, or online, using Microsoft's NetFabb service.

There are several extensions meant to help with 3D printing. MeshWrapper provides a way to simplify complex geometry into a single surface and smoothly fill in holes. There are several STL and OBJ exporters, which are common file types for 3D printers to accept. MakePrintable is a nice one because it examines your model and repairs it.

keep going until the file is closed. If you're planning to insert the animation into another application for presentation, such as PowerPoint, be sure to un-check this option.

Once you click *Export*, SketchUp will go through scene by scene, and we'll add in those transition times and calculate the total number of frames in your project. In fact, some advanced users will export individual frames instead of an animation file to get the highest fidelity and resolution. When you do this, you can export file formats such as TIFF, which are uncompressed, but also take up vastly more space than a JPEG or PNG file. A full 1080p HD animation will take about 1 minute for every hundred frames, more or less, depending on your computer. That translates to about a 15-minute export time for a 1-minute animation.

3D printing

There are now quite a few different 3D printers out there, each with its own parameters for acceptable 3D models and its own favorite types of software to use. In a general sense, the relative detail level and complexity of your model should relate to the medium of the printer you're planning to use. A large model made from PLA plastic, for example, can have a great deal of detail, down to textures on, say, a piece of furniture. A model that prints on paper will have trouble creating objects with voids, whereas a printer using a powder-setting material should be able to create voided objects, although only small ones.

Any type of 3D print will benefit from geometry optimization, however. You will want to remove any extraneous geometry that is not meant to be printed from the model, including text and dimension strings. Exploding the model will also help, especially if you intend to send the geometry onto a specialized 3D printing application, such as

Figure 18.14 *Export time estimate.*

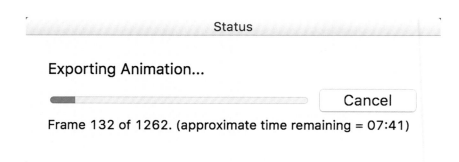

MakerBot Desktop. Most 3D printers will come crashing to a halt if even one tiny face is missing somewhere, so you'll want to make sure the model is **watertight**, which is to say, without any holes in the exterior skin of the model. Most 3D printers are also sensitive to face orientation. To see the face orientation in your model, you first need to remove any textures or colors that you might have added, from both sides of faces. Some 3D printers will also require export into a file format that they can read—check your manual.

Unwrap and Flatten Faces is a handy app for breaking down simple objects into their constituent faces. It's not always effective for complex pieces of furniture, but it can be fun to make folding models for kids!

1. Open your coffee table model.
2. Choose *File > Save As* and name the copy something clever, like *For 3D Printing*.
3. Select all the objects in your model, either by using a selection window or typing ⌘A.
4. Right-click on the objects and choose *Explode* from the context menu.
5. Repeat until *Explode* is no longer an option—this means that the model has been broken down to its simplest pieces.
6. Select all objects again.
7. Right-click on the objects and choose *Entity Info* from the context menu.
8. Click on the materials icon—it will probably be a question mark, indicating that the different sides of the faces are painted a variety of materials.
9. Click on the *Home* button to see all the colors in the model. The default materials are shown first.
10. Click on the default paint color in the materials dialog box.
11. The default material has a different color for the inside and outside of faces. If the faces are different colors, select one, right-click on it, and choose *Orient Faces* from the context menu. This should orient all the faces the same way.
12. Save your model one last time.
13. If needed, export your model to a file format that your 3D printer can read. Choose *File > Export > 3D Model*.

At this point in time, there don't appear to be any 3D printers that work directly with a SketchUp file, so it may take some experimentation with using other file types to get the best results. Most 3D printers will require that you import your OBJ file into their software for final preparation.

Figure 18.15 *Entity info for faces painted different colors.*

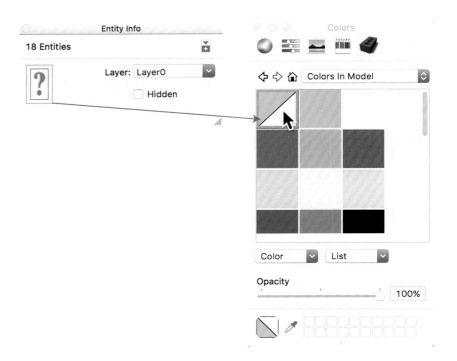

Figure 18.16 *The export 3D model dialog box.*

Each file type has many options, including how scened and layers are handled

The OBJ file type can generally be imported in 3D printer software

3DS File (*.3ds)
COLLADA File (*.dae)
FBX File (*.fbx)
IFC File (*.ifc)
Google Earth File (*.kmz)
✓ OBJ File (*.obj)
AutoCAD DWG File (*.dwg)
AutoCAD DXF File (*.dxf)
VRML File (*.wrl)
XSI File (*.xsi)

If you are starting a new model, you can always use a 3D printing template, although the main difference is that it is in metric, and has a model of a MakerBot in it instead of a scale figure.

Preparing for a laser cutter

It's generally not possible to laser cut directly from a SketchUp model, and it's probably not a good idea to try anyway—there is too much 3D information that could cause problems. A better strategy is to export a 2D graphic in a format that will successfully drive your laser cutter—you'll have to check and see the manufacturer's recommendations for which file formats will be best. The basic choice is between a raster image, like a JPG, and a vector-based drawing, such as DWG. When configuring a view to export, such as an elevation, remember that a laser cutter can only cut a 2D piece of material, so make sure you think through the shape and dimension of the material that you're cutting. A typical problem is to cut out too much and end up with very little left. Be aware that most laser cutters can etch as well, so there will almost certainly be some configuration in another application before printing to identify what each element will be doing in the laser cutter.

Once you have created the view you need to laser cut, export that view in the correct file format. If you have an active section plane in your model, right-click on it and choose *Export Section Slice* from the context menu. This will give you a DWG file that has lines where the section plane slices through the different parts of the model. One simple project is to create laser cut-out scale figures to place in your model—here's how:

1. Open a new drawing—it should have the default scale figure in it.
2. This scale figure has too many lines—it would end up being a jig-saw puzzle if it was laser cut. Delete it and open the Components Browser.
3. Type in *Outline People* in the search bar.
4. Insert one that looks like it has simple models—there's one called *White People* that works well, even if the name is somewhat unfortunate.
5. Explode the component and choose your favorite scale figure—delete all the rest.
6. Choose *Camera > Parallel Projection*.
7. Choose *Camera > Standard Views > Front*—most of these components will always face the camera.
8. Choose *File > Export > 2D Graphic*.
9. Choose DWG from the drop-down list. The exported file will not have any fill.
10. Be sure to size the drawing to print at the correct size for whatever scale your model is at. Click on the *Options* button if you plan to scale the export here rather than in the software that drives your laser cutter.
11. Type in the scale information—the logic is the same as when printing orthographic views to scale.
12. You will also probably want to eliminate section lines, even though it's doubtful that there are any.
13. Turn off extension lines also—these will just leave stray marks on the figure.
14. Open this file in whatever software you need to drive your laser cutter.

These cutouts can be glued into a model, and once you've set it up, they can be printed at any scale you happen to need.

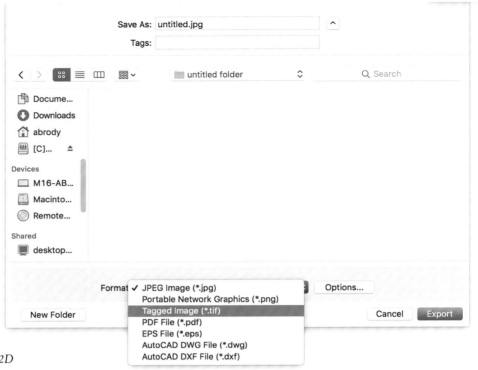

Figure 18.17 *The export 2D graphic menu.*

Figure 18.18 *AutoCAD export options.*

Try it out!

- Configure your café project to use your local printer. Print all of the perspective views on 8.5 x 11 paper and print the plan at 1/4" = 1'0".
- 3D print your coffee table from the previous chapter.
- Laser cut a scale figure to put next to your coffee table.
- 3D print an open view of your entire project, with the ceiling printed separately so the model can open up.
- Using black museum board, laser cut the walls of your floor plan and also the section view. Apply those cutouts to your floor plan drawings to give them depth.

Key terms

- Alpha channel
- Post-processing
- Raster
- Transparency
- Vector
- Watertight

CHAPTER
19

Interoperability

LEARNING OBJECTIVES

- Identify the major types and formats of files that can be imported into SketchUp.
- Create a rendering of a SketchUp model in Revit.
- Configure your coffee table model for viewing in augmented reality.
- Configure your coffee table model for viewing in virtual reality.

Interior designers are, more often than not, working with other design professionals in the course of their work. To collaborate effectively, each person must be able to interpret drawings and other information, incorporating elements and feedback into their own work. Alas, sometimes it's necessary to leave the comfort of the SketchUp environment and work with other applications, especially when working on larger projects, where the speed, simplicity, and affordability of SketchUp are less important. Engineers and architects in particular are more likely to use BIM-based applications to manage their projects. Fortunately, there are a number of different ways to import geometry and metadata into SketchUp or out to a file format others can read. These formats include AutoCAD and also augmented and virtual reality standard file types.

Import options

SketchUp allows the import of 2D raster graphics, which are used on their own and as textures. As we saw in the section on editing a material in Chapter 5, image-based textures can be modified within the Sketch-

Up interface, or new ones created from imported images. Using Photo Match, images of buildings can be converted into scaled 3D volumes; however, this technique doesn't work well for interior models, so we will not cover it here.

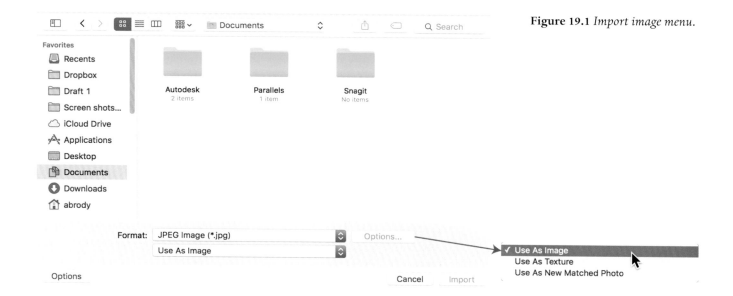

Figure 19.1 *Import image menu.*

3D models can also be imported in a number of formats. There are often options associated with each, which determine how certain types of geometry are simplified, or not. Even if SketchUp can't read a file directly, such as an OBJ file, there are often extensions that can convert the file type.

Figure 19.2 *Import options.*

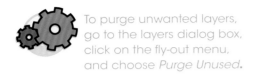

To purge unwanted layers, go to the layers dialog box, click on the fly-out menu, and choose *Purge Unused*.

The typical AutoCAD drawing uses inches or millimeters and all geometry is usually drawn at 1:1 scale. If the CAD file was not created near to the origin, which is the intersection of the X, Y, and Z axes, you may have trouble finding the geometry upon import. In that case, un-check *Preserve Drawing Origin*, which will center the geometry on your cursor and allow you to place it wherever you please in the SketchUp file. CAD files can have quite a few layers too, which can cause visibility problems in saved scenes. If you're having trouble turning off certain objects from the imported file, you can delete the imported layers from SketchUp—any elements on the deleted layer will be moved to the current layer.

Revit

Revit is a big part of the architecture and engineering market, so it makes sense that SketchUp would try to play nicely. Sadly, there can be some issues using SketchUp geometry within Revit, especially when rendering. Using Revit files within SketchUp also has problems, mainly to do with the extraneous geometry that needs to be purged. Revit objects are placed automatically on layers, some of which are named in recognizable ways and others that have more obscure names. The best way to purge these files is to figure out which layer extra objects, such as furniture, are on, so that they can be isolated and deleted. Even if you don't need to delete many objects, you can simplify the model by deleting extra layers. Objects on those layers will be placed on the current layer and then the cleared layers can be purged.

EXPORT FROM SKETCHUP TO REVIT

You can import SKP files directly into Revit and also into most types of Revit families. They can't be exploded, however, and unless they're in a family, they cannot accept any parametric information. Preparing a SketchUp model for use in rendering within Revit requires some slightly different strategies than you would normally use.

1. Open your coffee table model in SketchUp.
2. Choose *File > Save As* and give the new file a clever name like *Table for Revit*.
3. Explode all elements of the model to remove any sub-groups and sub-components.
4. Purge all extra layers.
5. Don't paint anything in SketchUp, and remove all paint from both sides of all surfaces.

6. Create layers for each different material you would like to render in Revit (don't arrange objects by what function they are for or some other scheme).

7. Select a single face.

8. Right-click on the face and choose *Orient Faces* from the context menu.

9. Save the model.

10. Open Revit.

11. Go to the *Insert* ribbon.

12. Click on the *Import CAD* button—linking a file just doesn't work well with the SketchUp file format.

13. Set the colors to black and white—otherwise, Revit will color by layer, which is a little annoying.

14. Browse for your file and import.

Changes to a linked
SketchUp file will
update within Revit

Changes to an
inserted SketchUp file
will not update in Rivit

Figure 19.3 *The* Insert *ribbon in Revit.*

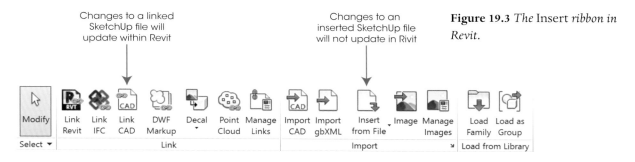

Figure 19.4 *The* Import *menu.*

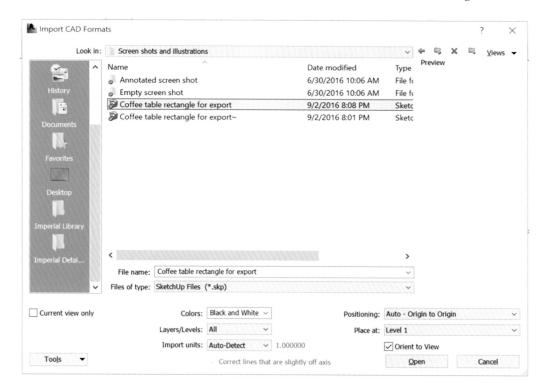

15. Go to the *Manage* ribbon.
16. Click on the *Object Styles* menu and then the *Imported Objects* panel.
17. Find the layer that you want to paint. Click in the cell for material to expose the ellipsis that indicates a menu is available.
18. Click on the ellipsis to open up the Materials Browser, where you can assign materials that, hopefully, will render properly.

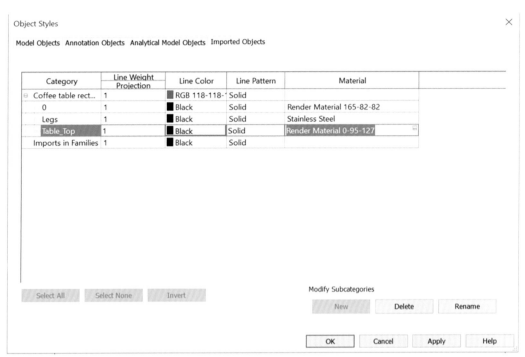

Figure 19.5 *The* Object Styles *menu.*

Figure 19.6 *The coffee table rendered in Revit.*

Revit files have a tremendous amount of information in them, but SketchUp can really only make use a of tiny portion of it. It's a good idea to try to limit Revit files in some way. If you only need a single room or a small part of a larger project, use Revit's *Section Box* tool to crop away absolutely every part of the model that you don't need. Then, click the *Application* button and choose *Export > CAD Format*—be sure to choose AutoCAD as the file type. Once the model is imported into SketchUp, there are extra lines that may appear as mysterious cobwebs on the walls and floors. These can be hard to delete, but you can use the *Smooth/Soften* menu to try to remove them. Another peculiarity of models exported from Revit is that scenes will often not update all of the typical properties—be sure to have the details visible in the *Scenes* menu and check off all options.

Well, this is actually an extension for Revit that will export your entire 3D model in SketchUp file format, including materials. Try the exporter from SimlabSoft—it's very good, if a bit pricey.

AutoCAD

SketchUp models can be exported in DWG and DXF format in all their 3D glory, as a section slice, or as a collection of the lines visible in any particular view. Note that these files can be imported directly into a number of different applications, but one that is very useful is Adobe Illustrator. This software is frequently used to render floor plans for presentations and has a number of tools for advanced graphic controls.

Trimble Connect

The owner of SketchUp, Trimble, has an online platform for collaboration between different designers within the architecture, engineering, and construction (AEC) industry. The main idea behind this relatively new system is to create a catch-all organizational structure to coordinate drawings and models from all sorts of different consultants, no matter what design platform they're using. For example, an architect might be using AutoDesk Revit, while the interior designer might be using SketchUp, and the mechanical, electrical, and plumbing (MEP) consultants might have their own systems.

If all goes well, these models can be overlaid with each other in the Trimble Connect platform, which allows coordination of design intent, services, structural elements, and the like. These overlaid drawings can be viewed on the computer or even a tablet device on the construction site. It's necessary for everyone to have a Trimble account for this system to work, and uploading the document couldn't be easier: just choose *File > Trimble Connect > Publish Model*, and you'll be prompted to log in to your system and choose a shared location for the model.

Augmented reality

Ask anyone who has walked into a park bench or wall trying to capture a Pokémon, and you'll find out that **augmented reality** has arrived. It is basically a way to overlay images of objects or scalable 3D models with a live camera view. For example, a design option for, say, an office system layout, can be superimposed on a view of the empty office space so that the client can evaluate the design. It is possible to save your SketchUp files in a special format that allows you to overlay your electronic creations with a view of the physical world. Upload your coffee table model to a website called Augment, and they will send it to their simple, free augmented reality app on either a phone or tablet. This can be a very powerful way for a client to visualize, say, a furniture layout within the actual space that they plan to use.

1. Open your coffee table model.
2. Choose *File > Save As* and give the copy a clever name, like *Table for 3D Printing*.
3. Choose *File > Export > 3D Model*.
4. Set the file type to COLLADA (*.DAE).
5. Click on the *Options* button.

Figure 19.7 *Export options.*

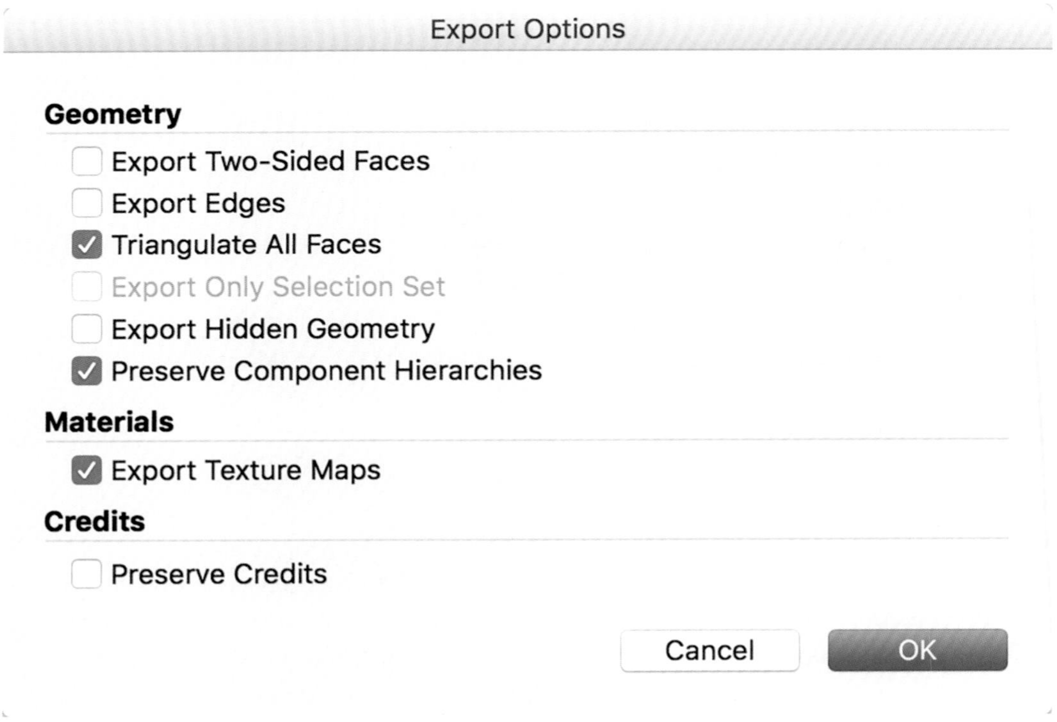

Export Options

Geometry

☐ Export Two-Sided Faces
☐ Export Edges
☑ Triangulate All Faces
☐ Export Only Selection Set
☐ Export Hidden Geometry
☑ Preserve Component Hierarchies

Materials

☑ Export Texture Maps

Credits

☐ Preserve Credits

Cancel   OK

6. Since this object will only be seen from the outside, it's fine to uncheck the *Export Two-Sided Faces* button.
7. Click OK to exit the options dialog box.
8. Create a new folder to save the file for convenience.
9. Give the file a name and hit OK to save.
10. Browse for the folder where you saved the file—you should see the DAE file and a folder with image files of the materials from your model.

For more control of the model behavior, install Augment Desktop, which is free and has quite a few additional tools and options, including animations.

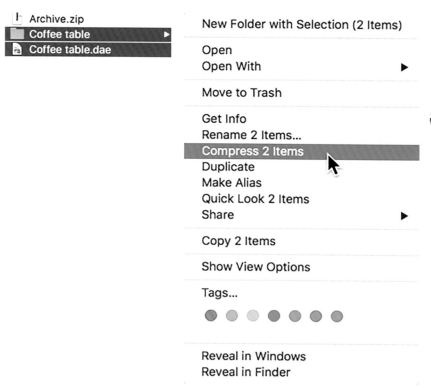

Figure 19.8 The exported file and supporting images.

Want to be able to walk around the table? Augment makes a printable pattern—place it in the room where you want the table to be, scan it with the software, and any model you upload will be glued to that spot.

11. Right-click on the selected items and choose *Compress 2 Items* from the context menu. This will create a file called Archive.zip, which is what you need to use the augmented reality app from Augment.
12. Browse to www.augment.com and sign up for a free account.
13. Navigate to the *My Models* section.
14. Click the *Add Model* button.
15. Browse for your Archive.zip file and select it for upload.
16. Give the 3D model a more clever name—*Coffee Table*, perhaps.
17. Open up a smartphone or tablet.
18. Install the Augment app and log in to your account.
19. Once logged in to the app, you can navigate to your models and choose the coffee table uploaded in a previous step.
20. You can now see your model placed in the room depicted in the camera view.

Figure 19.9 *The Augment online interface.*

Augment detects corners and edges in the view of your space to develop a model of the geometry. It may not work well if you can't see any corners or edges, so you might have to move around.

Click to upload your archive folder

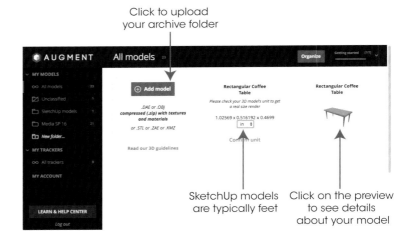

SketchUp models are typically feet

Click on the preview to see details about your model

Figure 19.10 *View of the model in the space.*

21. Click and drag with one finger to move the model in the view of your space—it should appear more or less foreshortened.
22. Use two spread fingers on the model to make it larger or smaller.
23. Rotate two spread fingers to rotate the model.

Virtual reality

While augmented reality views allow you to place a model into whatever is visible through the camera, **virtual reality** offers an opportunity to completely remove the real world from your 3D viewer, showing you a representation of a wholly artificial environment. Thanks to the advent of some pretty inexpensive hardware (Google Cardboard is less than $20), it is now possible to have access to a virtual reality view of your model—to visually surround yourself (or your amazed client) with your design. As with augmented reality, it's a matter of converting the model to something the hardware can read. In this case, all you need to do is load on an extension called qrVR Exporter, from Kubity.

See the Online Resources for video demonstrating the augmented and virtual reality views.

1. Open the model of your café design.
2. Load the qrVR Exporter extension.
3. Choose *Extensions > qrVR > qrVR Exporter*.
4. The extension will convert your model into a stereoscopic 3D PDF—browse to save the file somewhere that you'll remember.
5. Open the file (if it doesn't open automatically).
6. On your phone, install the Kubity app.
7. Scan the QR code. The model might take a few minutes to load.
8. You will see a mini version of your model on the screen that you can manipulate and navigate around.
9. Click on the Google Cardboard icon in the app and then turn your phone to the landscape position, if it wasn't already.

You will see a **stereoscopic** view of your model, which is two still images composed as if they were taken by two camera lenses spaced a small distance apart. It is meant to mimic the configuration of your eyes, where having two, slightly separate views allows us to perceive spatial

Figure 19.11 *The model loaded in the Kubity app.*

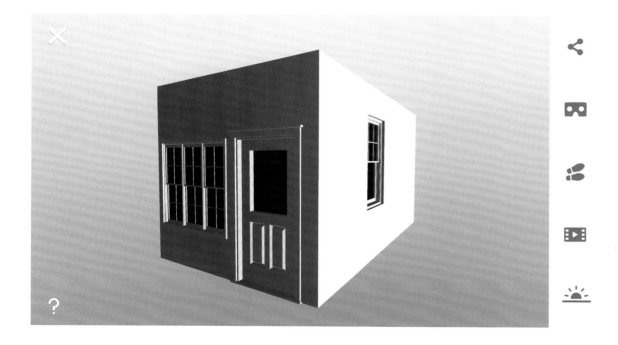

depth. Place your phone into a Google Cardboard set and begin wandering around your model. The sensors in your phone will detect when you move, look one direction or another, or look up and down.

Google Cardboard is expedient for viewing a model like this, but it's hardly impressive for a client. If you have the money, you'll probably get better fidelity from one of the fancier VR goggles out there.

Figure 19.12 *The virtual reality version of your model.*

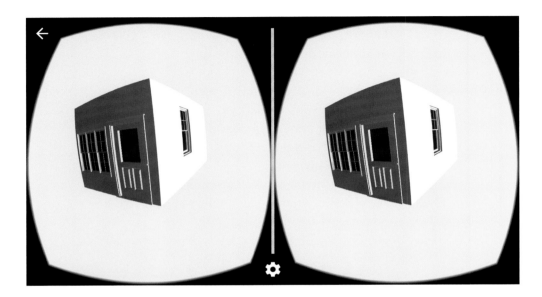

Try it out!

- Create a new texture using textile images from a well-known manufacturer. Apply to a piece of furniture that you've designed.
- Render your coffee table in Revit.
- Open your coffee table model in augmented reality and move, scale, and rotate to place it within a room. Have someone stand next to it for scale.
- Open your model in virtual reality and walk inside. Determine if the space seems any different viewed this way, as opposed to the modeling interface that you've been using up until this point.
- Develop three different furniture arrangements for a large space near you. Load each into your augmented reality view and take a vote among your peers about which one is the best design.

Key terms

- Augmented reality
- Stereoscopic
- Virtual reality

Photo-Realistic Rendering

LEARNING OBJECTIVES

- Identify different rendering options for SketchUp.
- Produce renderings using an internal rendering engine.
- Explain the pixel dimensions needed for different purposes.

By default, SketchUp graphics are, for lack of a better term, sketchy. The display of lines, colors, and textures are at relatively low resolution, which is what allows such quick drawing and interactivity. In terms of lighting, SketchUp does not display anything other than daylighting in its models. Architectural designs are often just fine viewed using daylighting settings, which are integral with SketchUp.

Interior designs, however, rely much more heavily on electronic lighting to bring a project to life. That's where a **rendering engine** is needed: it takes the model geometry, applies materials at a higher resolution and clarity, and then does calculations to simulate how lighting would behave in that space with those particular materials. This is how you can produce snazzy photo-realistic renderings and animations for your clients. Which types of rendering engines you choose, however, depends on quite a few different factors, including cost, workflow, and the types of drawings you want to produce.

Rendering engine comparison

To **render** a view in SketchUp is to take the model and apply photo-realistic representation of the lighting and material behaviors as they would occur if it was a physical space. A rendering engine is an extension or application that uses the SketchUp geometry, and sometimes SketchUp textures, to generate the photo-realistic view. As we have seen for other tasks, there are extensions that you can add for producing photo-realistic renderings right within the SketchUp interface, which has the advantage of allowing quick design iterations. These are generally, although not always, cheaper than stand-alone versions, and are not going to have as many features.

The highest quality renderings are likely to be produced using stand-alone rendering engines, which are completely external to the SketchUp interface. These can be very, very complicated (although not always), quite expensive, and require a great deal of training to use. It's also important to consider the type of work your office does. Some of these applications are more suited for cinematic work, while others are better at still rendering, while still others excel at physical lighting calculations, which can be handy if your office does a lot of lighting design. The overall cost also needs to be considered, for the software, the system that runs it, and the personnel needed to actually create the drawings. Here's a simple comparison of some of the main rendering engines that are used with SketchUp—my apologies to those that I may have missed!

Rendering is a notoriously complicated process, and there really isn't a good measure for the complexity of an application. For the purposes

TABLE 20.1 COMPARISON OF SKETCHUP RENDERING ENGINES				
Rendering engine	Platform	Operation	Cost	Complexity
Arielvision	Windows	External | linked	$$$	😊😊
Artlantis	Windows | Mac	External	$$ | Free for students	😊
Blender	Windows | Mac	External	Free for all	😊😊😊😊
Caravaggio/Studio	Windows | Mac	External	$$ / $$$	😊😊
Cinema4D	Windows | Mac	External	$$$$ | Free for students	😊😊😊😊
Indigo Renderer	Windows | Mac	External	$$ | Free for students	😊😊😊😊
iRender nXt	Windows	Internal	$$	😊
Kerkythea	Windows | Mac | Linux	External	Free for all	😊😊😊
LightUp for SketchUp	Windows | Mac	Internal	$$	😊
Maxwell Render	Windows | Mac | Linux	External	$$$$	😊😊😊😊
SU Podium	Windows | Mac	External | linked	$$$ | Free for students	😊😊
3ds Max	Windows	External	$$$$$ | Free for students	😊😊😊😊
Twilight Render	Windows	External	$$	😊😊😊
VRay	Windows	External	$$$$$	😊😊😊😊

of this chart, we used a less-than-scientific metric: the total number of buttons and menu options. Many professional renderers swear by whichever software they've learned, claiming it to be the easiest or most effective and generating the highest quality content, but most options will produce good results, once they are mastered. The cost is also relative and is more or less in $100 units. Some software has perpetual licenses, while others are on a monthly or annual subscription model. It's best to check out the websites of those apps that you're interested in, as prices vary and there are discounts from time to time.

Choosing a platform is often based on what one of your employees learned in school, so that the office can get going immediately on projects. This book has an emphasis on building the capabilities of SketchUp with native tools and extensions, so let's opt for a relatively simple, internal rendering engine, LightUp. The biggest advantage of this extension for interior design is that it handles electric lighting very well, which is something interior rendering relies on more than exterior rendering. LightUp can generate accurate illuminance calculations based on physical lighting and show illuminance maps interactively on the live SketchUp view. These are things interior design students need to do in lighting design class and studio, and that professionals will do in lighting-critical situations.

See the Online Resources for an in-depth chart with links to the websites for all of these programs.

A good website for learning more about how different rendering engines actually work with SketchUp is www.sketchupartists.org.

Internal rendering

Whichever tool you use, it's a good idea to save a nice clean file before starting the rendering operation. This includes purging the model of extraneous geometry, components, and annotation.

1. Open your file and choose *File > Save As*.
2. Save a copy, naming it something clever, like *For Rendering*.
3. Delete any unused design options.
4. Delete scenes that were saved for things like construction drawings, as they are not really necessary for rendering.
5. Set the current style as one that displays the textures on objects.
6. If you plan to use daylighting, make sure the model is geolocated.
7. Purge unused components.
8. Compose perspective views for any rendered views that you will want.
9. Save again.
10. Go to the Extension Warehouse and find LightUp.
11. Install the trial version for 30 days, or fork over for a license fee.

Figure 20.1 *The LightUp toolbar.*

Preferences dialog   Tour tool

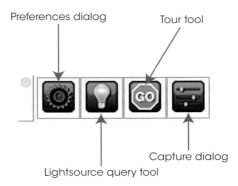

Lightsource query tool   Capture dialog

LightUp takes the geometry and materials visible in a view and applies **ambient lighting**, which is non-directional light that fills the space, and **physical lighting**, which is lighting based on a mathematical representation of actual light sources. It then generates a quick rendering of the view, to give a rough sense of the conditions in the space. It's also possible to render the entire model, which is known as a complete bake. This takes longer, but allows you to navigate the rendered model using standard SketchUp navigation tools. These settings can be adjusted for quality level as well, so that they can be rendered in a reasonable amount of time.

Quickie rendering

A quick rendering is a good place to start, to see the character of the space, the materials, and the ambient lighting used by default. The preferences can be configured to render only the current view and can be optimized for interiors.

1. Click on the *Preferences* button on the LightUp toolbar.
2. This menu has links to examples, video tutorials, and a written guide. Once we've gotten started, however, we can un-check the button for *Show on Startup* and then click OK.
3. Click on the *LightUp Preferences* button.
4. This simplified menu is fine for a first effort. Set the quality level towards the left and select *Quick Realtime* from the drop-down menu. The other options can remain as-is.
5. Click the green *Go* button to render the model. This is also known as the *Tour Tool*.

Figure 20.2 *The LightUp splash screen.*

Figure 20.3 *The simple GUI.*

Start with lower quality, for speed

Baked: renders the entire model

Baked: renders the entire model
Quick Realtime: very fast
Clay: ignores textures

Controls line visibility and weight

Many additional controls

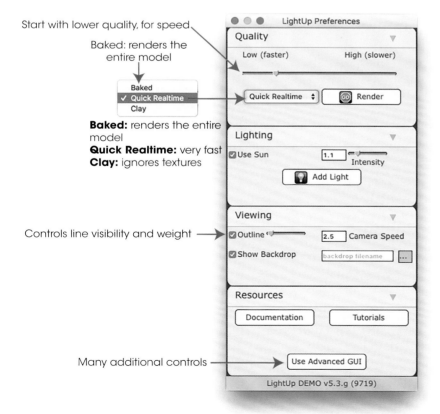

6. Keystrokes for changing the view are specific to LightUp and are displayed when you first render. If you choose to navigate through the model using your mouse and the usual view tools, LightUp will render each new view.

The rendering quality here is pretty low, because we haven't put in any physical lighting yet—all of the materials that you see are lit either by the sun, if was on already in your model, or ambient light, which is just enough to allow the material to be visible. You will also see some gray "visual noise" in the view, which is just a factor of the rendering resolution—the system is optimized for speed rather than quality at this point.

Figure 20.4 *A simply rendered interactive view.*

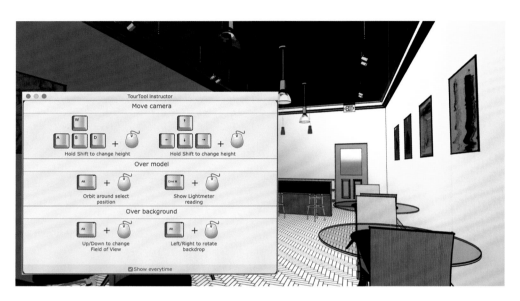

Interior rendering settings

The basic settings are actually quite powerful, but it is possible to have much more subtle control using the advanced settings—click on the *Use Advanced GUI* button to switch over. This is needed to make the rendering more amenable to interiors.

1. In the LightUp preferences, click the *Use Advanced GUI* button to switch the interface.
2. Click on the *Interior Rendering Mode* button.
3. If it's a complicated model, type 0.5X for the resolution—interiors have a lot of different materials and the potential for some fairly complex lighting.
4. Scroll down in the menu by clicking and dragging on a blank area.
5. Use the Stroke Selector to control how dark the edge lines are. They can also be eliminated entirely.
6. Close the menu.

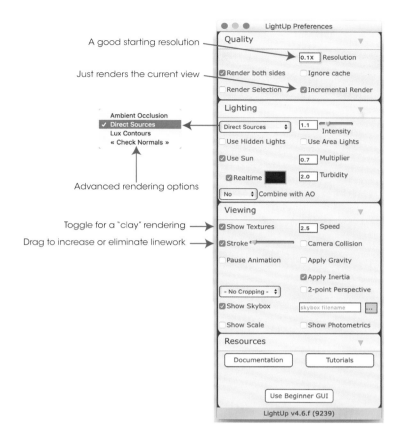

A good starting resolution

Just renders the current view

Ambient Occlusion
✓ Direct Sources
Lux Contours
« Check Normals »

Advanced rendering options

Toggle for a "clay" rendering

Drag to increase or eliminate linework

Figure 20.5 *Advanced GUI.*

Did that run very slowly? Drag the quality slider to the left. Is there no roof on your model yet? Turn off the sun.

7. Click the green *Tour* tool to re-render the space.
8. To exit the *Tour* tool, just hit ↻ or activate the *Select* tool.

Every model is going to be different in terms of the reflectivity of materials and how the light bounces around the space, so adjust these settings to find a level that works well for your project.

Figure 20.6 *Re-rendered with new settings.*

Lighting

Complex lighting is what makes interior rendering so challenging. Building exteriors often look just fine under daylighting alone, or with simple area lights. Interiors, however, need artificial lighting to function, even during the daytime, which means a lot more design needs to happen than just simple modeling. Clever and accurate lighting techniques can help make a design rich and interesting, but only if they can be modeled successfully.

LightUp has all the tools you need to model, render, and calculate lighting in a project, including virtual light bulbs and the ability to use physical lighting, which accurately represents the light output of real luminaires. Using the *Light Query* tool, we can place individual bulbs or repeated ones that are inside components. The sphere that you manipulate when you insert these lights is for reference only—it doesn't show up in the rendering and its size actually makes no difference in the light output characteristics. If it's inside a light fixture component, however, it's a good idea to make it smaller, as it can obscure the object geometry. Let's try rendering the café.

1. Navigate to an interior view of your model and click on the *Light Query* tool. A little light bulb will appear magically next to your cursor.
2. Click to place a bulb. Keep clicking in other places to add more bulbs.

Figure 20.7 *Floating bulb in the space.*

3. Click on the *Select* tool.
4. Double-click on a recessed can in the ceiling.
5. Zoom in on the can.
6. Click on the *Light Query* tool again and place a bulb inside the can.
7. Adjust the position of the bulb as needed to place it in the middle of the can using the *Move* tool.
8. Hit ↻ twice to exit the *Light Query* tool.
9. Tap on the tab of your saved scene to return to an overview of your space.
10. Click on the *Tour* tool to re-render your space.
11. Need to adjust the light level of a bulb? Click on the *Light Query* tool again.
12. Click on the offending bulb. A menu pops up with the light properties.

 For a lens flare effect, check the box next to *Corona*. Its strength can be controlled in the value box. This is also good for effects such as a crystal chandelier or string lights.

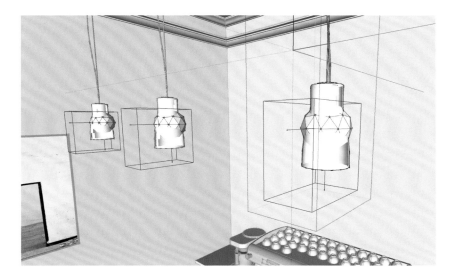

Figure 20.8 *Placing bulbs in a component.*

Figure 20.9 *The space re-rendered with physical lighting.*

Model not rendering at all?
Try selecting just objects that
are in view and then check
the *Render Selected* button
in the LightUp Preferences.
The problem geometry may
be hidden, or the model
may render if certain components are left out.

Lumen output of lamp

Click to apply an IES file

Color temperature

Light loss factor can,
which effectively dims
an IES light

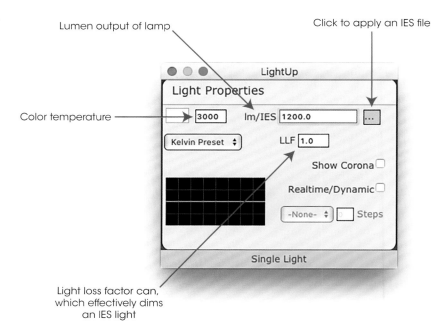

Figure 20.10 *Light source properties.*

13. Modify the light output up or down, and also the color tempera-ture, if desired. If it's a bulb in a component, the properties will change all of the components.

14. For more realistic lighting, it is possible to choose an **IES file**, which is a geometric representation of the light distribution prop-erties of a physical luminaire. Using physically based lighting is the most realistic way to render a space, although it requires more research.

15. Close the selection menu and the *Light Query* tool.

16. In the LightUp Preferences menu, choose *Clay Render* and also check the box to *Display Light Sources*.

17. Click the *Tour* tool to re-render.

18. To measure the illuminance level that LightUp calculates, just hold down ⌥ and move your mouse over any surface. A mini light meter will indicate the calculated value in lux.

19. Refer to the recommended light levels from a respected standards organization, such as the Illuminating Engineers Society of North America (IESNA), and modify your lighting design appropriately.

Adding electric lighting gives a much more realistic rendering, but can also lead to issues balancing day, electric, and ambient light sources. Go back to the LightUp Preferences menu to make general adjustments to these settings.

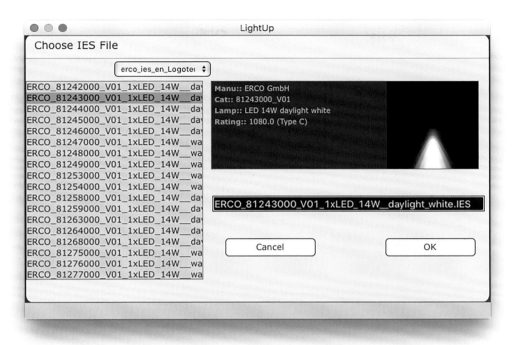

Figure 20.11 *IES selection menu.*

Figure 20.12 *A clay render with light sources visible.*

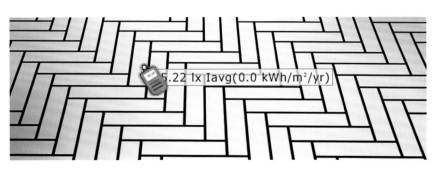

Figure 20.13 *The light meter making a measurement on the wall.*

Some of the default textures in SketchUp are fairly low resolution. For better results, look for high-quality, seamless textures to use in your models.

The *Capture menu*

No rendering is ever perfect the first time around, although most rendering engines do a pretty good job of guessing what sort of lighting balance you want. Further adjustments can be made in real time, using the *Capture* menu at the end of the LightUp toolbar.

Each space will render slightly differently, and the personal preference of the designer is also a big factor. The best thing here is to try out each of these effects and see which ones work well with your particular view. If the rendering seems too dark or light, adjust the exposure. *Bloom* will force bright points to become fuzzy, softening the overall image and giving it the look of a miniature model. *DOF* stands for depth of field and will blur the view both in front of and beyond the point that you have designated as the focal point. With the *Tour* tool active, the focal point shows up as a red dot at roughly the geometric center point in the model. This point can be moved by toggling the *Unlock* button and then adjusting the location of the red dot. Toggle the *Unlock* button again to keep the new focal point, and return to your original view composition. *Vignette* makes the perimeter of the perspective darker, forcing the visual focus of the composition more toward the center. These simple adjustments are instantaneous and can really liven up your rendering. The strength of the effects can be varied using the sliders.

Figure 20.14 *The* Adjust Color *panel of the* Capture *menu.*

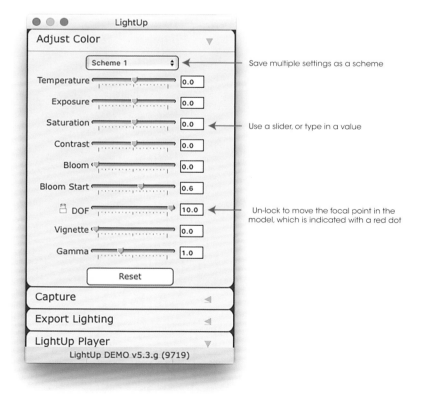

Materials

Once the *Tour* tool is activated, you can double-click on any material to bring up the *Materials* menu. That will allow you to modify some of the basic characteristics of the material, including reflectivity and refraction. There are a number of pre-set materials, and these are generally the best place to start, especially for shiny materials like tile and metal. Another property worth looking at is *Fresnel*, which adjusts how the material behaves when seen at a sharp angle. Making this darker can have a very realistic effect on the rendering.

Using image maps for *Bump* and *Specular* reflections can add a good deal of subtlety to a material—this is great when it's an object, such as a table, that is prominent in a view. LightUp takes whatever image was used for the texture in SketchUp as the base for the map. De-fringing image-based textures is sometimes needed when there is an alpha portion, which is meant to be transparent. De-fringing eliminates areas where the pattern is partially transparent, due to a softening of the color along the edges. Just ALT-click on the material with the *Query* tool and un-check *De-Fringe*.

Exporting rendered still images

So far, we have been rendering at a low, draft resolution. For presentation drawings, however, it's necessary to produce renderings with enough pixels that they can show materials and lighting precisely when printed. To do

Figure 20.15 *Comparison of different adjustments. Clockwise from top left: vignette, DOF (depth of field), gamma, and bloom.*

Transparency can only be controlled within the SketchUp materials editing panel.

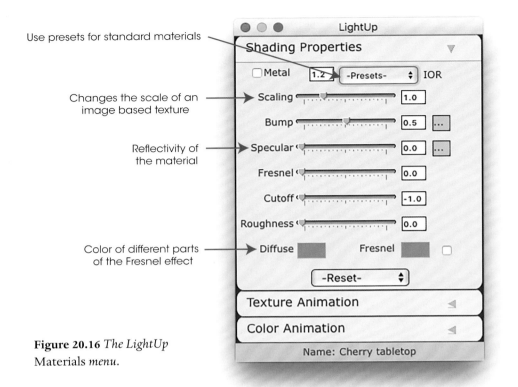

Use presets for standard materials

Changes the scale of an image based texture

Reflectivity of the material

Color of different parts of the Fresnel effect

Figure 20.16 *The LightUp Materials menu.*

this we need to change some settings in LayOut and then prepare for the render to take a good deal more time—this is referred to as a **final bake**. This operation will fully render all parts of a model, so there won't be any delay when navigating around the space using the *Tour* tool.

1. Open your model and click on the tab for the scene that you'd like to render.
2. Click on LightUp Preferences.
3. Change the resolution settings to 4X.
4. Un-check Incremental Render and check Ignore Cache.
5. Close the Preferences.
6. Click the *Tour* tool and wait for LayOut to render the model. Depending on how complicated the model is (e.g., spoons with 50,000 polygons), this can take a few minutes or half an hour.
7. Once completed, test with a thermometer to see that the model is baked all the way through. OK, that's a geek joke—once fully rendered, you can navigate around the model and to any scene without having to wait for LightUp to process the new view. Mouse and keyboard navigation controls are available.

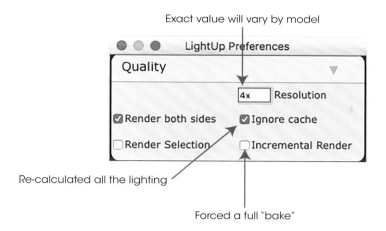

Exact value will vary by model

Re-calculated all the lighting

Forced a full "bake"

Figure 20.17 *Settings for a final bake.*

See the Online Resources for a spreadsheet that will do this calculation for you.

Each pixel can also have a bit depth, which is basically how much information about the particular color it saves. More depth, in theory, means more sophisticated colors.

8. Click on the *Capture* menu.
9. Make adjustments to the rendering as needed.
10. Scroll down to the sections on stills and animations.
11. Choose an image size from the drop-down menu.
12. Click the *Still* button.
13. Browse to save the file on your computer, preferably in a file location that you'll remember. You will need to specify the file extension in order for the export to be successful. JPG, PNG, and TIFF are all valid formats, from smallest file size to largest.

Once exported, it's likely that you'll want to do some post-processing in Photoshop. No rendering is ever quite perfect in terms of composition, lighting, materials, or line work, and a few simple techniques can make a big difference.

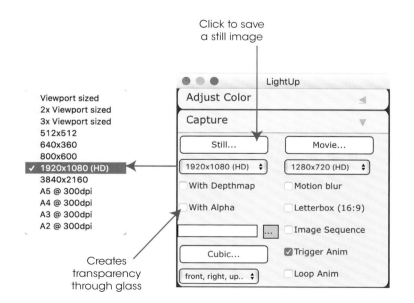

Click to save a still image

Creates transparency through glass

Figure 20.18 *Still export settings in the* Capture *menu.*

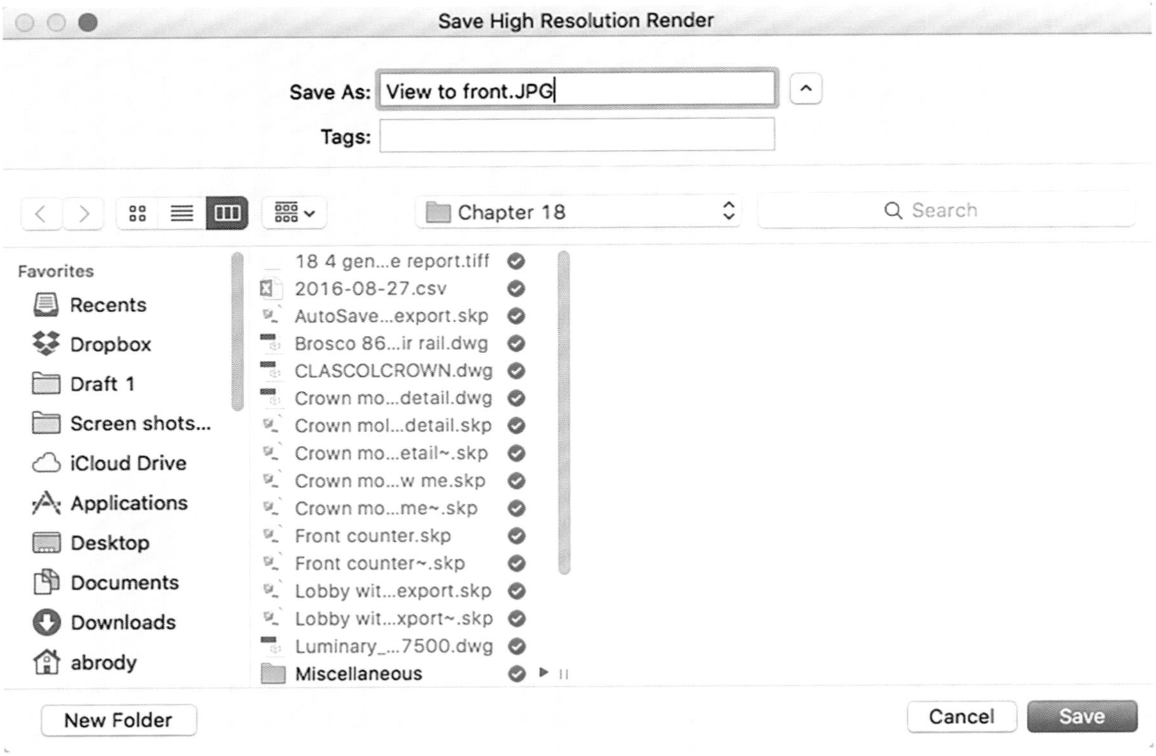

Figure 20.19 *The save as dialog box.*

Printing target resolution

One subject that often causes confusion is **resolution**. Electronic images are measured in pixels, which are basically little dots, each with a color, arranged in a grid that makes up the image. The more pixels, the more details you can see in the image. The trick is that, in the physical world, we need to decide how many pixels we plan to squeeze into an inch—too few, and the image looks dotty, or pixilated. Too many, and, well, it just makes creating the image and printing it slower. So, to figure out how many pixels we actually need, we need to calculate the size of our intended print with the number of pixels per inch that works well with our printer. Most printers will max out at about 220 pixels per inch, which is really the threshold at which our eyes will probably not be able to perceive much more detail. So, if we want a 20" print, we multiply that times the printer resolution.

TABLE 20.2 TARGET PIXEL DIMENSION CALCULATION		
Printer resolution	**Physical print size**	**Target pixel dimension**
220	20	4400

Exporting animation files

Once you have completed a final bake, exporting an animation is almost as easy as exporting a still. You should be sure to check your saved scenes first, so that the animation doesn't walk through any walls or zoom in on a door knob by mistake. It's best to export a non-rendered version of the animation first, just to get a better sense of the timing—see the section on animations in Chapter 7 for more information on export settings. It there are no instances of walking through walls or spaces that are completely dark, export the higher resolution rendered version.

Once you start exporting an animation, it's a good idea not to mess around with SketchUp at all, as this can cause crashing. If the animation just won't work, try breaking it into two batches of scenes, exporting each separately.

1. Create the scenes needed for your animation.
2. Export a non-rendered animation to make sure that the timing and views are acceptable.
3. Change your LightUp Preferences to *Final Burn*.
4. Click the *Tour* tool.
5. When the rendering is done, go the *Capture* menu.
6. Choose a resolution based on how you plan to present. On a laptop, 1900 pixels is plenty.
7. Un-check *Trigger Anim*.
8. Un-check *Loop Anim*.
9. Click *Movie* and browse to save the file.
10. This can take a while. If you forgot to un-check *Loop Anim* and *Trigger Anim*, you will see the animation loop endlessly on your screen.

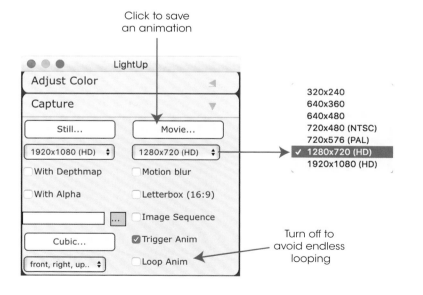

Figure 20.20 *Animation capture settings.*

Try it out!

- Think of an office where you might have worked. Choose a rendering engine for their use, based on one of the rationales discussed. List the reasons for your choice.
- Render your café space, adding lighting and detail to the materials to make the image look photo-realistic.
- Calculate the pixel dimension needed to print your perspectives at 10" wide.
- Model a stained-glass window and render it with different lighting conditions.

Key terms

- Ambient lighting
- IES file
- Final bake
- Physical lighting
- Render
- Rendering engine
- Resolution

Compositing SketchUp Views

LEARNING OBJECTIVES

- Prepare a variety of view types for compositing.
- Combine and blend drawing elements for dramatic effect.
- Create lighting effects in Photoshop.

SketchUp has some really interesting styles that can make views of your model look hand-sketched or even water-colored. This approach, which makes reference to manual drawing techniques of the past, doesn't always produce interesting and rich illustrations that capture the design aesthetic of a project. To add more richness and intent to presentation drawings, it's best to add some post-processing using a photo editor. This process is known as **compositing**, where different graphical elements are combined in various and interesting ways to produce a creative and expressive composition. This allows for easier blending of styles and the ability to easily tweak colors and saturation to help focus attention on the important aspects of your design. For the purposes of this book, we will use Adobe Photoshop, but there are several other photo editors out there that have the same capabilities.

Preparing the ingredients

Compositing is the process of selectively layering bits and pieces of drawings to produce a view that is compelling and rich. It's hard to know exactly which types of views are going to be the most useful in this process, since what you want to say about each project can be quite

You can export all the scenes at once, although it takes some advanced planning. Choose *Window > Model Info* and go the *Animations* panel. Remove scene transitions and make the scene delay 1 second. Then, go to *File > Export > Animation.* The frame rate should be 1 FPS. Make the file format *.JPG instead of a movie file, and you'll get a folder full of images of each scene.

See the Online Resources for a demonstration of these techniques and the files used in their creation.

different. But, in general, there are a few standard views that are most handy. Most of these can be exported together or individually.

1. Open up your schematic design for the café.
2. Choose *File > Save As*.
3. Name it something clever, like *Model for Rendering*.
4. Choose a perspective view that you would like to create a composite for. Delete all of the other scenes.
5. The exported image will be the exact size of your SketchUp window, so adjust its size as part of your composition. This type of cropping can also be done in Photoshop, if you'd prefer.
   If you have a Mac, it's possible to have SketchUp remember the size of your viewport window. This is especially important if your window is not maximized to fill your screen entirely. Choose *SketchUp > Preferences* and navigate to the *Workspace* panel. From there, click the *Save Current Windows Size* button. Windows users should just maximize the application before exporting and count on having to crop in Photoshop.
6. Apply the default simple style to the current view.
7. Edit the style and turn off axes and section planes to get a clean view.
8. Update the style and scene.
9. Without changing the view, apply a black-and-white sketchy style to the scene, such as one of the pencil styles, although they don't always look great if there are a lot of curves in the model.
10. Save a new scene.
11. Repeat steps 10 and 11 for at least two more styles. Interesting ones include white lines on a black background and almost any of the Style Builder Competition winners. You should now have four scenes.
12. Add a layer called *Scale Figures* and make it the current layer.
13. Without altering the view, import some silhouette scale figures. It's good to have one each in the foreground, middle ground, and background, but compose them as you think shows off the space best.
14. Back in the layers dialog, turn off all other layers.
15. Save a scene with just the scale figures visible. This can also be done with any element that you might want to highlight in the final composition, such as furniture or a decorative light fixture.
16. Choose *File > Export > 2D Graphic*.

Figure 21.1 *The different scenes.*

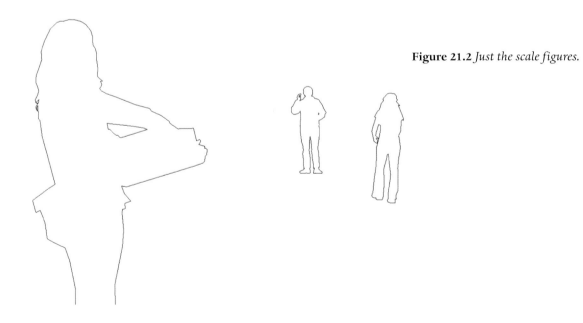

Figure 21.2 *Just the scale figures.*

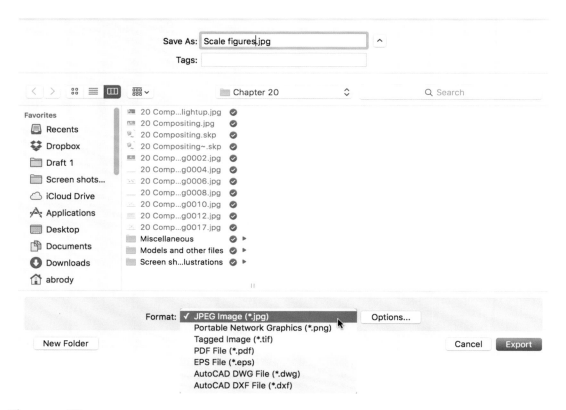

Figure 21.3 *The export 2D graphic dialog box.*

Other ingredients for this rendering recipe might include things like photographs of the view outside the window and of people. Try to find images that match the resolution of the SketchUp export. You'll also want to make sure that the camera angle is the same as what you see in the SketchUp view.

17. Make the file type tagged image (*.TIF)—this file format is the least loss-y, and so will result in the best quality image overall. If your computer is older and slower, use JPG instead, as the smaller file sizes will be a bit easier on the processor.
18. Click on the *Options* button.
19. Set the resolution based on the size you plan to print. You may need to un-check *Use View Size* and type in a value, so be sure to leave the dimensions as proportional.
20. Repeat these steps for each of your saved scenes.
21. A rendered view is also handy, especially if you've put in lighting already. Render the view and then export a still image. LightUp does not allow you to enter a custom value, but it will allow you to use the viewport size and multiples of the viewport size.

Just as a kitchen recipe can only turn out as good as the ingredients, a composite rendering is only as good as the quality of the original imagery.

Rendering recipes

This is where you get to channel your inner illustrator, since so much of rendering is artistic judgment. There are a few basic recipes that are

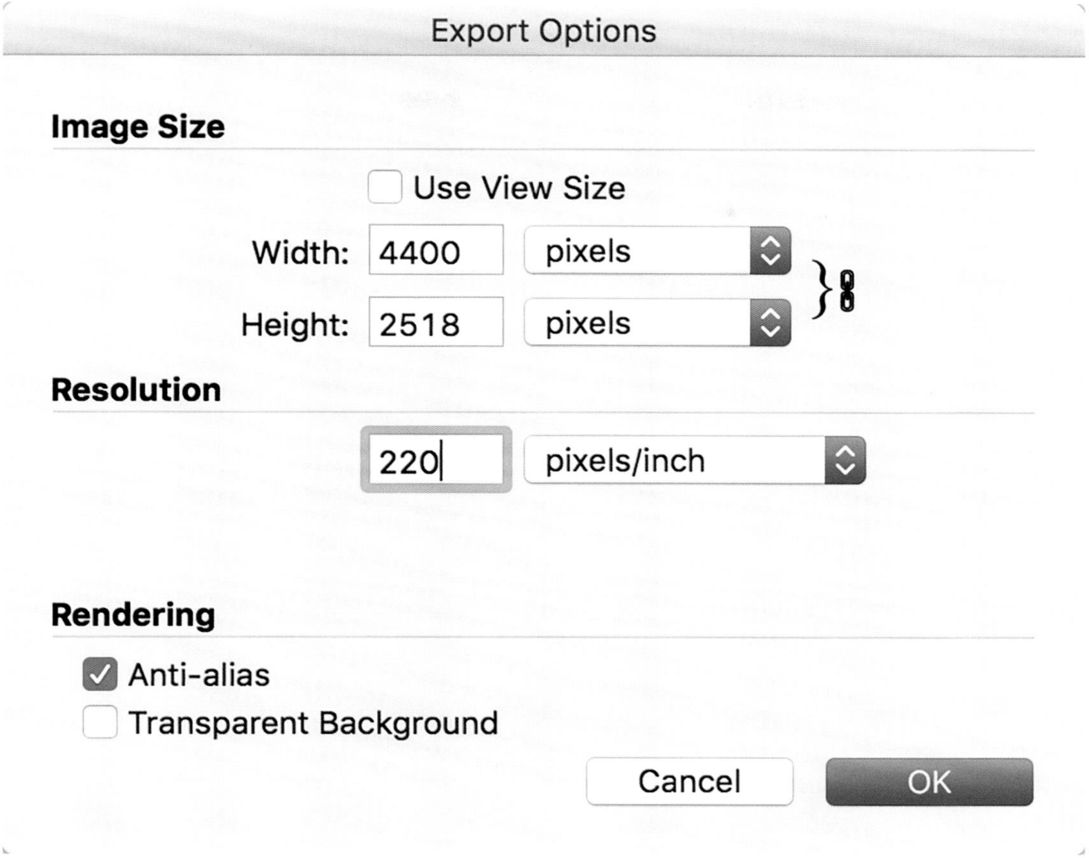

Export Options

Image Size

☐ Use View Size

Width: 4400   pixels ⌄

Height: 2518   pixels ⌄

Resolution

220   pixels/inch ⌄

Rendering

☑ Anti-alias

☐ Transparent Background

Cancel   OK

Figure 21.4 *The image options dialog box.*

commonly used, and of course they can be combined, modified, or ignored entirely. Let's assume that, if you're reading this chapter, you've got a functional working knowledge of Photoshop, so the basic operation of each tool will not be explained here. You'll have to look for a different book for that, if you need it—the techniques described here will be in more general terms.

THE FADE

This is where you blend one layer with another in different ways. The most typical types of fade go from a black-and-white image to a color layer, which helps focus the eye on the center of the image.

1. Open up one of the images you just created in Photoshop.
2. Place each of the other images so that they are all stacked up as layers, with the black-and-white line drawing on top and the rendered view just below it.

This operation deletes pixels from the foreground image, but it is also possible to use a layer mask, which will not destroy the original layer. The technique you choose is just a matter of personal preference.

Clipping masks can themselves be faded by changing the opacity of the clipping layer.

See the Online Resources for a video showing exactly how these images were created.

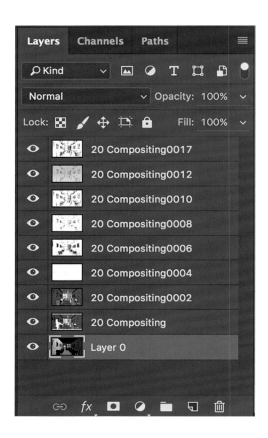

Figure 21.5 *The stack of layers in Photoshop.*

3. Select all the layers and rasterize them so that they can be edited.

4. Save the drawing somewhere that you'll be able to find it later—the project folder is a good place.

5. Turn off all of the layers except the top two.

6. Create a new layer below the color layer. This will be the clipping layer, where we define the areas to be hidden and areas to show through.

7. On the new layer, select a rectangular area around the center of the view. Such a sharp edge to the change in style is a bit jarring, so let's ease the transition a bit.

8. Right-click on the selection and choose *Feather* from the context menu.

9. Type in 50↵ to soften the edge of the selection.

10. Choose *Edit > Fill*.

11. Click OK to fill the selected area with color.

12. Select the top layer.

13. Right-click in the selection and choose *Create Clipping Mask* from the context menu. You should see only the portion of the view remaining that was within the black area.

14. Clipping different layers or using different shapes can create some very interesting images—the rule here is to experiment and evaluate!

Figure 21.6 *The feather dialog box.*

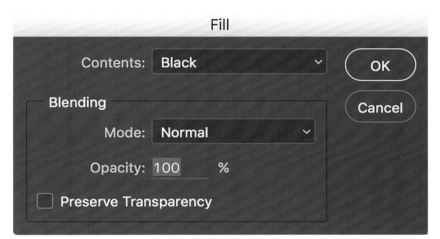

Figure 21.7 *The fill dialog box.*

Figure 21.8 *The clipped layer.*

Figure 21.9 *Examples of these types of effects.*

Once it's been feathered, it's easier to delete the clipping shape and re-draw, rather than trying to fix part of it.

FILTERS

Looking to waste an entire day fiddling on the computer? Photoshop filters are just what you're looking for, because there are quite a large range of options and each one has parameters specific to that tool that can be modified for a different appearance. Filters will permanently modify the layer that they are applied to, which is known as **destructive editing**, so be sure to work on a copy of your base image.

There are quite a few filters that are provided with the base installation, and it's even possible to purchase additional ones. Each filter will behave differently on different types of images, and there are even controls to tweak how the filter behaves. Add a bit of blur to the back of a space for a perception of spatial depth. Interesting effects can be had by blending the photo-realistically rendered layer with a heavily filtered layer to get some texture into the image.

1. Open the Photoshop drawing with all of the layers.
2. Right-click on the photo-realistic layer and choose *Duplicate* from the context menu.
3. Select the layer and move it to the top.
4. Choose *Filter > Filter Gallery*.
5. Go to the artistic group and choose *Colored Pencil*.
6. In the preview area, zoom in on part of the drawing to get a good idea of the effect of the filter.
7. Adjust the sliders to get more or less of the pencil effect—a bright paper and a heavy stroke pressure often works well.

Figure 21.10 *The filter gallery with enlarged preview.*

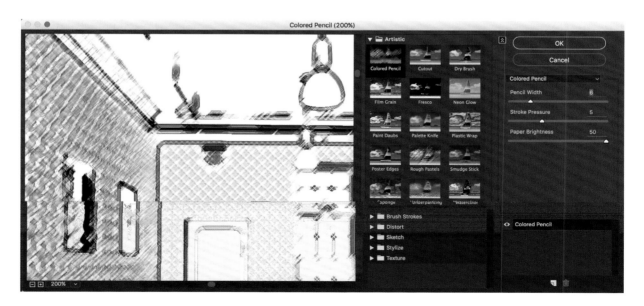

8. Click OK to apply to the entire layer.

9. This effect works to create some visual "noise," which feels a bit less aggressive. Choose *Layer > New Adjustment Layer > Hue/Saturation*.

10. In the new layer dialog box, check the *Use Previous Layer to Create Clipping Mask* button.

11. Drag the saturation value all the way to the left so that the image becomes monochromatic.

12. In the *Layers* palette, select the filtered layer and the adjustment layer.

13. Right-click on them and choose *Merge Layers* from the context menu.

14. Change the blending mode for this layer to *Multiply* and you should see the rendered layer wherever the top layer is white.

15. Adjust the opacity of the top layer to lessen the effect to your liking.

Figure 21.11 *The filtered layer.*

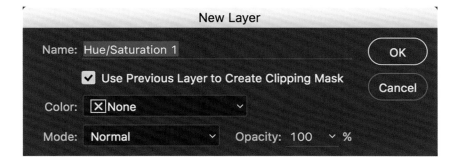

Figure 21.12 *The new layer dialog box.*

Figure 21.13 *The rendering with some texture.*

 An alternative to Photoshop filters is a Windows-only app called FotoSketcher, which has a number of very artistic options.

16. Aggressive filters tend to wash out any line work you might have in the drawing. Drag the black and white layer to the top of the stack.
17. Select the layer.
18. Click on the *Layer Mode* drop-down list and choose *Multiply* to get just the black lines to display.

This technique, with or without the hue adjustment, can produce a great variety of image types and can be a relief from the omnipresent photo-realistic rendering style.

THE OVERLAY

Adding in furniture and scale figures on top of heavily filtered images can be an interesting stylistic flourish. This technique, for a change, is quite simple.

1. Open up the Photoshop document again.
2. Drag the layer with the scale figures to the top.
3. Change the opacity to roughly 75 percent—enough for a little bit of the architecture beyond to show through, but not so much that you lose a sense of the figures.

LIGHTING AND LIGHTING EFFECTS

If you don't have the time or wherewithal to create a photo-realistically rendered image with physical electric lighting modeled, it's possible to fake in some pretty convincing electric lighting effects. Let's create a wall-washing effect on the side wall and a lens flare off of the picture in the back.

Figure 21.14 *Examples of these types of effects.*

Figure 21.15 *The scale figures.*

1. In Photoshop, open up the textured image created from SketchUp.
2. Select the side wall using one of the lasso tools.
3. Choose *Filter > Render > Lighting Effects*.
4. On the *Presets* drop-down list on the toolbar, choose *Five Lights Down*.
5. Drag the lights into a row along the back wall.
6. Adjust their distribution by dragging the handles so that they appear to recede as you get farther back in the room.
7. Adjust the light level of each so that they don't wash out the wall too much.
8. Click OK to apply the lighting effect.
9. Select the entire drawing by typing ⌘A.
10. Choose *Filter > Render > Lens Flare*.
11. Move the focus of the lens flare over a shiny surface at the back of the space—there's a picture frame there.
12. Adjust the style and intensity of the flare.
13. Click OK to apply.

Figure 21.16 *The* Lighting Effects *palette and toolbar.*

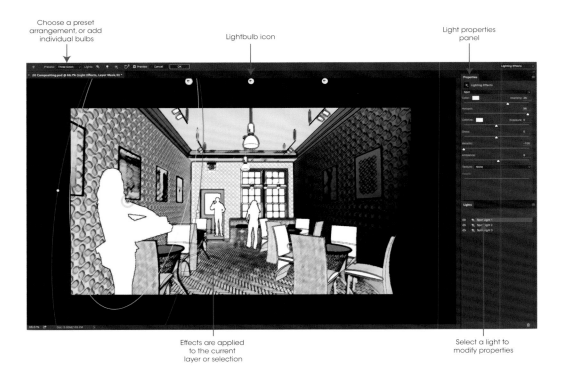

Choose a preset arrangement, or add individual bulbs

Lightbulb icon

Light properties panel

Effects are applied to the current layer or selection

Select a light to modify properties

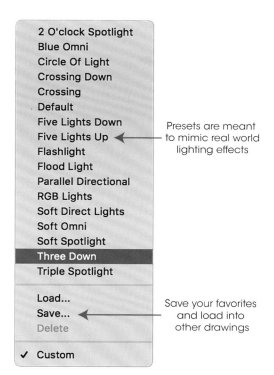

2 O'clock Spotlight
Blue Omni
Circle Of Light
Crossing Down
Crossing
Default
Five Lights Down
Five Lights Up — Presets are meant to mimic real world lighting effects
Flashlight
Flood Light
Parallel Directional
RGB Lights
Soft Direct Lights
Soft Omni
Soft Spotlight
Three Down
Triple Spotlight

Load...
Save... — Save your favorites and load into other drawings
Delete

✓ Custom

Figure 21.17 *Several different lighting effects.*

Intensity : 36

Figure 21.18 *Adjusting the light distribution.*

Figure 21.19 *The completed lighting effect.*

Figure 21.20 *The lens flare dialog box.*

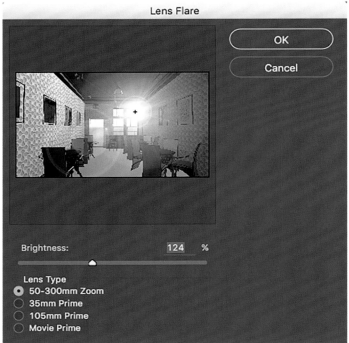

Presentations

Nothing is worse than spending hours tweaking your masterpiece to have just the right composition, color, and lighting, and then having the print come out radically different than what you were looking at on your screen. Screen calibration is the first step toward getting output that matches your intent: it will force a much more accurate display of colors, which for this process is invaluable. Calibration requires a physical device that scans your screen and compares the result to a known standard. The calibration software will then adjust the color.

A soft proof of a physical print is the best way to preview what it is going to look like. You'll need to load the profile for your exact printer and the exact paper that you plan to use, which is not an insignificant task. This is important because the range of colors that your printer can print, known as the gamut, needs to match the range of colors that you're showing on your computer.

For electronic presentations, you are at the mercy of the equipment available to you, so it helps to do your homework. If you're on a laptop, get it calibrated—it will then match any other calibrated machine that you work with. If you are using a projector or large monitor, you are going to have more trouble calibrating them, especially if they are not your own. The best strategy in that case is to bring along some high-quality prints, either as boards or handouts. Because lighting and materials are at the heart of interior design, you don't want to have to make excuses about the poor quality of your imagery—it's difficult for clients to shift colors in their heads.

Try it out!

- Compose a rendering of your space that emphasizes the seating groupings. Use at least three different techniques described above.
- Fake in lighting for daytime and nighttime views of your project.
- Write down the steps needed to create your favorite rendering recipe. Apply that recipe to several different views so that the end results have a consistent graphic look.

Key terms

- Compositing
- Destructive editing

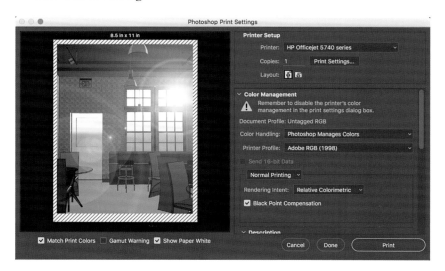

Figure 21.21 *Printer settings for a soft proof.*

APPENDIX

Performance Issues

Sometimes good models go bad—it's just the way of things. Interiors models in particular have quite a lot of geometry from all the furniture and entourage, and also a large number of photo-based textures. All of those can make model sizes large and put a strain on system resources. The various problems that can arise include everything from a general slowdown in your model to frequent crashing. Many of these features have been mentioned briefly in other parts of the text, but they are collected together here.

System settings

The biggest thing you can do to improve system performance is to close unnecessary applications and application windows—this is often the culprit. You can always open them up later. You can also try shutting down your computer for a few minutes and then restarting. Processors and other components sometimes heat up when you're working them hard and need a rest. Finally, updating your operating system, especially your graphics card drivers, will help a great deal.

The Mac comes with a number of built-in animations applied to operations in the OS, such as opening applications with different effects. It's nice to have a snappier interface, however, so turn them off under *System Preferences > Dock* and un-check the *Animate Opening Applications* button. Windows has even greater control. Go to the *Advanced Graphic Settings* menu and check the box next to *Performance*.

Highly complex models will slow down rendering significantly. Strategize about whether you need the objects in the model, for shadows or scale, or if they can be Photoshopped in later.

Choose *Optimize for Performance* to get rid of all these effects or pick and choose from the list.

Windows allows you to optimize the performance of your computer in a number of ways that Mac does not. Under *Control Panel > Display Options > Advanced Display Options*, on the performance panel, you can check the *Optimize for Performance* button. Also, under the power options, change the battery power setting to maximize for performance. This will eat up your battery much faster, but model performance will be greatly improved. Update your anti-virus software and firewall, if those programs don't do it automatically.

Having a large number of extensions can also slow down SketchUp, especially the application launch time. Extensions can be turned off in the *Toolbars* menu or unloaded completely under the *Preferences* menu. If they were installed using the Extension Warehouse, they will remain part of your account, so you'll be able to load them back in later.

SketchUp settings

SketchUp models can slow down for a number of reasons, some of which have to do with application settings, while others are more specific to an individual file.

GENERAL SETTINGS

Adjusting your OpenGL preferences can make a difference, especially on older machines that may not be compliant with the standards for hardware acceleration. It can seem counterintuitive to turn *off* hardware acceleration to improve performance, but life is full of little mysteries. You can also turn off and unload unused extensions. On Mac, you can have several documents open in one application window. In Windows, you can have several windows open at the same time. Either way, close any that you don't absolutely need.

MODEL SETTINGS

There are style settings that have a huge impact on the speed of your model. Here are some steps you can take, in order of how much relief they might give you:

- Turn off the display of daylighting.
- Turn off sketchy lines and extension lines under the style settings.
- Turn off the display of textures under *Face Styles*.
- Or, just choose a fast style—one with the little green clock on the icon.

Make sure to update any scenes in which you'd like the objects to remain hidden.

Instead of proxy objects, you can use special components created for rendering from a company called ArchVision. They have an extension which, for a fee, allows you to import their high-resolution people, trees, and other types of entourage directly into SketchUp. Many rendering engines, including LightUp, will recognize these components, too.

- Turn off animation scene transitions under the animation settings.
- Clean up extra, unused geometry that might have been created unintentionally, which often happens with the *Push/Pull* tool.

Hiding your problems

The largest contributor to model slowdown is having too many objects in the model, because this makes the graphics processor work too hard. The culprit here is typically a component with a high number of polygons, which are the basic geometric building block of SketchUp models. Some components in the 3D Warehouse are actually described as having a low **polygon count** for this exact reason, while the higher polygon models often look smoother. The simplest solution is to hide all that extra geometry. Right-click on the object and choose *Hide* from the context menu. Once hidden, you can choose *View > Hidden Objects* and then right-click on it again to unhide it.

You can also go *Edit > Unhide > Unhide All* and anything that you've hidden in the model will reappear. Model performance will improve, even though all those components are still there, but hidden, so this is only a short-term solution. A similar method is to put the extraneous objects on layers and then turn off those layers. This is handy if you still want those objects around for, say, testing out furniture layouts, but they are high polygon or have large images attached.

Proxy objects

Some SketchUp components have a tremendous amount of geometry in them, and these so-called polygons can really slow down a model. This is particularly true for components loaded from furniture libraries created in other applications, and while we won't name names here, some of the big furniture companies based in the Midwest have been slow to clean up their models. Besides causing ugly meshes that are hard to hide, these manufacturer's components will slow down the model. The other big culprit is meshes created using the sandbox tools or other mesh editing tools. A good practice while modeling a complex project or one with a lot of complex, historical finishes is to avoid putting in those high-polygon items, such as crown molding or complex furnishings, until they are critical.

Another strategy is to use proxy objects in place of the final ones so you can still visualize them without bogging down your system until the very end. Swap out the problem entities with simpler ones, and then swap them back before rendering or creating other types of output. Plants are among the worst offenders, as they can have literally tens of thousands of polygons, so that's what we'll replace with a proxy object.

It can be hard to find an image that has enough pixels to look convincing in a rendering, but not so many that it slows down editing and the rendering process. Use the extension Goldilocks to analyze your model for that resolution sweet spot.

1. Create a simple shape, such as a tube, that is the same size and scale as the offending plant.
2. Choose *File > Save As* and name the file *Planter Proxy*, or something clever like that.
3. Open the problem model—in this case, there is a plant component placed in my café project, so let's use that one.
4. Right-click on the plant and choose *Reload* from the context menu.
5. Browse to find the *Planter Proxy* model and select it. All of the plants should be simplified now.
6. Before going to render or export images, be sure to change the plants back.

If you just want to **purge** components that you're not using, there is a purge option in the fly-out menu of the Components Browser.

Texture sizes

While the default textures in the SketchUp materials palette are generally adequate to get started, a good designer will try to use images that are based on actual photos of an exact manufacturer's product, especially when presenting options to a client. These image files are easy enough to find on, say, the Shaws Carpet or Maharam upholstery websites, but their size may slow down your SketchUp model. It's handy to have these images available if you're planning to render, but the highest resolution is not always needed while developing a model. One general setting that you can change is under the *Preferences > OpenGL* menu, where you can un-check the box for *Use Maximum Texture Size*. This will help SketchUp to ignore some of the extra pixels in very high resolution textures and other images used in the model.

If the model is still slow, you can swap out the offending texture in the *Materials* palette—just edit the material and choose *Load* from the action fly-out menu. Use a photo editing application such as Photoshop to reduce the size of your image to the bare minimum needed—1024 x 1024 is the maximum that SketchUp will display, but 400 x 400 should be plenty for general modeling. You can swap the higher resolution images back in later, since it will make a difference in rendering, if you are rendering within SketchUp.

For more information about the world of splatted bugs, take a look at https://help.sketchup.com/en/article/114285.

Purging the model

All sorts of detritus can pile up in a big project with lots of design options and components: old components that aren't used, layers, and bits of geometry. This can lead to some pretty big files—anything over 50 MB is sure to tax even the most robust computer. The *Purge* command will remove anything that is not actively used in the model. Getting rid of components and layers that you're not using will reduce the file size, often dramatically, if you have just swapped in a few proxy objects. Choose *Window > Model Info* and select the *Statistics* panel. From there, click *Purge*, and wait while SketchUp removes anything it considers unused: empty layers, components that have no instances in the model, and even paint colors and textures that are no longer being used.

While you are at this point in the dialog box, you can also click the *Fix My Model* button. It won't make a bad design any better, but it will alert you about any noncompliant geometry and try to repair it. SketchUp checks models in this way when it first opens them and will automatically try to fix them before allowing you to proceed. If there is a problem, it's typically noncompliant geometry—SketchUp can usually fix the geometry and also check any other models you open up.

You'll also want to check for any unused geometry in your model. Click *Zoom Extents* and your model should fill the screen. If it zooms way out and your model is a tiny spec, it means that there's something out there that SketchUp is zooming to. Display hidden geometry and try to select and delete anything you find. Even inside your model, there may be options or pieces of furniture that you hid a long time ago and have no intention of using. Those elements would be good candidates for deleting as well.

What is a Bug Splat?

SketchUp uses an error-reporting system called Bug Splat. If you've been having troubles with your model, you've seen this unhappy message before. It's always a good idea to send the error report, just in case there's actually something wrong with SketchUp. Often, however, one of the techniques mentioned above will fix the model.

Generally, there is nothing that can be done once you've gotten a Bug Splat. If the original model has been corrupted in some way, so that it will no longer open, try using the backup file. It is saved in the same location as your main file and will have the SKB file extension. Rename the corrupted file first, and then change the extension of the backup to SKP. SketchUp will then recognize it and open it per usual.

Figure A.1 *Nobody likes to see this message.*

Try it out!

- Check for updates in your operating system and install all that are needed.
- Update your anti-virus software and firewall, if those programs don't do it automatically.
- If you're in Windows, maximize your computer for performance.
- Purge your SketchUp model and fix any problems.
- Create components for scale figures using photographs instead of geometry. Crop the components around the edges of the images.

Key terms

- Polygon count
- Purge

GLOSSARY

Alpha channel A layer within a graphics file that represents the degree of transparency.

Ambient lighting In electronic rendering, the minimum level of illumination to view a given scene. The light does not typically appear to come from any particular source or location.

Application programming interface (API) A system of tools and resources in an operating system enabling developers to create software applications.

Array Multiple copies of a drawing entity with a specified spacing and number of instances. An array can be rectangular or circular.

Augmented reality A live camera view from an electronic device that has non-real elements, such as furnishings, overlaid on the screen.

Auto-fold The SketchUp feature that generates new geometry to keep a volume enclosed when moving some edge or point of that object.

Base point The first point used to define a linear dimension or angle in any number of different drawing and editing commands, such as *Move* or *Rotate*.

Browser An interface that allows the selection of some drawing element or feature from a temporary window, typically with multiple options.

Bubble diagram A graphical representation of the architectural program requirements, adjacencies, separations, circulation, and the line.

Building Information Modeling (BIM) A method of designing a building with parametric elements combined into a single database. Views of the model can be graphical or in the form of schedules.

Call-out An architectural symbol used to indicate an enlarged or detail drawing, such as a wall section, in some other location in the drawing set.

Caret A symbol used in the text to indicate holding down the shift key.

Central Processing Unit (CPU) The brain of a computer, often referred to as the chip or chipset.

Circular array See Array; a series of copies of a drawing entity or entities with a specified spacing and limit.

Collections The organization of components in the component browser into thematic folders, such as windows or doors.

Component A single, selectable entity within SketchUp that contains a number of different types of SketchUp base objects, such as lines, arcs, individual surfaces, and multi-surface elements. Useful for repeated objects, such as furnishings

Component properties Information about the selected component, typically found in the entity info dialog box. This may include geometric information and also metadata about the object's manufacturer or catalogue number.

Compositing Creating a single rendering in Photoshop by combining pieces of other drawings

Construction details Large-scale drawings that indicate the configuration and construction of some element of a project.

Context menu A menu accessed by right-clicking on some object, area, or selection set.

Destructive editing In Photoshop, the type of editing that modifies the original image. This is as opposed to using a filter layer or blending mode, which do not modify the original image.

Dialog box The menu that pops up during certain operations. It is necessary to answer whatever question or check off the feature the dialog box is prompting you about.

Docked menu When a menu is snapped into one edge of the screen or another, or the top or bottom, making the drawing area smaller. This is as opposed to a floating menu.

Entourage In composing a drawing, these are elements, such as people and plants, that may not be critical to the design, but illustrate how the space will be used.

Face A two-dimensional surface in a SketchUp model, defined by a continuous loop of linear elements.

FF&E The type of contract most frequently associated with interior designers and interior architects: finishes, fixtures, and equipment.

Field measurements A drawing with a set of dimensions that are taken to create the existing conditions of a project.

Field of view The angle of the extent of a drawing that is visible from the station point, as measured in degrees.

File extension The three-letter code appended to a file name that indicates to the computer which type of file a given document is.

Final bake In computer rendering, this indicates the calculation intensive process of generating the highest quality photo-realistic rendering.

Floating menu A menu that can occur over any point on your screen. This is as opposed to a docked menu.

Fly-out menu A menu, typically indicated with a right arrow, that when clicked produces another sub-menu of options off to the side.

Frustum A three-dimensional representation of the focus area of a particular virtual camera. Useful when composing a video animation.

Graphics Processing Unit (GPU) The physical part of your computer that is designed to handle graphics editing tasks. Critical when using SketchUp.

Grip A point along a model or drawing element that allows selected elements to be modified by clicking and dragging.

Group A collection of SketchUp entities, similar to a component. Unlike a component, however, a group is a unique instance, where copies of the group will not be modified if the original is changed.

Horizontal array The type of array that is linear, with the spacing and angle of the object copies and number of copies being specified.

IES file A file format created by the Illuminating Engineering Society of North America to specify the strength of light sources in different directions. Used for modeling a physical representation of electric lighting in a project.

Industry Foundation Classes (IFC) A standardized classification system for keeping track of architectural elements in a building information modeling.

Inferences Guesses made by your "smart cursor" as to what you would like to select or do with an object. Typically, they pop up when you mouse over different geometric parts of objects.

Information windows Menus that pop up that have information about the selected object.

Inspector The term for certain types of menus that display information about a selected object or tool, more commonly seen on the Mac interface.

Instance A copy of a component or group.

Interoperability The ability of different software applications to share or read files produced in other applications.

Jitter The shakiness of a given line. Tends to make lines look hand-drawn.

Key A chart showing each icon in a drawing and describing what it signifies.

Keyboard shortcut A keystroke or a combination of keystrokes that activates a command or some other feature.

Layers A way of organizing a model in which objects are collected onto a layer, which can be turned on or off.

Legend On a set of construction drawings, a key to the symbols used on a particular drawing or series of drawings.

Life safety plan A reduced-size floor plan indicating compliance with the major egress requirements of a particular project.

Material take-off Measurements of a particular material for a schedule. Varies by the type of material; for something like carpet, it may be yards, whereas paint may be measured by the gallon.

Menu The verbal list of commands that appears at the top of your user interface.

Metadata Information about non-geometric aspects of a given component, such as the manufacturer or the catalogue number.

Nested The condition where a group or component has been inserted into another parent group or component. Sub-objects will copy, paste, and paint as per their type, and will not take on the properties of the parent object.

Open Graphics Library (OpenGL) Programming interface for rendering 2D and 3D vector graphics.

Operating system The system your computer uses to run applications and the user interface. The main operating systems currently available are Windows, Mac, and Linux.

Organic The type of geometry that is nonlinear, typically with plenty of curves.

Origin The geometric home point of a drawing or component, which is typically 0,0,0 on the orthogonal grid.

Orthographic A drawing without perspective distortion, including plans, sections, elevations, and axonometrics; typically set to some reference scale.

Palette A collection of drawing options, as in the *Materials* palette.

Pan Moving the virtual camera left to right or up and down, without changing the distance from the visual target.

Parameters In building information modeling, elements of an object that can be changed by entering values in a menu.

Physical lighting Modeling electric lighting that is closely representative of the characteristics of an actual light source, typically using IES files.

Poché The fill patterns within cut objects, such as walls, on-floor plans, and section views.

Polygon count The total number of individual faces in a model, which is a measure of geometric complexity.

Post-processing Modifying a computer-generated image using software such as Photoshop, instead of the originating application, such as LightUp.

Preferences The settings and configuration for a particular application.

Pull-down menu The verbal listing of commands and tools that typically occurs at the top of the user interface.

Purchase order A list of items to be obtained for an interior design project.

Purge To remove unused elements (such as lines, faces, or components) and settings (such as styles or textures) from a model.

Raster A type of image file that is a grid of pixels with different values. These are typically edited in a photo editing software, such as Photoshop.

Reference line A linear element of the drawing that is not meant to be printed, but instead used as a reference for placing other objects.

Render The process of taking the geometry of a model and adding lighting and materials. Can be photo-realistic or a stylized, non-realistic type of view.

Rendering engine A software application, either embedded in the main application or as a stand-alone, that renders the model.

Report In SketchUp, a written tabulation of selected elements and their parameter values.

Resolution The precision of an image, measured either in pixels per inch for an electronic image or dots per inch for a printed image.

RGB color A color working environment defined by the red, green, and blue values within each pixel.

Rubber band line When drawing elements in Sketch-Up, a line that connects the cursor to the base point.

Sampling The process of copying a material off of a given entity in SketchUp for the purpose of then adding that material to some other object.

Section plane The SketchUp object that slices away part of the model so that you can see inside.

Selection set Using the *Select* command, the series of objects that are available all at once.

Solid color A paint material that is based on a combination of red, green, and blue values, as opposed to one based on an image file.

Solid modeler A three-dimensional modeling environment in which shapes have fill inside of them, as opposed to being hollow.

Space planning The design process wherein furnishings, interior partitions, and other interior elements are organized and distributed on a floor plan.

Station point In perspective drawing, the position of the viewer.

Stereoscopic In rendering, the type of image that can be viewed using a 3D virtual reality device, such as Google Cardboard.

Strokes When creating a custom line type, strokes are copies of a particular line length used to generate the sketchy views.

Studio Method The traditional method of perspective drawing using a floor plan and elevation or section.

Surface modeler The type of 3D modeling environment that produces surfaces that bound hollow objects. SketchUp is this type of modeler.

Template A blank drawing preconfigured with a number of different settings typically used in a particular project type.

Texture Representation of finish quality of a material; can be either a solid color or image based.

Tile A repeated pattern, where an image can cover a surface in a grid pattern based on the image size.

Tool tip Small descriptive tags that pop up when the mouse moves over different elements of a project and at different points in tool operation.

Transparency The feature of a texture, on a scale of 0 to 100, that indicates how much light will pass through it.

Tray On the Windows user interface, the collection of menus in SketchUp.

User interface (UI) The way in which operating systems and applications accept input and information from the user.

Vanishing point In perspective drawing, the point at which coplanar linear elements converge.

Vector The type of drawing that is created using algorithms and other types of mathematics to describe how elements appear. Typical of computer-generated 3D modeling.

Viewport A window in LayOut that contains a view of a given SketchUp model.

Virtual reality A completely visually immersive way of viewing a SketchUp model or other content.

Watertight In 3D printing, the future of a model where there are no openings or gaps in the three-dimensional geometry.

Zoom Moving a camera in and out of a given scene.

INDEX

3D modeling software
  printing, 248–49, 250
  SketchUp, 1, 4
3D Warehouse, 42–43, 132, 141

A

alpha channel, 242
ambient lighting, 268
animation
  composing a linear walkthrough,
    243–44
  configuring and playing, 244, 245
  creating an, 242–48
  exporting, file from SketchUp,
    246–48
  exporting files, 281
  scenes for, 245
  types of, 245–46
application programming interface
    (API), 93
Applications panel, 91
Architectural Team, The, Chelsea,
    MA, 11
arc tools, 26

array, 30
  arraying the, 135–36
  circular array, 134
  horizontal array, 134
@Last Software, 1
augmented reality, 260–62
AutoCAD
  arrays, 135
  export options, 252, 256, 258
  file formats, 241, 254, 259
  importing drawings from, 233–35
  layers, 82, 141
  SketchUp, 9, 80
  software, 5
auto-fold, 162–63
axes
  color-coded, 37
  model, 36–37

B

base point, 30, 64
Beganyi, Mike, 203, 204
Boolean modeling, 164
browsers, 12, 18

bubble diagram, 128
Bug Splat, error-reporting system,
    302, 303
building. *See* complex building elements
Building Information Modeling (BIM), 5–6

C

call-outs, drawing, 212–13
Capture menu, 276, 279, 281
caret, 25
case studies
  The Architectural Team (Chelsea,
    MA), 11
  framing exploration by Mike
    Beganyi, 204
casework drawings, 232–33
Central Processing Unit (CPU), 10, 93
circular array, 134
Classifications panel, 96, 97
collections, 41, 76
colors, menu on Mac and Windows, 41
complex building elements
  dynamic components, 157–61
  handrail, 151–52

hiding/showing components during editing, 152–53

layering and grouping, 143–44

modeling interior, 144–47

stair from scratch, 147–50

stair using an extension, 153–55

view tools, 151

walls and openings, 155–57

component, 64, 136

dynamic, 157–61

management, 137–38

properties, 157

Components Inspector, 75, 76

Components panel, 96, 97

compositing, 283

preparing the ingredients, 283–86

presentations, 296–97

rendering recipes, 286–95

construction details, 229

casework drawings, 232–33

enlarged floor plan, 229–30

enlarged section, 230, 231

importing drawings, 233–34

construction drawings using LayOut, 194

dimension strings, 201–3

dimensions, elements, 201, 203

finishes plan, 201, 202

notes, 205–6

overlaying viewports, 197–200

preparing, 195

refining floor plan, 195–201

room names, 204–5

template, 195

context menu, 12

Credits panel, 96, 98

curves

complex, 169–71

drawing, 25

D

design presentations using LayOut, 175–76

creating and editing background graphics, 182–85

Document Setup menu, 182, 183

editing the title block, 189, 190

exporting file to print, 191–92, 193

grid settings, 182, 183

handles, 186, 187

inserting images, 189

layers, 186, 188

LayOut drawing and editing tools, 186, 187

pages, 190–91

paper settings, 184

preparing SketchUp model, 176–77

presenting using LayOut, 191

References panel, 184, 185

Send to LayOut button, 177–80

setting views to scale, 181–82

Shape Style, 186, 187

text and titles, 188, 189

Units panel, 185

viewport, 182

viewport graphics controls, 180

destructive editing, 290

dialog box, 12

dimensions, 137

Dimensions panel, 98, 99

dimension strings, 103, 160, 201–3, 248

Display Secondary Selection Pane, 56

docked menus, 19

Document Setup menu, 182, 183

doors

cleaning up the frame, 84

interiors project, 77–78, 79

drawing, 24

basic tools, 24

curves, 25

lines, 24–25

shapes, 25–27

drawing panel, preferences, 91, 92

E

editing tools, 29

Move, 30

Offset, 31–32

Push/Pull, 30–31

Scale tool, 32–33, 34

tool modifiers, 30

electronic workflow, 3

elevation drawings, 113–14

entourage, 138

Eraser tool, 24, 28

Esch, Joe, 1

exporting images, 241–42

Extensions, 6, 8, 92

Extension Manager, 44–45

Extensions panel, 92

Extension Warehouse, 43–44

managing, 173–74

external applications, 42–45

Eyedropper tool, 42

F

faces, 23

field measurements, 73

field of view, 60, 108, 110

file extension, sketchup, 69

File panel, 98, 99

final bake, 278

floating menus, 18

floor plan. See also construction drawings using LayOut

composite plan view, 199

configuring layers, 196–97

creating enlarged, 229–30

graphic standards, 201

legends, 210–12

overlaying viewports, 197–200

refining, 195–201

reflected ceiling plan (RCP), 196, 199, 200

fog, 57, 58

fonts dialog box, 129

Freehand tool, 25

frustum, 108

furnishings, finishes, and equipment (FF&E), 73

furniture. See table

G

General panel, 92–93
Geographic Information System (GIS), 2
Geolocation panel, 98, 100–101
geometry, advanced
    auto-fold, 162–63
    complex curves, 169–71
    groin vault, 166
    intersecting objects, 167
    managing extensions, 173–74
    overlapping, 165
    sandbox tools, 167–69
    solid tools, 164–66
    warped surfaces, 171–73
Google, 43
Google Cardboard, 263–64
graphical controls
    applying a style to new scene, 52–53
    creating an exterior backdrop, 57, 59
    fog, 57, 58
    launching Large Tool Set, 46–49
    scene management, 53–55
    section planes and section cuts, 51–52
    shadows, 55–56, 57
    slicing open the model, 49–50
    styles, 52
Graphics Processing Unit (GPU), 10, 93
graphic symbols, keyboard, 11
grid, 182, 183
grips, 180
groin vault, 166
group, 64, 136

H

Handy Dandy LayOut file, 215
horizontal array, 134

I

IES file, 274

Illuminating Engineers Society of
    North America (IESNA), 274
images, exporting, 241–42
Industry Foundation Classes (IFC), 96,
    104, 219, 221, 222
inferences, 37–38
information windows, 18
inspector, 12, 18
installation, SketchUp software,
    13–14
instance, 157
Instructor, The, 20–21
interface, customizing, 90
    creating a template, 103–5
    Model Info menu, 96–103
    SketchUp preferences, 91–95
interior designers, SketchUp using, 3–5
interiors project, 71–72
    back door, 79
    building volume from outside, 75
    documenting the existing
        conditions, 72–73
    FF&E, 73
    floor plan, 74
    inserting ready-made components,
        75–76
    layer assignments, 80–82
    modeling exterior volume, 73–74
    model of retail site, 72
    positioning the door, 77–78, 79, 81
    saving views of model, 85–88
    wall thickness, 83–85
    windows, 78–80
interoperability, 96
    augmented reality, 260–62
    AutoCAD, 259
    import options, 254–56
    Revit, 256–59
    Trimble Connect, 259
    virtual reality, 262–64

J

jitter, 121

K

key, 216
keyboard graphics shortcuts, 10–12

L

Large Tool Set, 46–49
    customizing Mac toolbar, 47
    customizing Windows toolbar,
        48–49
laser cutter, preparing for, 250–51,
    252
layer, assigning for interiors project,
    80–82
Layers Inspector, 81, 82, 188
LayOut, 175–76. *See also* construction
    drawings using LayOut; design
    presentations using LayOut
    adding own scrapbook,
        214–15
    construction drawings, 194,
        197, 199
    Create Clipping Mask, 213–14
    creating a schedule within,
        226–28
    creating cover page, 215–17
    display graphics, 180
    drawing and editing tools, 186, 187
    exporting file to print, 191–92
    images, 189
    interface, 179
    layers in, 186, 188
    pages, 190–91
    preparing SketchUp model,
        176–77
    presenting masterpiece using, 191
    Scrapbook, The, 208–9
    Send to LayOut button,
        177–80
    text and titles, 188, 189
    tip of the day, 178
    title block, 189
leader lines, 40

legends, 206, 210–12
life safety plan, 216
lighting
    rendered image, 292, 294,
       295, 296
    rendering, 272–74, 275
lines, drawing, 24–25

M

Mac version
    customizing toolbar, 47
    inspectors and, 75
    SketchUp and LayOut, 177
    solids toolbar, 165
MakerBot Desktop, 249, 250
Make and Pro versions, SketchUp,
    comparing, 9
Make version, SketchUp, 7, 9,
    44, 221
managing content
    3D Warehouse, 42–43
    Extension Manager, 44–45
    Extension Warehouse, 43–44
    Send to LayOut tool, 44
Materials menu, 277
material take-off, 225
measurement, 38
menu, 18
metadata, 2
model. *See* interiors project
model axes, 36–37
Model Info menu
    animations, 96
    Classifications panel, 96, 97
    Components panel, 96, 97
    Credits panel, 96, 98
    Dimensions panel, 98, 99
    File panel, 98, 99
    Geolocation panel, 98, 100–101
    Rendering panel, 101, 102
    Text panel, 101, 102
    Units panel, 103

N

nested, 135

O

object
    object snap points, 39
    Object Styles menu, 258
    selecting, 28–29
Offset tool, 31–32
OpenGL (Open Graphics Library)
    panel, preferences, 93, 94
operating system (OS), 6
organic, 171
origin, 37, 74
orthographic drawings, 44, 60
    adding own scrapbook, 214–15
    advanced, 207–18
    creating a clipping mask, 213–14
    creating cover page, 215–17
    drawing call-outs, 212–13
    floor plan legend, 210–12
    Scrapbook, The, 208–9
    section and elevation symbols,
       209–10
orthographic views
    creating, 111–12, 113
    creating style for, 116–18
Outliner, 139

P

Paint Bucket tool, 41–42, 68, 112, 129,
    136
palette, 12
pan, 21
parameter, 6, 157
Pencil tool, 24
performance issues
    error-reporting system, 302, 303
    hiding problems, 300

proxy objects, 300–301
    purging the model, 302
    SketchUp settings,
       299–300
    system settings, 298–99
    texture sizes, 301
perspective view, printing,
    236–38
Photoshop, 69, 124
    compositing, 283–84,
       287–88
    layers, 290, 292, 294
    LayOut and, 175, 192
    photo editing, 301
    post-processing, 192, 241, 279
physical lighting, 268
poché, 112, 196
Polygon tool, 27
polygon count, 300
post-processing, 241
preferences, SketchUp
    Applications panel, 91
    Drawing panel, 91, 92
    General panel, 92–93
    OpenGL (Open Graphics Library)
       panel, 93, 94
    Shortcuts panel, 94
    SketchUp, 91–95
    Template panel, 95
    Workspace panel, 95
presentations, 296–97
printing
    3D, 248–49, 250
    exporting images, 241–42
    perspective view, 236–38
    presentations, 296–97
    scaled view, 238–41
    target resolution, 280
Pro version, SketchUp, 3, 7, 9, 175,
    194, 207, 221
pull-down menus, 13
purchase order, 220
purge, 301
Push/Pull tool, 30–31, 32

R

raster, 241
Rectangle tool, 26
red, green, and blue (RGB) color, 66
reference line, 38, 77
References panel, 184, 185
reflected ceiling plan (RCP), 196,
     199, 200
render, 265
rendering
     Capture menu, 276
     exporting animation files, 281
     exporting rendered still
          images, 277–79
     interior settings, 270–71
     internal, 267–68
     lighting, 272–74, 275
     Materials menu, 277
     printing target resolution, 280
     quickie, 268–70
     rendering engine comparison, 265–67
     Rendering panel, 102
rendering recipes, 286–95
     the fade, 287–88
     feather dialog box, 289
     fill dialog box, 289
     filters, 290–92
     lighting and lighting effects, 292,
          294, 295, 296
     the overlay, 292, 293
report, generating a, 222–225
resolution, 280
Revit, 6, 11, 175, 254, 256–59, 264
     export from SketchUp to, 256–58
     import from, to SketchUp, 259
Ropefall, 24
Rotated Rectangle, 26
rubber band line, 25

S

sampling, 42
Sandbox tools, 167–69
satellite map preview window, 100

Scale tool, 32–33, 34
scaled view, printing, 238–41
scene management, 53–55
     composing interior perspectives,
          107–9
     creating orthographic view,
          111–12, 113
     creating section view, 112–13, 114
     elevation drawings, 113–14
     transverse view, 114, 115
     updating, 109–10, 111
Scenes Manager, applying style to new
     scene, 52–53
scheduling, 219
     counting components, 220
     creating components with
          embedded metadata, 221, 222
     creating within LayOut, 226–28
     generating a report, 222–25
     measuring surface area, 225–26
Schell, Brad, 1
scrapbook, 208–9
section cuts, 51–52
section planes, 49–50, 51–52
section view
     creating, 112–13, 114
     creating enlarged, 230, 231
selection set, 28
send to LayOut, 44, 177–80, 195
shadows, 55–56, 57
shapes, drawing, 25–27
Shape Style Inspector, 203, 206
Shape Style menu, 187, 216
shift, 49
Shortcut panel, preferences, 94
SketchUp, 1–3
     Building Information Modeling
          (BIM), 5–6
     error-reporting system, 302, 303
     Extensions, 6, 8
     exterior backdrop, 57, 59
     features, 9
     file extension, 69
     installing the software, 13–14
     Instructor, The, 20–21
     for interior design, 3–5
     interoperability, 9–10

keyboard shortcuts, 10–12
Large Tool Set, 46–49
Make and Pro versions, comparing, 9
menus and dialogs, inspectors and
     palettes, 12–13
office-wide decisions, 6–8
platform of, 10
scenes management, 53–55
settings, 299–300
shadows, 55–56
using a template, 17–18
SketchUp Model Inspector, 180, 181,
     182, 191
Smoove tool, 168–69
Soap Skin & Bubble tool, 171–72
software interface, 19
solid color, 66
solid modeler, 23
Solids tools, 164–66
space planning, 127
     analyzing the program, 127–31
     arraying the array, 135–36
     circular array, 134
     coloring by layer, 141, 142
     component management, 137–38
     design options, 131–32, 140–41
     difference between block and
          component behavior, 136
     dimensions, 137
     losing objects, 141
     placing a painting on the wall,
          138–39
     populating the model, 132
stairs. See two-story model
station point, 57
Statistics panel, 220, 302
stereoscopic view, 263
strokes, 121, 124
Studio Method, 108
Style Builder, 121–23, 124
styles, working with, 52
Styles Browser panels, 118
styles management
     applying dramatic styles, 118–19
     applying styles to multiple scenes, 125

creating a style for orthographic views, 116–18
creating your own, 124
inserting a new style, 125
mixing and matching characteristics, 120
Style Builder, 121–23, 124
Styles menu, 104, 117, 120, 122
surface modeler, 23

T

table, 61–62
copying the legs, 64
creating legs, 62–63
tabletop, 64–66
texture, 66–69
Tape Measure, 38, 77, 78
template
creating a, 103–5
SketchUp, 17–18
Template panel, preferences, 95
Text panel, 101, 102
Text tool, 40
texture, 17, 66–69
Texture Palettes, tab, 42
tile, 67
toolbar, 20

tools, types of, 20
tool tips, 20, 39
transparency, 242
tray, 12, 19, 179
Trimble, 3, 8
account, 18, 43
SketchUp owner, 259
web-based app, 10
Trimble Connect, 259
two-story model
creating stair from scratch, 147–50
creating stair using extension, 153–55
extruding a handrail, 151–52
hiding/showing components, 152–53
modeling existing interior, 144–47
view tools, 151

U

units panel, 103, 185
user interface (UI), 1, 18–19

V

vector, 241

viewport, 180, 197–200
View tools, 21–23
virtual reality, 262–64

W

walls and openings, creating, 155–57
wall thickness, interiors project, 83–85
warped surfaces, 171–73
watertight, 249
windows, interiors project, 78–80
Windows version
customizing toolbar, 48–49
inspectors and, 75
SketchUp and LayOut, 177
solids toolbar, 165
workspace panel, preferences, 95

Z

zoom, 21
Zoom Extents, 22